SPACE MARINES

By Matthew Ward

CONTENTS

Written by: Matthew Ward.

Previous Editions by: Rick Priestley, Andy Chambers, Pete Haines, Andy Hoare, Jervis Johnson, Graham McNeill, Anthony Reynolds and Gavin Thorpe.

Cover art: Alex Boyd. **Sub-editor:** Andrew Kenrick

Illustrations: John Blanche, Dave Gallagher, Alex Boyd, Paul Dainton, Robin Carey.

Graphic Design: Neil Hodgson. **Production Lead:** Carl Dafforn.

Photography: Stuart White & Ian Strickland. **Production:** Kris Jaggers, John Michelbach, Melissa Roberts, Rachel Ryan, Sean Turtle.

Hobby Material: Dave Andrews, Mark Jones, Chad Mierzwa, Chris Peach.

Miniatures Design: Colin Grayson, Mark Harrison, Martin Footitt, Dave Thomas, Jes Goodwin, Seb Perbert, Neil Langdown, Dale Stringer, Tom Walton, Chris Catton.

'Eavy Metal: Fil Dunn, Darren Latham, Neil Green, Keith Robertson, Kirsten Williams, Anja Wettergren, Joe Tomaszewski.

Special thanks: James Karch, Graham Davey, Alan Merrett, Jeremy Vetock.

PRODUCED BY GAMES WORKSHOP

UK	US	CANADA	AUSTRALIA	NORTHERN EUROPE
Games Workshop Ltd., Willow Rd, Lenton, Nottingham, NG7 2WS	Games Workshop Inc, 6711 Baymeadow Drive, Suite A, Glen Burnie, Maryland, 21060-6401	Games Workshop, 2679 Bristol Circle, Unit 3, Oakville, Ontario, L6H 6Z8	Games Workshop, 23 Liverpool Street, Ingleburn, NSW 2565	Games Workshop Ltd., Willow Rd, Lenton, Nottingham, NG7 2WS

INTRODUCTION

Forged by forgotten science and driven by their eternal duty, the superhuman Space Marines are Mankind's foremost defence against a dark and brooding universe.

The Warhammer 40,000 rulebook contains the rules you need to fight battles with your Citadel miniatures in the war-torn universe of the 41st Millennium. Every army has its own Codex that works with these rules, allowing you to turn your collection into an organised force ready for your games of Warhammer 40,000. This particular Codex details everything you need to know about the Space Marines.

WHY COLLECT SPACE MARINES?

Space Marines are the heroes of the Imperium, and one of the deadliest fighting forces of the 41st Millennium. A Space Marine's characteristics equal or better those of other armies' elite troops, combining both excellent close combat skills and shooting accuracy. As a result, even the most basic Space Marine trooper is a formidable opponent in his own right!

The Space Marines' combat prowess is backed up by the best weaponry and equipment the Imperium can provide, from the legendary boltgun and impenetrable power armour, to devastating heavy bolters, assault cannons and Whirlwind missile launchers. Nowhere in Warhammer 40,000 will you find an army so mobile, durable and, above all, destructive.

HOW THIS CODEX WORKS

Codex: Space Marines contains the following sections:

- **The Space Marines:** The first section introduces the mighty Space Marines and their part in the Warhammer 40,000 universe. It details their creation, their battles and their mission to safeguard Mankind. It includes the full history, organisational details and uniform guides of the proudest and noblest of all the Space Marines – the Ultramarines Chapter – as well as colour schemes and background information for many other Chapters.

- **Forces of the Space Marines:** Each and every character, troop type and vehicle in the Space Marine army is examined in this section. Firstly, you will find a full description of the unit, describing its role within the army and its specialised combat abilities. Secondly, you will find complete rules for the unit and details of any unique skills, wargear or abilities they can bring to bear against the enemies of Mankind.

- **Wargear:** This section contains full details and rules for the battle heirlooms, armour and weaponry used by the Space Marines, including annotated illustrations.

- **Space Marine Showcase:** This section contains colour photographs of the extensive range of Citadel miniatures available for your Space Marine army, gloriously painted by Games Workshop's famous 'Eavy Metal team. Colour schemes for the various Chapters are included, as well as tips and techniques for constructing and painting your own Space Marine strike force.

- **Space Marines Army List:** The army list takes all of the units presented in the 'Forces of the Space Marines' section and arranges them so you can choose an army for your own games. Each unit type also has a points value attached to help you pit your force against an opponent's in a fair match.

FIND OUT MORE

While Codex: Space Marines contains everything you need to play a game with your army of Space Marines, there are always more tactics to use, scenarios to fight and painting ideas to try out. The monthly magazine White Dwarf contains articles about all aspects of the Warhammer 40,000 game and hobby, and you can find articles specific to the Space Marines on our website:

www.games-workshop.com

In addition, you'll find more advice and information about painting your Space Marine army in the books How To Paint Citadel Miniatures and How To Paint Space Marines.

THE SPACE MARINES

The 41st Millennium is an age of war, but it is also an age of heroes. One force stands between humanity and annihilation, a warrior brotherhood by whose valour civilisation endures. They have known betrayal. They have known tragedy. They have fought the most thankless of wars against the most terrible of foes, winning impossible victories when all around them have fallen. They are Mankind's foremost defence against a dark and brooding galaxy, and the beneficent Emperor's greatest gift to his people. They are the Space Marines, the Angels of Death, and they know no fear.

A Space Marine is no mere man. He is a superhuman being, born of scientific manipulation and genetic modification, as different from humankind as steel is from iron. Through years of the most exhaustive and rigorous training, the rough firmament of the Space Marine's mind and body are forged into that of a warrior supreme, with battle-skills and faculty of reason that far surpass those of the common man. Thus transfigured, the Space Marine is forevermore separate from those he protects. He is no longer mortal in the truest sense, for a part of his heritage is now that of the immortal Emperor, and a spark of that same majesty flows within his veins.

The paternal link, though incredibly faint, forever seperates the Space Marine from those he protects. Where the Emperor is both deity and saviour to the common man, he is a revered ancestor to the Space Marine. Where the man worships a beneficent god, the Space Marine venerates an ancestral patriarch.

Even fighting alone, each Space Marine is a formidable foe, with might enough to defeat many times his own number. He bears the power armour and boltgun of those who have come before him - noble burdens that serve as constant reminder of the duty that gives him purpose and strength. Yet a Space Marine seldom fights alone. Each is but one brother in a Chapter of a thousand warriors. Where one Space Marine stands, his brothers stand with him - by the score, by the hundred or by the thousand. There are only a thousand such Chapters spanning the galaxy, one thousand fortress-monasteries on scattered worlds, standing as bastions throughout the Imperium of Man. There is thus one Space Marine for each of the million worlds in the Imperium, a small number to be sure, yet still sufficient for the task at hand.

It is rare for an entire Chapter to fight as one. Only by dividing their might can the Space Marines oppose the many dangers to humanity. Most threats to the Imperium can be settled by the intervention of a relative handful of Space Marines, but such threats are many and the Space Marines few. Should a Chapter stand together in battle, its roster of heroes united in common cause, then the assembled might is sufficient to bring liberation or destruction to entire star systems.

Space Marines strike with the precision and fury of a thunderbolt. Drop Pods scream down from orbit at impossible speeds, slamming into the battlefield to disgorge squads of Space Marines into the heart of the foe. Terminator-armoured veterans teleport into areas of the heaviest resistance, wading unharmed through firepower that could topple buildings, and unleashing the fury of storm bolter and power fist upon all in their path. Thunderhawk Gunships roar through the skies, deploying indomitable Predator and Land Raider battle tanks to vital locations before turning the fury of their guns upon the foe.

Not for Space Marines the steady advance or the holding of fortifications. To them fall the most arduous and dangerous of duties: crippling strikes at the very heart of the enemy, the daring seizure of heavily fortified positions and nigh-hopeless battles against an infinitely outnumbering foe. Few are the enemies that can withstand such an assault. By breaking the enemy where he is strong, so do the Space Marines harness surprise and dismay as their weapons. Few opponents can weather the terrible storm of the Space Marines' onslaught, and most campaigns end in victory shortly thereafter. On those occasions where the enemy survives the initial dolorous blow, the Space Marines press the attack. With bolter and chainsword they scour the enemy from his strongholds, often fighting many times their number with a dedication that is as unceasing as it is terrible to behold.

Only when the foe is beaten do the Space Marines set aside their weapons, but they do not rest, do not take time to celebrate their glorious victories. For every battle won, another awaits. The Space Marines are the heroes of the Imperium, and they live in a time when Mankind needs heroes as never before. For such men there can be no rest - only an eternity of battle in the Emperor's name.

ORIGINS OF THE SPACE MARINES

The earliest days of Mankind's expansion to the stars is a time of dark myth and legend, unremembered by all save the Emperor of Mankind. Terrible wars and anarchy engulfed the galaxy at this time, and as human civilisation fragmented, alien races and vile creatures of the Warp seized their chance to plunder unprotected worlds and enslave their populations. Planets were sacked, their peoples slaughtered, and those that survived the onslaught were dragged into barbarism. Alone and beset by internal strife, the human worlds that survived were pitiful shadows of what they had once been. Humanity was on the brink of annihilation and never more were great heroes needed to stave off the hordes of darkness.

From the ashes of the Age of Strife arose a mighty leader, the man who would be known only as the Emperor. His origins are unrecorded and unknown, but it was on Terra, the cradle of humanity, that he founded an empire that would unite the worlds of the galaxy. From the outset of his campaigns, the Emperor employed genetically engineered warriors, the earliest precursors of the Space Marines. Within shrouded vaults far beneath the surface of Terra, the Emperor began the creation of the next generation of super-warriors. These were the Primarchs, twenty extraordinary individuals who would be his generals – great leaders who would conquer thousands of worlds in his name. Each Primarch would have powers and skills beyond those of any

other warrior, rivalling even those of the Emperor himself. Disastrously though, in the early stages of their development, the Emperor's great work was almost undone when the Primarchs vanished, scattered throughout the galaxy by an unknown force.

Conquest of the Galaxy

All was not lost, for the Emperor still had the genetic records of his beloved Primarchs and from these were created the Space Marines – the Angels of Death. Mustered into the great, ten thousand strong Legions of the First Founding, they were warriors of immense strength and unbreakable willpower, with an unflinching loyalty to the Emperor. Together with his Space Marine Legions, the Emperor set out from Terra to conquer the galaxy. Fighting for their master without fear or doubt, it was the Space Marines who first referred to their mission as the Great Crusade. World after world was reconquered, alien oppressors routed or annihilated in a series of epic wars and worlds infected with the taint of the Warp cleansed with apocalyptic orbital barrages.

During the Great Crusade the Space Marine Legions were reunited with their lost Primarchs, and the planets on which they had been raised (and now dominated) became the Legions' new homeworlds. With the Primarchs at the fore, the power of the Legions was at its zenith. Like gods they smote the battlefields of the Crusade and their names and legends would endure forever. Each was engineered to be a leader of men, a warrior and a hero; a mighty warlord whose martial fortitude was only matched by his charisma and mental prowess. Nothing could stand in the way of the Emperor and his mighty armies. The heroic dream of a united galaxy was almost within the Emperor's grasp. But in an act of vile treachery that echoes from a past of ten thousand years ago to the present day, the galaxy was soon to be damned forever.

The Great Betrayal

Horus, Primarch of the Sons of Horus and trusted Warmaster of the Emperor's armies, cast aside his oaths of loyalty and offered his fealty to the Dark Gods of Chaos, driving the Legions to turn upon one another as the Emperor stood on the very brink of his ultimate triumph. In what should have been their finest hour, brother fought brother and warriors that had stood shoulder to shoulder to carve the Emperor's realm from the flesh of the stars butchered one another in a civil war that set the galaxy afire. Worlds burned in the name of the Chaos Gods and a terror unlike any seen before was unleashed. Much of the truth of these times has been lost, obscured by the mists of time or embellished to the point where giants bestrode worlds with thunderous steps and the planets themselves cracked and split at their tread.

The traitorous forces of the rebel Warmaster drove all before them until the warriors still loyal to the Master of Mankind stood at bay within the walls of the Emperor's Palace on Terra itself. Blind hate and malice met courage and steel on the blood-slick ramparts of the Emperor's last bastion, the corrupted Primarchs horrifyingly revealed as the abominations they truly were. The forces of darkness pressed in around the guttering flame of Humanity, but desperate times called for desperate solutions and the Emperor and his most trusted warriors took the fight to Horus upon his starship, facing the traitor in his inner sanctum. Sanguinius of the Blood Angels, most beatific of the Primarchs, was slain and the Emperor cast down, broken and wounded almost unto death. But the Emperor was infused with unimaginable power and struck Horus down with the last ounce of his strength, destroying the traitor utterly and breaking the power of his Legions.

The followers of the Ruinous Powers were defeated, but it was victory won at terrible cost. The brotherhood of the Primarchs was no more. The Emperor's dream lay in ruins and the last, best hope of its achievement lost for all time. The conflict with Horus had shattered the Emperor's body; his immortal existence was now sustained for all eternity by constant sacrifice and the baroque machineries of the Golden Throne. The galactic empire he had forged was all but destroyed and it was to take many more years of brutal warfare before all the traitor forces were defeated and driven into the Eye of Terror. The death toll numbered in the billions. Uncounted worlds had been left as little more than corpse-haunted wastelands as the raging inferno of the Heresy was finally extinguished. In these dark times of anarchy and confusion, many human renegades and predatory aliens sought to plunder the reeling and mournful worlds of the Emperor.

The Scouring

Mankind teetered on the very brink of annihilation. It seemed that the Emperor's realm had weathered the storm of the Horus Heresy only to collapse in flames and blood in its aftermath. Without the Emperor's guidance, the greatest heroes of Mankind came to the fore to unite in the defence of his realm.

Roboute Guilliman, Primarch of the Ultramarines, rallied the surviving loyalist warriors and, together with his Legion of Space Marines, stood as a bulwark against the tide of enemies that sought to deliver the deathblow to the Emperor's dominion. Tutored on the world of Macragge, Guilliman understood the logistics of warfare better than any man alive. Together with his surviving brother Primarchs and their Legions, Guilliman held the scattered defenders of Humanity together through the nightmare that followed.

Knowing of Guilliman's lethal efficiency in war, Horus had masterfully planned his rebellion to begin while the Ultramarines were fighting far in the galactic south. As a result, the Ultramarines had come through the terrible wars largely unscathed. Yet even these mighty warriors were stretched to the limit in buying time for other loyalist forces to regroup and rearm. Legends tell that Guilliman was everywhere in these times, rallying defenders on one world and leading them to victory before moving on to another where his awe-inspiring skills might best serve humanity. Though invaders circled like vultures, the Space Marines and their Primarchs stood firm. Darkness looked sure to overwhelm them at every turn, but not one amongst them took a backwards step. So began the Age of the Imperium.

The Codex Astartes

With the threat of extinction held at bay, Guilliman turned to ensuring that such a catastrophe could never happen again, distilling his formidable wisdom into a mighty tome known as the Codex Astartes. This sacred text became the cornerstone upon which the future of the Imperium would be based.

For all its multitudinous topics, the most lasting and contentious decree of the Codex Astartes was that the existing Space Marine Legions be broken up into smaller organisations known as Chapters. Though many of his brother Primarchs initially railed against Guilliman's decree, almost all eventually accepted the necessity of the Codex. Thus were the Space Marine Chapters of the Adeptus Astartes born.

Upon the Codex's implimentation, each old Legion became a Chapter named for its forebear plus a number of other new Chapters. These new Chapters are known as the Second Founding. Each Chapter would take for itself a homeworld or fortress-monastery, and stand ready to defend the Imperium from all threats. The Codex decreed that each Chapter would be a thousand battle-brothers strong and look to its own recruitment, training and equipment. Though Chapters have often exceeded their basic fighting strength of one thousand souls during times of prolonged war, the desired effect was achieved. Never again would one man be able to command the awesome, terrifying power of a Space Marine Legion.

Legion	Primarch	World	Second Founding Chapters
Dark Angels	Lion El'Jonson	[Caliban]	Angels of Absolution, Angels of Redemption, Angels of Vengeance
All Records Expunged from Library... Order Origination: **UNKNOWN**			
Emperor's Children	Fulgrim	[Chemos]	Excommunicate Traitoris
Iron Warriors	Perturabo	[Olympia]	Excommunicate Traitoris
White Scars	Jaghatai Khan	Mundus Planus	Marauders, Rampagers, Destroyers, Storm Lords
Space Wolves	Leman Russ	Fenris	Wolf Brothers
Imperial Fists	Rogal Dorn	Terra	Black Templars, Crimson Fists
Night Lords	Konrad Curze	[Nostramo]	Excommunicate Traitoris
Blood Angels	Sanguinius	Baal	Angels Encarmine, Angels Sanguine, Angels Vermilion, Blood Drinkers, Fleshtearers
Iron Hands	Ferrus Manus	Medusa	Red Talons, Brazen Claws
All Records Expunged from Library... Order Origination: **UNKNOWN**			
World Eaters	Angron	No Record	Excommunicate Traitoris
Ultramarines	Roboute Guilliman	Macragge	Novamarines, Patriarchs of Ulixis, White Consuls, Black Consuls, Libators, Inceptors, Practors of Orpheus, Genesis Chapter
Death Guard	Mortarion	[Barbarus]	Excommunicate Traitoris
Thousand Sons	Magnus the Red	[Prospero]	Excommunicate Traitoris
Luna Wolves	Horus	[Cthonia]	Excommunicate Traitoris
Word Bearers	Lorgar	[Colchis]	Excommunicate Traitoris
Salamanders	Vulkan	Nocturne	None Known
Raven Guard	Corax	Deliverance	Black Guard, Revilers, Raptors
Alpha Legion	Alpharius	No Record	Excommunicate Traitoris

LEGION: Name of Legion when founded.
PRIMARCH: Name of Primarch from which Legion allegedly drew its gene-seed.
WORLD: Where Legion was based. Worlds in parentheses subsequently destroyed.

SECOND FOUNDING CHAPTERS: Chapters named in Apocrypha of Davio [M.33].
EXCOMMUNICATE TRAITORIS: Those Legions who turned during the Great Heresy as reported in the Grimoire Hereticus [M.35]

DARK ANGELS. For reasons undisclosed, the Dark Angels and their Second Founding successors refer to themselves as the Unforgiven.
Source: Mythos Angelica Mortis (M.36)

SPACE WOLVES. "The Space Wolves encourage genetic deviancy [re: extraordinary growth of canines] and show extreme unorthodoxy in their tactics and organisation."
Source: Personal Comment Inquisitor Horst (M.37)

BLOOD ANGELS. Blood Angels and their successors follow unconventional and deviant gene-replication practices which has led to the debasement of their gene-seed.

Rumours of 'Red Thirst' and 'Black Rage' still abound where the Blood Angels are concerned, despite investigation on numerous occasions.
Source: Authorised Report - Inquisitor Damne (M.34)

ULTRAMARINES. These are the named Successors to the Ultramarines Legion (Apocrypha of Davio), though the Apocrypha of Skaros states there are 23 Second Founding Chapters but fails to name them.
Source: Compiler Atreax (M.41)

The Ultramarines Legion is responsible for nearly 3/5ths of the gene-core of the current Space Marine Chapters. The Ultramarines Chapter rules large empire in Galactic South-East, known as Ultramar, one of the most powerful institutions on the Eastern Fringe.
Source: Liber Astartes (M.37)

LUNA WOLVES. The Luna Wolves were renamed Sons of Horus (c.125.M30). After the death of Horus, they became known as the Black Legion.
Source: Grimoire Hereticus (M.35)

The Horus Heresy had revealed weaknesses in the gene-seed of several Space Marine Legions. These defects had been exacerbated by the accelerated gene-seed cultivation techniques needed to keep the huge Space Marine Legions up to strength. The Chaos Powers were able to exploit the resultant physical and mental corruption to turn Horus' troops against the Emperor. So had the Emperor's great plan contained the seeds of its own downfall.

One of the key objectives of the new Codex Astartes was to recognise and expunge these genetic weaknesses. The Codex decreed that Space Marines would be created and trained slowly. The genetic banks used to create implants would be carefully monitored. Cultivated organs would be subject to the most stringent tests of purity. Young initiates were to undergo trials of suitability before they were accepted, and only those of the very sternest character would be chosen.

Each of the Second Founding Chapters was derived directly from an original First Founding Chapter and initially shared the same gene-seed. Subsequently the new Chapter's gene-seed was isolated, forming a new genetic line.

On Earth the Adeptus Terra set up genetic banks to produce and store Space Marine gene-seed. These banks were used to provide all new gene-seed for Space Marines. To prevent cross-contamination, the genetic stock of each Legion was isolated and henceforth the new Space Marine Chapters would receive gene-seed only from their own genetic stock. The gene-seed of the Traitor Legions was placed under a time-locked stasis seal, although at the time many believed these dangerous gene stocks had been destroyed. By taking direct control of the genetic stocks, the Adeptus on Earth could ultimately control the Space Marines. They alone had the power to destroy or create Space Marine armies at will.

It is not certain how many new Chapters were created during the Second Founding. Many Imperial records were lost during the later Age of Apostasy, a troubled time that lies across the history of the Imperium like a veil. In all likelihood some of the Chapters created during the Second Founding have since been destroyed, leaving no record of their deeds and glories. Others have been lost in most recent times, and their names are now all that remain of them. Some survive to this day, proud inheritors of the traditions of the Great Primarch and First Lord of the Ultramarines.

The Codex Astartes further defines the tactical roles, equipment specifications and uniform identification markings of the Space Marines. These guidelines have been much modified over the centuries, and the Codex Astartes of the 41st Millennium is a highly developed treatise combining the wisdom of hundreds of military thinkers throughout history. Some of its contents seem petty and restrictive, hardly worthy of the great mind of the Primarch. Others describe actual battles together with comments on the tactics employed and the decisions of the commanders on the spot. As such the Codex Astartes is revered as a holy text in many quarters. Some Chapters even regard the recommendations as sanctified by the Emperor himself.

The Codex Chapters

Most Chapters stick rigidly to the Codex patterns laid down for organisation, tactical roles and other processes. Others are largely organised according to the Codex but have slight variations, such as the Blood Angels and Dark Angels. A small number of Chapters are utterly different from the Codex, and owe nothing to it at all. The most famous of these wild Chapters is the Space Wolves. The Space Wolves have never followed the Codex Astartes – their strong willed Primarch moulded his Chapter very much in his own image, irrespective of other influences and doctrines.

Those Chapters that adhere rigidly to Guilliman's teachings are sometimes referred to as Codex Chapters. These Space Marines adhere to the Codex as the model for their organisation and identification markings. Of all the Codex Chapters the oldest and most famous is the Ultramarines, the Chapter of the Primarch Roboute Guilliman himself. Many of the other Codex Chapters are descended from the Ultramarines' genetic line.

The Adeptus Terra has never felt it necessary to enforce the Codex absolutely. Indeed it is doubtful if it could. However, with subsequent foundings they have always favoured the Ultramarines' gene-seed and created new Codex Chapters from their line. With the passage of years some of these Chapters have subsequently strayed from the strict letter of the Codex, introducing new variations but remaining broadly faithful to the principles of Roboute Guilliman.

Subsequent Foundings

The history of the Imperium since the Heresy is not a continuous story. There have been periods of rebellion and anarchy; times when the balance of power has suddenly changed and history has been quite literally re-written.

Many of the subsequent foundings of Space Marines belong to these troubled times, making it impossible to ascertain when some Chapters were created. Indeed, it is impossible to say for certain how many Chapters have been created. All that is known is that there are approximately a thousand Chapters in existence today, scattered throughout the galaxy. Of these, more than half are descended from the Ultramarines, either directly or indirectly through one of the Primogenitor Chapters. By their reverent obedience to the tenets of the Codex, these Chapters do honour to their forebears, to Roboute Guilliman, and to the immortal Emperor himself.

THE CURSED FOUNDING

The Twenty First Founding was the largest since the Second Founding. It took place in the 36th Millennium, sometime before the Age of Apostasy, a time of civil war which almost destroyed the Imperium. The new Chapters were dogged by bad luck right from the start. Several disappeared mysteriously whilst in action or voyaging through Warpspace.

Surviving Chapters of the founding are affected by spontaneous genetic mutation of their gene-seed. As a result these Chapters have gradually dwindled in size as their inability to raise and induct recruits means that casualties cannot be replaced. Worse still, some have developed genetic idiosyncrasies, mutations that strain the tolerance of the Inquisition and threaten the Chapter's survival.

Few Chapters have suffered as ignominious an end as the Flame Falcons, whose spontaneous and extreme physical corruption turned them into a race no longer human nor sane. Eventually the entire Chapter was declared Excommunicate and driven from its home world of Lethe by the Grey Knights. Surviving brotherhoods remember the Flame Falcons with a mix of sorrow and shame, and pray that they will not share the same fate.

THE MAKING OF A SPACE MARINE

The blood and sinew of legendary heroes, forged anew for an age of war.

Every Chapter of Space Marines must induct new warriors into its ranks in order to survive. Most have recruited from their Chapter Planets and nearby worlds since the foundation of their brotherhood. This explains why many Chapters are based on feral or otherwise deadly worlds – the recruiting stock is far stronger on planets where every day is a struggle to survive. Aspirants must always be chosen when they are young, before they become too mature to accept the gene-seed that will turn them into Space Marines. Each gene-seed comprises a series of genetically tailored organs that are carefully implanted into the recruit's body. These act upon the body's natural chemistry in conjunction with hypnotherapy and physical training. For example, the implantation of a small organ called the biscopea greatly accentuates the effects of hormones controlling muscle growth, and so is the foundation of a Space Marine's prodigious strength.

Gene-seed is a finite resource, for it is a direct delineant of the bio-manipulations that created the Emperor's Primarchs. In a very real sense, the blood of the Primarchs flows through each Space Marine's veins. It is without doubt a Chapter's single most valuable possession, for it alone allows the continued recruitment and development of Battle-Brothers. Gene-seed implants work in conjunction with body tissues to stimulate natural abilities or create abilities that are wholly new. The implants rely on the body's natural growth process to incorporate them into the Space Marine's physiology. This organ implantation goes hand in hand with a harsh routine of physical and spiritual training. This is achieved by means of hypnotic suggestion, prolonged meditation, vigorous spiritual tests, and gradual initiation into the cult rites of the Chapter. All of these processes serve to harden the Space Marine's mental prowess and sharpen his instinctual senses.

Mucranoid – The Weaver
This organ responds to chemical stimuli, causing the Space Marine to secrete a waxy substance that seals his skin. Marines are cocooned in this way before they enter suspended animation, and the process can even protect them from vacuum and extremes of temperature.

Larraman's Organ – The Healer
When a Space Marine is wounded, the blood forms an instant layer of scar tissue, staunching blood flow and protecting the wound. This organ is responsible for producing the special blood cells called Larraman cells that make this possible.

Omophagea – The Remembrancer
Space Marines can gain part of a person or creature's memory by eating its flesh. This special organ is implanted between the thoracic vertebrae and the stomach wall. It works by absorbing genetic material from the meal itself.

Occulobe – The Eye of Vengeance
Thanks to this organ, Space Marines have eyesight that is far sharper and more capable in low-light environs than a normal man's.

Secondary Heart – The Maintainer
Situated on the right side of their chest, this secondary heart is capable of boosting the blood supply or maintaining full life functions with the primary's destruction.

Biscopea – The Forge of Strength
This organ is implanted into the chest cavity where it releases special muscle-building hormones, greatly increasing the Space Marine's strength.

Oolitic Kidney – The Purifier
This emergency detoxificaton organ allows a Space Marine to survive poisons and gases that are too powerful for even his rugged system.

Preomnor – The Neutraliser
Space Marines have a second or pre-stomach that allows them to eat otherwise poisonous or indigestible materials. Deadly poisons are either neutralised or isolated from the digestive tract.

Interface – The Black Carapace
The hardened and shell-like ribcage of the Space Marine is covered with a stiff membrane. Neuron connectors from the membrane penetrate the Space Marine's spine and connect his motor nervous system to the interface. Connectors on the interface link up to the Space Marine's armour, equipment controls or monitors. This allows the Space Marine to control an armoured suit with all the speed and precision of his own body.

Haemastamen – The Blood Maker
The Haemastamen alters the constituent make-up of the host's blood, making it considerably more efficient than that of an ordinary human.

Multi-lung – The Imbiber
Space Marines can close off their normal lungs in favour of the bio-engineered multi-lung. The multi-lung enables the host to breath poisonous atmospheres or even water.

Lyman's Ear – The Sentinel
The internal organs of the normal human ear are removed and replaced with the Lyman's Ear. As a result, a Space Marine's hearing is not only sharper, but they can filter out or enhance specific sounds. The organ also affects balance, so a Space Marine is unlikely to become disoriented as a result of motion.

Sus-an Membrane – The Hibernator
This brain implant allows a Space Marine to enter a voluntary state of suspended animation in which he can survive for centuries if necessary.

Betcher's Gland – The Poison Bite
A Space Marine can synthesise acidic poison in this modified salivary gland which he can spit at foes or use to burn away the strongest of metals.

Ossmodula – The Ironheart
This small implant made into the lower part of the brain affects bone growth. As a result, Space Marines have a tremendously strong and fast-healing skeleton and their rib cage is fused into a solid protective shell.

Neuroglottis – The Devourer
By chewing, tasting or smelling a substance a Space Marine can test it for toxicity and nutritive content. The organ also allows the Space Marine to identify subtle odours in the same way as a tracker dog.

Catalepsean Node – The Unsleeping
Space Marines can rest half of their brain at once, and thus stay awake for days at a time. The Catalepsean Node which makes this possible is implanted into the brain where it controls circadian rhythms of sleep and the Space Marine's response to sleep deprivation.

Progenoids – The Gene-seeds
Every Space Marine has these organs, one implanted in the neck and another in the chest. The organs respond to the presence of other implants in the body by creating germ cells corresponding to those implants. These germ cells grow and are stored in the progenoid organs. Mature progenoid organs can be removed and new implants artificially cultured from them. This is the only way new implants can be created, so a Chapter depends upon its Space Marines to create other Space Marines.

HISTORY OF THE ULTRAMARINES

According to legend the Emperor created the Primarchs from artificially engineered genes, carefully imbuing each of them with unique superhuman powers. Legend goes on to tell how the Dark Gods of Chaos spirited away the Primarchs within their incubator capsules, scattering them widely throughout the Warp. More than one of the capsules was breached whilst it drifted through Warpspace – the forces of the Warp leaked in, wreaking havoc to the developing genetic material inside the capsule. Undoubtedly damage was done, although the nature of that damage would not become apparent until the Horus Heresy.

The Youth of Roboute Guilliman

After drifting for decades, or in some cases even hundreds of years, the twenty incubation capsules came to rest on human worlds throughout the galaxy – distant planets inhabited by a variety of human cultures. The capsule containing the developing form of one Primarch fell upon the world of Macragge. This was a bleak but not inhospitable world that Mankind had inhabited for many centuries. Its industries had survived the Age of Strife and its people had continued to build spacecraft throughout the period of intense Warpstorms. The people of Macragge had successfully maintained contact with neighbouring systems, despite the loss of many ships and crews.

The Primarch's capsule was discovered by a group of noblemen out hunting in the forest. They broke the capsule's seal to reveal a striking child surrounded by a glowing nimbus of power. The amazing infant was brought before Konor, one of a pair of Consuls who governed the civilised part of Macragge. Konor adopted the child as his son and named him Roboute.

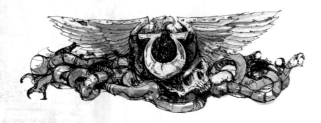

The young Primarch grew quickly, and as he did so his unique physical and mental powers became obvious for all to see. By his tenth birthday he had studied and mastered everything the wisest men of Macragge could teach him. His insight into matters of history, philosophy and science astonished his elders, but his greatest talent lay in the art of war. A genius for military organisation prompted his father to give him command of an expeditionary force in the far north of Macragge. This mountainous area was called Illyrium, a barbarous land which had harboured bandits and brigands for as long as anyone could remember. Although many wars had been fought against them, no-one had ever pacified the region for long. Roboute fought a brilliant campaign and won not only the submission, but also the respect, of the fierce Illyrian warriors.

Returning home Roboute found the capital in turmoil. During Roboute's absence his father's co-Consul, a man called Gallan, had crafted a conspiracy against Konor. Gallan was one of many amongst the wealthy nobility who were jealous of Konor's power and popularity. These malcontents were accustomed to easy living on their vast estates where they were supported by the toiling of impoverished slaves. Konor had changed all that, forcing the old aristocracy to provide their vassals with reasonable accommodation and food. He had also passed legislation which obliged them to contribute to an ambitious programme of improving and enlarging the city. All these reforms were of great benefit to the people of Macragge, but were unpopular with all but a few of the more far-sighted aristocrats.

As Roboute and his army approached Macragge City they saw the smoke from fires and hurried to investigate. From citizens fleeing from the city, Roboute learned that troops in the pay of Gallan had attacked the Senate House with Konor and his loyal bodyguard inside. The rebels surrounded the Senate, whilst drunken soldiers roamed the city looting and murdering at will.

Roboute hurried to his father's rescue. Leaving his troops to deal with the drunken mob, he fought his way into the Senate House. There he found his father dying of wounds inflicted by an assassin in Gallan's employ. For three whole days the Consul had directed the defence of the building, even as surgeons fought for his life. With his dying breath Konor told his son of Gallan's treachery.

Roboute crushed the rebels and quickly restored order to the city. Thousands of citizens flocked to the Senate House and amidst a wave of popular acclaim Roboute assumed the mantle of sole and all-powerful Consul of Macragge. The new ruler acted swiftly to crush the old order. Gallan and his fellow conspirators were executed and their lands and family titles taken from them. New, honest, hard-working settlers were given their old farms and property. With super-human energy and vision the Consul reorganised the social order of Macragge, rewarding the hard-working, placing men of honour in high office, and building the armed forces into a powerful and well equipped force. Macragge flourished as never before.

The Emperor Reaches Macragge

While the capsules containing the Primarchs drifted through the Warp, the Emperor and his armies advanced across the galaxy. This Great Crusade liberated many worlds from alien domination and re-established contact with human planets which had endured isolation and danger for untold thousands of years.

As the young Roboute Guilliman waged war against the Illyrian bandits in the northern mountains of Macragge, the Emperor and a force of Space Marines reached the planet of Espandor in a neighbouring system. From the Espandorians the Emperor learned of Macragge and the astounding son of Consul Konor. He immediately realised that he had found one of the long lost Primarchs.

Though the Emperor took ship to Macragge his vessel ran into a sudden and unexpected Warp-squall, a brief but intensely strong disturbance that threw the craft far off-course. By the time the Emperor reached Macragge, Roboute Guilliman had ruled for almost five years. In that time the world had undergone a transformation. Its people were well-fed and prosperous, its armies well-equipped and its cities had been rebuilt in glittering marble and shining steel. Vessels from Macragge plied regular trade with the local systems, bringing raw materials and more people to the flourishing world. The Emperor was astounded to find a world so well-ordered and prosperous, and realised at once that Roboute Guilliman was a Primarch of unsurpassed ability and vision.

The Ultramarines Legion of Space Marines was assigned to the control of Roboute Guilliman and its forward base relocated to Macragge. The Primarch quickly assimilated the many wonders of the Imperium and set about his new role with skill and enthusiasm. Guilliman's chief talents, as ever, lay in war, and he led the Ultramarines to fresh conquests in the galactic south. He succeeded in liberating more worlds during the Great Crusade than any other Primarch, and the worlds he brought within the Imperium were to benefit from his organisational skills and passion for efficient government. Whenever Roboute Guilliman freed a world from tyranny, his first priority was to set up a self-supporting defence system. Once a world was safe he could move on, leaving behind enough advisers to ensure that industry would be created, trading routes set up with the Imperium, and government directed towards the prosperity of the people.

Fortress Macragge

Meanwhile, the fortress of the Ultramarines grew on Macragge. Some Ultramarines remained behind to supervise the work, which progressed rapidly thanks to the trading network and advanced industries of the planet. Within a year a training base was established, and recruiting began on the planet Macragge and surrounding worlds. It was not long before the Ultramarines Legion received its first influx of warriors born and bred on Macragge. Thanks to the thoroughness of their organisation, the Ultramarines were able to receive constant recruits throughout the Great Crusade. Because of their strong recruitment base and Roboute Guilliman's tactical expertise, the Ultramarines soon became the largest Space Marine Legion, having more recruits and suffering fewer casualties than any other Legion.

After the Heresy

Whilst the Horus Heresy plunged the Imperium into savagery and civil war, the Ultramarines were engaged on the southern edge of the galaxy. Their very success had carried them far from Earth and isolated them from the conquering armies of Warmaster Horus in the north-east. News of Horus's treachery did not reach the Ultramarines until the attack on Earth was underway. Thanks to the speed of Horus's attack there was little that Roboute Guilliman could do in support of his Emperor. None of the worlds already liberated by the Ultramarines were in serious danger from the forces of Chaos. Consequently, the Ultramarines were poorly placed to contribute during the early stages of the Horus Heresy.

As fate would have it, the Ultramarines were therefore largely untouched by the fighting of the Horus Heresy. Other loyal Space Marine Legions had lost thousands of troops during the fighting, and half of the original Legions had sided with Horus. As a result the number of Space Marines left was very few, yet never were they more needed.

The confusion and disorder following the Horus Heresy had left the Imperium weak and vulnerable. Everywhere the enemies of mankind prepared to attack. Many worlds remained in the grip of Chaos. Into this breach stepped Roboute Guilliman and the Ultramarines. Always the largest Legion, the Ultramarines found themselves divided and dispatched all over the Imperium in a desperate effort to stem the tide of invasion and unrest.

The Ultramarines successfully held the Imperium together during a time of intense danger. Macragge was able to supply new recruits at such a rate that before long the Ultramarines alone accounted for more than half the total number of Space Marines, and few were the systems where their heroism went unnoticed.

Within a decade, order was restored to the Imperium. Even as the Ultramarines reconquered, a new theory of warfare was emerging. Under the guidance of the Ultramarines' Primarch, the Codex Astartes was taking shape. Its doctrines would reshape the future of all Space Marines and forevermore dictate the foundation for the Imperium's military strength and the ultimate survival of Mankind.

The Second Founding

The Second Founding of the Space Marines was decreed seven years after the death of Horus. Most of the old Legions divided into fewer than five Chapters, but the Ultramarines were divided many times. The exact number of Chapters created from the Ultramarines is uncertain: the number listed in the oldest copy of the Codex Astartes gives the total as twenty three, but does not name them.

With the Second Founding, the size of the Ultramarines force was much reduced. Most of the Space Marines left Macragge to establish new Chapters elsewhere. The Ultramarines fortress was built to accommodate more than ten times as many Space Marines as now remained on their homeworld. As a result its arsenals and weapon shops were partially dismantled and taken by the new Chapters to found their own bases. The genetic banks of the Ultramarines, and the huge recruitment organisation, were similarly reduced.

As a result of the Second Founding, the Ultramarines' gene-seed became pre-eminent. The new Chapters created from the Ultramarines during the Second Founding are often referred to as the Primogenitors, or `first born'. The lasting heritage of Guilliman was not only genetic, but spiritual. Even to this day all the Primogenitor Chapters venerate Roboute Guilliman as their own founding father and patron, and hold the ruler of Ultramar, whoever he be, as the exemplar of all that it means to be a Space Marine. So did the Ultramarines rise to become preeminent amongst their brother Chapters.

Ultramar

One aspect of the Ultramarines Legion that survived the Second Founding was the close relationship between the Space Marines and the populations of the surrounding planets. During the Great Crusade the worlds around Macragge provided young recruits for the Ultramarines. They also supplied raw materials, armaments and spacecraft. Although the need to recruit from these worlds diminished almost to vanishing point with the reorganisation, the tradition continued. To this day, the Ultramarines recruit not from a single world, but from the whole of local space. This area around Macragge is called Ultramar, the stellar empire of the Ultramarines.

Ultramar is unique amongst the domains of the Space Marines. Where other Chapters rule over a single planet, asteroid or, in some cases, a mobile space fleet or orbital fortress, the Ultramarines have a larger domain. They control no fewer than eight local systems, each with its own worlds and governments loyal to the Chapter. All the worlds of Ultramar share a common cultural heritage with Macragge, so it is not surprising that their styles of architecture, government, and traditions are similar.

After the Horus Heresy all eight worlds benefited from the improving reforms of Roboute Guilliman and its citizens are disciplined, productive and loyal. As a result, Ultramar is a wealthy empire that knows little unrest and no rebellion – a somewhat unique distinction in the desperate days of the 41st Millennium. The population live in sprawling cities, but these cities are surrounded by extensive farmlands and seas that teem with fish.

Each of Ultramar's worlds are self-sufficient in raw materials and food. Trade between the planets is active, and each planet has its specialities and delicacies. Each world is balanced as a society and also as an ecosystem - although composed of primarily industrial worlds, Ultramar has none of the nightmarish toxic wastelands that are common phenomena throughout the galaxy. It is therefore little wonder that many system governors and planetary lords regard Ultramar with an envious eye.

The worlds of Ultramar are by no means identical. Macragge itself is mostly bleak and rocky, with more than three-quarters of its land mass formed from mountainous upland almost entirely devoid of life. The people of Macragge do not live in this inhospitable region, but the fortress of the Ultramarines is built here upon a craggy peak surrounded by impenetrable mountains. Within this mighty fortress, inside a vast temple, is the shrine of the Primarch himself. This is where his body sits upon a huge throne of ornately carved marble. He is preserved in death by a stasis field impervious to the decaying effects of time. This is one of the holiest places in the Imperium, and thousands come from all over the galaxy to look upon the face of the ancient Primarch.

Other worlds are quite different from Macragge. Talassar is a planet of storm-tossed seas and rocky islands whose single continent is known as Glaudor, which was the site of a major battle between the Ultramarines and invading Orks immediately after the Horus Heresy. In contrast to the oceanic world of Talassar are the three arid planets of Quintarn, Tarentus and Masali.

These small planets form a triple world combination orbiting around a common centre of gravity much like the Earth and its moon. Gigantic horticultural cities cover hundreds of square miles, capturing precious water in wind traps and storing it in massive underground tanks. The cities of the Three Planets are enclosed by gigantic domes under which flourish forests and gardens as lush as any in Ultramar.

Calth is an airless world whose inhabitants live in underground cities where the deadly light of Calth's blue sun cannot reach them. The caverns of Calth are constructed on such a huge scale, and with such grandeur, that they are as light and airy as any city of Macragge. Of all the local worlds Calth is the most specialised, for although its people grow vast quantities of food in nutrient vats, they prefer to import most of what they eat from the neighbouring system of Iax. Calth is famous for its shipyards, which provide the craft used by the Ultramarines as well as civil and military craft for wider use in the Imperium.

Iax is sometimes described as the Garden of Ultramar. Its climate and fertility have made it one of the most naturally productive worlds in the Imperium. The inhabitants have harnessed the planet's inherent verdancy, covering its surface with well-ordered farms and cultivated woodlands. There are no large cities on Iax, but many small towns dotted over the landscape, connected together by an efficient system of fast hydroways. The oldest and most urbanised area of Iax is the ancient city of First Landing, whose citadel has withstood the barrages of invaders over the centuries. Legend has it that Guilliman came to Iax many times, and that he treasured the world almost as much as his beloved Macragge.

Prandium once teemed with life. Settlers from Macragge established a colony on the planet after the Horus Heresy. Thanks to a mild climate and fertile virgin environment the people of Prandium prospered. The planet soon become the most beautiful jewel of Ultramar, a planet of markable prosperity and an incredibly rich native fauna. Prandium was destroyed by Hive Fleet Behemoth in the First Tyrannic War. The lifeless world is now reduced to bedrock, its atmosphere blown into space by the ferocity of the Tyranid attack.

Most distant from Macragge is the world of Espandor, a planet of extensive forests whose major cities are confined to the westernmost of its two continents. Espandor is a secondary settlement whose people are the descendants of explorers from Macragge and hold considerable pride in their rugged existence. Tradition has it that Espandor was settled during the Age of Strife by traders blown off-course and subsequently stranded by Warpstorms. It is the least densely populated of all the worlds of Ultramar.

The Military of Ultramar

Ultramar is the realm of the Ultramarines within the greater realm of humanity that is the Imperium. Its worlds do not pay the Imperium's tithes. Instead they contribute directly towards the upkeep of the Ultramarines Chapter. The rulers of the individual worlds of Ultramar are feudal lords of the Master of the Ultramarines. This is why the Ultramarines leader is also the Lord of Ultramar, with all the rights and responsibilities that such a title entails.

Just like other worlds in the Imperium, each world of Ultramar raises regiments for its own defence. Most worlds in the Imperium are obliged to provide regiments for the Imperial Guard when required, but Space Marine homeworlds are an exception. In the case of Ultramar, however, the Ultramarines rule so efficiently and are so prosperous that they maintain several hundred regiments ready and willing to join the Imperial Guard when the need arises. As a result, regiments from Ultramar have fought all over the galaxy, often in campaigns alongside the Ultramarines themselves.

Each world of Ultramar also provides Space Marine recruits for the Ultramarines Chapter itself. Throughout Ultramar, proud citizens point to public statues of famous Ultramarines who were born to local families. Amongst the older aristocratic dynasties it is a matter of considerable esteem to send recruits to the Ultramarines. For a family to have provided a renowned hero, perhaps even an actual Master of the Chapter, is a great honour that brings considerable fame and status for generations.

THE SHRINE OF THE PRIMARCH

The Shrine of Guilliman is one of the most holy places in the entire Imperium, and one which welcomes millions of pilgrims every year. It lies within the Temple of Correction, a vaulted sepulchre forming a small part of the Ultramarines' vast northern polar fortress.

The temple is a miracle of construction and typical of the attention to detail to which the Ultramarines apply themselves. Its proportions defy the human mind by the scope and grandeur of design. The multi-coloured glass dome that forms the roof is the largest of its kind. Even the Techno-magi of the Adeptus Mechanicus come to marvel at the structure said to have been designed by Roboute Guilliman himself. According to the Ultramarines there is enough marble within the temple to build a mountain, and sufficient adamantium and shining plasteel to construct a sizable warfleet.

Within this edifice is the great marble throne of Roboute Guilliman, and upon that throne sits a regal corpse. Though the best part of ten thousand years have passed since his death, the Primarch's body is perfectly preserved. Even his death wounds are visible upon his throat. His mortal remains are preserved from the ravages of time by means of a stasis field that isolates the Primarch from the time-stream. Everything encompassed by the field is trapped in time and can neither change nor decay.

There are some, however, who claim the Primarch's wounds do change. They say that Guilliman's body is slowly recovering and that his wounds show mysterious signs of healing. Others deny the phenomena, and point out the sheer impossibility of change within the stasis field. Yet enough believe the stories to come and witness for themselves the miracle of the Primarch.

CHAPTER ORGANISATION

A significant part of the Codex Astartes is given over to the organisation of a Space Marine Chapter.

Each of the ten companies that comprises a Chapter is led by a Space Marine Captain and includes supernumeraries such as the Company's Chaplain and Apothecary. The official fighting strength of each company is made up of ten squads each of ten Space Marines led by a Sergeant, though of course injury and other circumstances may mean that a company takes to the field with as little as sixty or seventy Brother-Marines.

Of the ten companies, one company, usually the 1st Company, consists of the Chapter's most experienced veterans. The veterans of the 1st Company are masters of all battlefield roles, and are permitted to fight as Sternguard or Vanguard squads as their proficiencies dictate, and can even fight in revered suits of Terminator armour should the mission goal require it. It is rare for the 1st Company to be fielded en masse – its units normally take to the field alongside the Chapter's Battle Companies.

The Codex decrees that the 2nd, 3rd, 4th and 5th companies should be designated 'Battle Companies'. These formations carry the main weight of the Chapter's combat duties. Each Battle Company consists of six squads of Tactical Space Marines, two of Assault, and two of Devastators. The Assault squads of the Battle Company may be deployed as Bike squadrons or Land Speeder crews, should theatre conditions require it. Most Space Marine deployments will consist of a single Battle Company, heavily reinforced by elements of the Veteran, Scout and Reserve Companies.

The 'Companies of Reserve' are entirely composed of squads of the same designation. They normally act in support of the Battle Companies and provide a source of replacements for any casualties suffered by the line formations. The 6th and 7th Companies are Tactical companies, each consisting of ten Tactical squads. These are intended to act as a reserve which may be used to bolster the main line, launch diversionary attacks, or stem enemy flanking manouevres. The 6th Company is also trained to use bikes, and the entire Company may be deployed as bike squadrons. Similarly squads of the 7th Company are trained to fight with Land Speeders and the Company commonly acts as a light vehicle reserve formation.

The 8th Company is an Assault Company consisting of ten Assault squads. This is the most mobile company and is often equipped with jump packs, bikes and Land Speeders.

The 8th Company is used in the assault role and wherever a strong hand-to-hand fighting force is needed – it is a truly fearsome and mobile foe.

The 9th Company is a Devastator Company, consisting of ten Devastator squads. It is the most powerfully equipped company in the Chapter and is used to bolster defence points and provide long range support.

The Chapter's 10th Company is its Scout Company consisting of a number of Scout squads. Scouts are youths who have been recruited and partially transformed into Space Marines. Until their physical transformation and training is complete they fight as Scouts. The Codex Astartes dictates no formal size for a Scout Company as the rate of recruitment is not a fixed amount.

All of the companies, except the Scout Company, maintain Rhino transports for each of their squads and officers. The 1st Company also has a permanent establishment of Land Raiders for carrying Terminator squads.

Many of the Battle Companies and Reserve Companies include a number of Dreadnoughts. It is customary for a Dreadnought to remain a part of the company in which he served before being interred in the metal sarcophagus, and his presence greatly bolsters the company's fighting strength.

A Chapter also includes a number of officers and specialists who stand aside from the company organisation. These individuals are known as the headquarters staff and they may be assigned to fight with a company in battle. Included amongst them are psychic Librarians from the Chapter's Librarius, Chaplains from the Reclusiam, and Techmarines together with their Servitors.

> "We follow in the footsteps of Guilliman.
> As it is written in the Codex, so shall it be."
>
> Marneus Calgar, Chapter Master of the Ultramarines

There are relatively few of these senior officers as most non-combatant roles within the Chapter are performed by the Chapter's human serfs. The two largest groups are the Librarians and the Techmarines. Consequently, these two are set aside from the other headquarters staff and considered as separate organisations.

Although the Codex describes a number of ranks and responsibilities within the headquarters staff, only a very few of these officers actually accompany the Chapter to war. Many are non-combatants of advanced years whose roles are to find and train recruits or administrate the Chapter, other titles are borne by the Chapter's Captains. Some ranks described by the Codex include the Chapter's Ancient (or Standard Bearer), the Chapter Master's Secretarius, the Lord of the Household, the Chapter's Armourer, the Master of the Fleet, Victuallers, the Master of the Arsenal, Master of Recruits and the Master of the Watch.

ULTRAMARINES CHAPTER ORGANISATION

This diagram represents the composition of the Ultramarines Chapter circa 999.M41. It should be noted that although the fighting strength of each squad is officially ten Space Marines, combat attrition dictates that squads may go into battle under optimal strength. Transport vehicles and special equipment (such as bikes, Land Speeders and so on) are not listed, as each company will draw such equipment contingent to mission parameters.

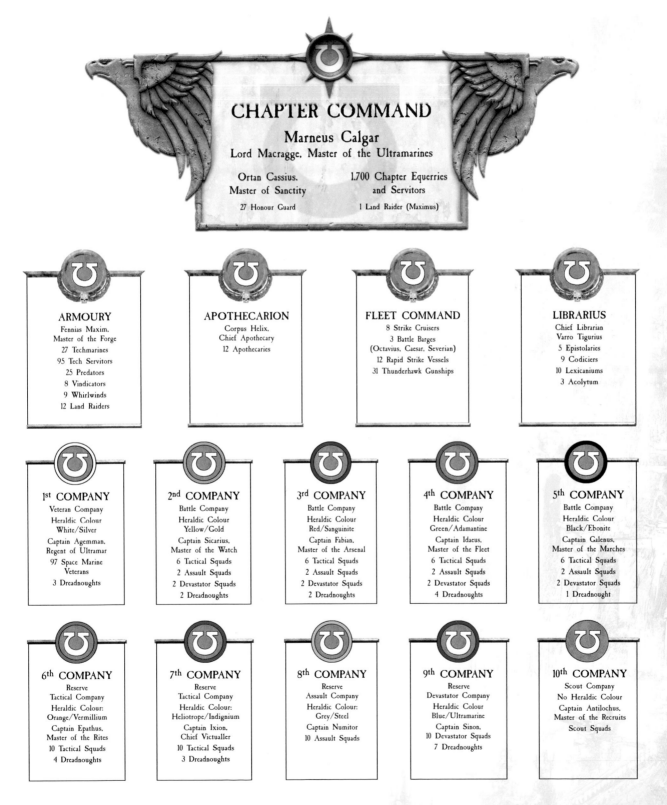

CHAPTER COMMAND

Marneus Calgar
Lord Macragge, Master of the Ultramarines

Ortan Cassius,
Master of Sanctity

1,700 Chapter Equerries
and Servitors

27 Honour Guard

1 Land Raider (Maximus)

ARMOURY
Fennias Maxim,
Master of the Forge
27 Techmarines
95 Tech Servitors
25 Predators
8 Vindicators
9 Whirlwinds
12 Land Raiders

APOTHECARION
Corpus Helix,
Chief Apothecary
12 Apothecaries

FLEET COMMAND
8 Strike Cruisers
3 Battle Barges
(Octavius, Caesar, Severian)
12 Rapid Strike Vessels
31 Thunderhawk Gunships

LIBRARIUS
Chief Librarian
Varro Tigurius
5 Epistolaries
9 Codiciers
10 Lexicaniums
3 Acolytum

1st COMPANY
Veteran Company
Heraldic Colour
White/Silver
Captain Agemman,
Regent of Ultramar
97 Space Marine
Veterans
3 Dreadnoughts

2nd COMPANY
Battle Company
Heraldic Colour
Yellow/Gold
Captain Sicarius,
Master of the Watch
6 Tactical Squads
2 Assault Squads
2 Devastator Squads
2 Dreadnoughts

3rd COMPANY
Battle Company
Heraldic Colour
Red/Sanguinite
Captain Fabian,
Master of the Arsenal
6 Tactical Squads
2 Assault Squads
2 Devastator Squads
2 Dreadnoughts

4th COMPANY
Battle Company
Heraldic Colour
Green/Adamantine
Captain Idaeus,
Master of the Fleet
6 Tactical Squads
2 Assault Squads
2 Devastator Squads
4 Dreadnoughts

5th COMPANY
Battle Company
Heraldic Colour
Black/Ebonite
Captain Galenus,
Master of the Marches
6 Tactical Squads
2 Assault Squads
2 Devastator Squads
1 Dreadnought

6th COMPANY
Reserve
Tactical Company
Heraldic Colour:
Orange/Vermillium
Captain Epathus,
Master of the Rites
10 Tactical Squads
4 Dreadnoughts

7th COMPANY
Reserve
Tactical Company
Heraldic Colour:
Heliotrope/Indignium
Captain Ixion,
Chief Victualler
10 Tactical Squads
3 Dreadnoughts

8th COMPANY
Reserve
Assault Company
Heraldic Colour:
Grey/Steel
Captain Numitor
10 Assault Squads

9th COMPANY
Reserve
Devastator Company
Heraldic Colour
Blue/Ultramarine
Captain Sinon,
10 Devastator Squads
7 Dreadnoughts

10th COMPANY
Scout Company
No Heraldic Colour
Captain Antilochus,
Master of the Recruits
Scout Squads

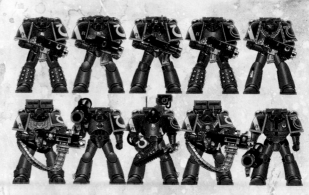

Assault Squad Ixion "Macragge's Avengers"

Squad Ixion swore vengeance for Macragge and have honed their Tyranid-fighting skills against Hive Fleets Leviathan, Kraken and Jormungandr.

Devastator Squad Tirian "Guilliman's Hammer"

Renowned across the segmentum for their steadfast and unwavering conduct in battle.

Brother Agnathio

Blessed with Dreadnought armour following the Fall of Chundrabad, 141.M36.

Tactical Squad Vandar "The Victors"

Veteran Sergeant Vandar is the youngest ever recipient of the Iron Halo, awarded for tactical brilliance during the Tamari rebellions of 929.M41.

Tactical Squad Solinus "The Indomitable"

Received Victorex Maxima honours during the retaking of Fort Telrendar, where they were first into the breach after Captain Sicarius.

Tactical Squad Manorian "The Shield Bearers"

Boasting many experienced and honoured warriors, Squad Manorian leads the vanguard of both Company and Chapter-level assaults.

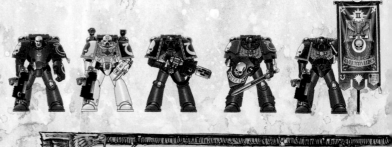

Command Squad "Lions of Macragge"

Comprising Veteran Sergeant Daceus, Apothecary Venatio, Honoured Brother Gaius Prabian, Brother Vandius (Company Standard Bearer) and Brother Malcian.

THE ULTRAMARINES

Heroes all, united in defence

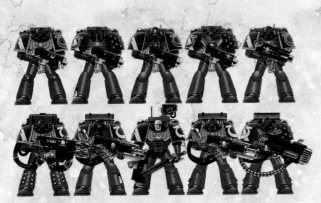

Devastator Squad Atavian "The Titan Slayers"
Awarded the Principex Maxima for their destruction of the Renegade Warlord Titan Soulmauler.

Assault Squad Strabo "The Heroes of Selonopolis"
Responsible for the death of Warboss Bonehamma and the rout of his horde amid the ash wastes of hive world Selonopolis.

Tactical Squad Octavian "Swords of Judgement"
Between them the members of Squad Octavian have earnt an impressive total of fifteen Marksman's Honour badges for their uncanny precision.

Brother Ultracius
Blessed with Dreadnought armour following the Pyra Crusades of 453.M39.

Tactical Squad Vorolanus "The Thunderbolts"
Squad Vorolanus conducts many of the Company's reconnaissance and deep-strike missions when dedicated Scout units are unavailable.

Tactical Squad Fennion "The Immortals"
Squad Fennion has not taken even a single casualty since its current roster was formed in 829.M41, despite performing many perilous frontline duties.

Captain Cato Sicarius
Master of the Watch, Knight Champion of Macragge.

Chaplain Elianu Trajan
Attached to the 2nd Company since 901.M41

"We are the slayers of kings, the destroyers of worlds, bringers of ruination and death in all its forms. These things we do in the name of the Emperor and in the defence of Mankind. Let none stay our wrath."

Cato Sicarius
Captain of the Ultramarines 2nd Company

SECOND COMPANY
of Macragge and all Mankind

SPACE MARINE POWER ARMOUR

Most humans who have any contact with Space Marines will know and recognise the most common types of Space Marine armour quite readily. However there are older types of armour (also known as marks) which remain in service to this day and whose design differs greatly. Indeed, many of the older variants have special associations for particularly old or honoured Chapters and so may be worn by ceremonial guards or by elite units. Other Chapters are less formal in their use of armour, mixing various types into their fighting units with little or no regard for conformity. The degree of uniformity within a Chapter varies a great deal and is often determined by historical precedent or tradition.

Each Chapter's power armour is maintained by skilled Artificers. These are not Space Marines, but dedicated servants who spend their lives working for the Chapter. Over the history of a Chapter, especially talented Artificers become famous and justly celebrated, and examples of their work are much sought after. When a Space Marine earns a combat honour it is the Artificers who fashion the honour badge and fasten it onto the Marine's armour. Similarly, the Artificers make rank badges, long service accolades and other awards of distinction.

Artificers religiously hunt down elements of ancient armour. Such pieces will be lovingly restored, often plated with silver or gold, and then painstakingly engraved with naturalistic scenes, abstract designs or Chapter badges. Older types of armour are associated with the past history of many Chapters and often with the deeds of heroic individuals. A piece of armour that belonged to an old Chapter hero is valued above all others, for it implies his presence on the battlefield, witnessing the deeds of his successors. In this way, a single armoured plate or helmet might be heir to a long and famous history, having belonged to a whole succession of Space Marine heroes and been worked on by many renowned Artificers.

As well as resurrecting old pieces of armour for notable Space Marines, the Artificers also decorate and modify armour to suit particularly revered individuals. As a result of the Artificers' efforts over the many thousand years a Chapter has been in existence, it is quite common to find suits which combine elements of the different marks as well as quite unique suits which have customised armoured plates or helmets. Some Chapters reserve such armour for special individuals, officers, or high ranking commanders. There is no fixed rule on this, it is a matter of Chapter tradition and preference how such armour is used. However, it is generally the case that very high ranking officials inherit special suits of armour, which they may then combine with their own existing suits so that their individual honours or personal pieces of armour are retained when they are appointed to a new position. So does a Chapter's power armour evolve down the centuries, each and every greave and gorget a recollection of mighty deeds and terrible battles won.

Mk1 "Thunder" Pattern

Mk2 "Crusade" Pattern

Mk3 "Iron" Pattern

Mk4 "Maximus" Pattern

Mk5 "Heresy" Pattern

Mk6 "Corvus" Pattern

Mk7 "Aquila" Pattern

Mk8 "Errant" Pattern

SPACE MARINE HERALDRY

Space Marines usually display their Chapter symbol on their left shoulder guard, and a symbol denoting their squad designation on their right shoulder guard. A Space Marine's helmet also frequently displays battle honours or rank, either through colour or insignia.

Tactical Space Marine of the Ultramarines Chapter.

Typically, Sergeants have red helmets. Veterancy is indicated by a white laurel.

This Space Marine's Veteran status is shown by a white laurel.

Here, Veteran status is indicated by the white helmet.

SQUAD MARKINGS

2nd Company Command squad
Heraldic colour: Yellow/Gold

1st Company, 9th Veteran squad
Heraldic colour: White/Silver

3rd Company, 4th Tactical squad
Heraldic colour: Red/Sanguinite

2nd Company, 8th Assault squad
Heraldic colour: Yellow/Gold

9th Company, 9th Devastator squad
Heraldic colour: Blue/Ultramarine

CHAPTER SYMBOL VARIANTS

2nd Company
Heraldic colour: Yellow/Gold

1st Company Veteran
Heraldic colour: White/Silver

3rd Company Sergeant
Heraldic colour: Red/Sanguinite

2nd Company
Heraldic colour: Yellow/Gold

9th Company
Heraldic colour: Blue/Ultramarine

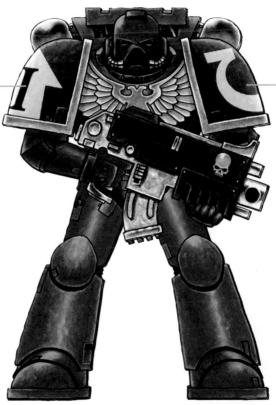

For a wealth of further information on Space Marine markings, heraldry and insignia, see Insignium Astartes (available from the Black Library) and How to Paint Space Marines.

HONOUR BADGES

Space Marines are awarded badges of distinction for all manner of heroic deed or worthy action. Though some honours are simply painted onto the armour, while others are elaborate carvings, all are highly regarded by the recipient and his Brother-Marines. Each Space Marine Chapter has its own variations of awards, ennoblements and honour badges, according to its history and traditions. The badges displayed below are amongst the most common accolades and see use in almost all Chapters.

THE IRON HALO
This simple badge has its origins in the earliest days of the Imperium. Often painted onto a Marine's armour as a red badge, the Iron Halo is the insignia for an exceptional leader and strategist. It is displayed on the shoulder armour or helmet of the Brother-Marine as a mark of rank.

THE IRON SKULL
A badge of ancient origin, the Iron Skull is awarded for leadership. It is the Codex insignia for a sergeant and is often displayed on the shoulder armour or helmet of a Space Marine of this rank. Classical convention is to represent the Iron Skull as a red device.

IMPERIAL LAUREL
Deeds of valour leading to great victory are rewarded with the Imperial Laurel. The wreath is often worn as a crown or sculpted onto the Brother-Marine's helmet. The Codex demands that Company and Chapter Standards be born into battle only by warriors awarded the Imperial Laurel.

PURITY SEAL
The Purity Seal is not so much an honour as a blessing. Before a campaign the Chapter's Chaplains pass through the ranks chanting litanies and invocations. Honoured individuals are marked by the Chaplains for special blessings recorded on the parchment streamers and affixed to their armour with the great wax seal.

THE MARKSMAN'S HONOUR
The Codex insists that those warriors who prove their combat accuracy should be singled out so that their skill may be instantly commanded. Marksman's Honour badges are believed to have been forged by encasing in gold bolter shell cases fired in battle by Roboute Guilliman himself.

SKULL AND MOTTO
In addition to the specific badge of the Iron Skull, there are many other icons and emblems which incorporate the skull. As honours these often have a multitude of uses and meanings. Often combined with simple mottoes, the skull honour can be seen on shoulder pads, helmets, kneepads and even on bolter cases or vehicles.

THE HONOURS OF CAPTAIN SICARIUS

Cato Sicarius has been awarded many honours over a long lifetime of service. All are borne upon his armour, whether as stylised representations or electrum castings. The armour itself is also a noble burden, for it incorporates elements borne by some of the Chapter's most notable heroes.

Aquila
Honour badge proclaiming great wisdom. Awarded at the commencement of the Dantaro campaign – Sicarius' first action as Captain of the Second Company.

Eternium Ultra
There are few such revered relics in Ultramar as these. They mark Sicarius as High Suzerain of Ultramar and defender of the eight systems.

Imperial Laurel
Awarded in the wake of the Crusat Minor planetstrike 733.M41.

Honorifica Valourum
In recognition of exceptional bravery when fighting Orks during the Battle for Dyzanyr.

Personal Heraldry
Sicarius' left shoulder pad originally hails from a suit of Mark II 'Crusade' armour worn by Captain Orar during the Scouring. The heraldry combines the Iron Halo, the Ultramarines Chapter icon and the golden aquila that marks Sicarius as the Grand Duke of Talassar.

The Valour Crest
The right to bear a crest must be earned through acts of near suicidal bravery. Sicarius won his crest during the nine-day battle for Fort Telendrar. The colours of the crest are those of the noble house from which Sicarius was recruited, countless decades ago.

Victorex Alpha
In recognition of exceptional valour during the Siege of Rynneth V.

ULTRAMARINES BANNERS

Each company – with the exception of the Scout Company – has its own banner that bears its heraldry and roll of honour. Especially heroic Captains or great victories may be commemorated by a devotional icon or litany woven into their sacred fabric.

The 1st Company are known as the 'Warriors of Ultramar'. Their banner bears a Crux Terminatus and honorific emblem for the fallen of the Battle for Macragge, while their shoulder guards display heraldry of one of the Chapter's greatest heroes, Captain Agemman.

The banner of the 2nd Company, the 'Guardians of the Temple', bears motifs, such as laurels and skulls, alongside the symbol of the Ultramarines. Captain Sicarius displays heraldry earned fighting the Tau as part of the Damocles Gulf Crusade.

Known as the 'Scourge of the Xenos', the 3rd Company's banner displays a battle honour won in the First Tyrannic War. To honour his warriors, Captain Ardias took his company colours and worked them into his own heraldry.

The 'Defenders of Ultramar', the 4th Company. The banner shows the Iron Gauntlet of its former leader, Captain Idaeus, which indicates he was a mighty hero. In the interim, they have an acting leader who bears Idaeus' heraldry.

The 5th Company are the 'Wardens of the Eastern Fringe' and Captain Galenus is also the Master of the Marches. The banner and his armour display the eagle that is his badge of office. It is a sign of honour to display such ranks on their armour.

Though one of the Ultramarines Reserve Companies, the 6th Company has won much honour, notably in the defence of the Gerio sector. Captain Epathus is the Master of the Rites, and his shoulder guard bears the skull insignia of his company.

The 7th Company are celebrated as the 'Defenders of Caeserean' in memory of their crushing defeat of Korus the Defiler.

The 8th Company are 'The Honourblades'. The crossed swords indicate the company's designation as a dedicated Assault Company.

The 9th Company's banner carries the traditional Ultramar lightning bolt blazon. They are known as the 'Stormbringers'.

The Ultramarines have several Chapter banners, although only one will be in use at any one time. The specifics of design vary greatly from banner to banner, but all will evoke one of the Chapter's greatest triumphs or some other key moment from its long history.

This banner, with lavish designs depicting the victory against Hive Fleet Behemoth, carries the names of the great heroes from the war, as well as the pivotal engagements.

CODEX CHAPTERS

Tradition dictates that there are always roughly one thousand Space Marine Chapters – a selection of which are shown on these pages. In truth, this number is little more than an approximation. Chapters are constantly being founded, disbanded or eradicated, and it is doubtful that any accurate record of the Adeptus Astartes is maintained.

It can be said that there are three categories of Space Marine Chapter. The first and largest group could perhaps be called the scions of Guilliman – those Chapters directly descended from the Ultramarines and their Primogenitors. These Chapters maintain their own traditions, as is to be expected, for the Codex Astartes insists that each Chapter should have its own name, badge and heraldry. Nonetheless, they honour Roboute Guilliman as Primarch and his successor, the ruler of Ultramar, as their distant liege. Should the Lord of Ultramar ever find himself in need of aid, he will find these Chapters ever willing and able to fight at his side. Such Chapters follow the Codex Astartes with as much dedication and passion as the Ultramarines, viewing its dictates as tactical doctrine and spiritual guidance in equal measure.

With the Ultramarines' gene-seed the favoured foundation for new Chapters, these scions of Guilliman are an ever more dominant force upon the galactic stage.

Chapters in the second category are disciples who owe their genetic inheritance to another Primarch, but follow the Codex Astartes as keenly as their divergent heritage allows. While primarily composed of successor Chapters, this group also includes several Chapters of the First Founding – notably the Imperial Fists, White Scars and Raven Guard. These Chapters can never be Ultramarines, for their gene-seed is not that of Roboute Guilliman. Nevertheless, they will ever aspire to the standards and teachings of the great Primarch.

The third and final group are aberrants; Chapters who, through quirk of gene-seed, mutation or stubbornness, eschew the Codex Astartes in favour of other structural and combat doctrines. Some, such as the Blood Angels and their successors, strive to be worthy of Guilliman's legacy, but their recalcitrant gene-seed drives them ever further from it. Others, such as the Space Wolves and the Black Templars, remain stubbornly independent, looking to their own founder's ways of war and caring little of how they fare in the eyes of others. These aberrant Chapters were always few in number and their presence diminishes further with each passing decade, for their gene-seed is no longer the source of fresh Chapters. Such divergent Chapters play little part in this volume, for this is the tale of the Ultramarines, and all those who follow their example.

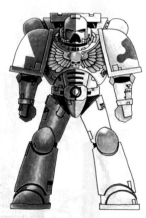

EAGLE WARRIORS
The Eagle Warriors are a fleet-based Chapter, continually on campaign in the systems conquered by Roboute Guilliman during the Great Crusade.

BLACK CONSULS
Recorded as annihilated at the Siege of Goddeth Hive, 455.M41. Current status unknown.

SILVER SKULLS
The Silver Skulls believe that the Emperor guides their purpose and take to the battlefield only when portents demand it. Such mercurial behaviour does not sit well with some Imperial commanders, but victory is seen as ample compensation by most of their allies.

GENESIS CHAPTER
First amongst the Primogenitors, the Genesis Chapter are dogmatically loyal to the memory of Roboute Guilliman, and can be counted upon to fight at the Ultramarines' side without hesitation.

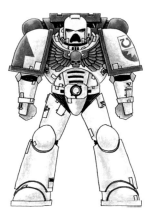

PRAETORS OF ORPHEUS
The technological lore of the Praetors of Orpheus is second only to that of the Adeptus Mechanicus. Many believe that the two are tied by more than shared service in the Emperor's name. The Praetors of Orpheus are highly active in systems neighbouring Pavonis.

THE SONS OF ORAR
Orar is a mythical figure in the histories of the Space Marines, an Ultramarines Captain who won great renown in the wake of the Horus Heresy. Details of the Sons of Orar's founding are lost to Imperial records. The legends of the Chapter claim Orar as spiritual patriarch.

AURORA CHAPTER
The armoury of the Aurora Chapter boasts more Predators and Land Raiders than three other Space Marine Chapters combined. Their name has become a byword for armoured assault across the entire Ultima Segmentum.

NOVAMARINES
The Novamarines are scattered throughout the galaxy, and have not fought together as a Chapter since the early years of M37.

RAVEN GUARD

The Raven Guard are masters of the unseen war, engaging in frontal battle only when no other option presents itself. In pursuit of their covert goals, the Raven Guard depend heavily on Scout forces able to act alone for extended periods of time, and rapid-reaction forces such as jump-pack equipped assault troops who can quickly capitalise on the foe's weaknesses. Thunderhawk strikes and Drop Pod assaults are commonly employed by the Raven Guard for much the same reason. Indeed, they have a great many more of these craft than any other Chapter. Deliverance, the Raven Guard's Chapter Planet and base of operations, has the production capacity of a small forge world, ensuring that the Raven Guard rarely lacks for the materiél to prosecute its campaigns.

Raven Guard Captains are fiercely independent, and it is incredibly rare for the Chapter to fight as a whole. Individual companies are completely autonomous and are quick to lend their aid to Imperial commanders across the galaxy, with or without the sanction of their Chapter Master. Such behaviour has led some to question the Raven Guard's soundness, but most recognise that such fluidity of command proves the presence of formidable discipline, not its absence.

"In the darkness all men are equal, save those that embrace it."

Captain Kayvaan Shrike
Captain of the Raven Guard 3rd Company

Personal Heraldry
Captain Ravenclaw

Lightning claws
'Hawk's Talons' pattern

SALAMANDERS

Born out of fire, the battle brothers of the Salamanders Chapter have jet-black skin and burning red eyes – a daemonic appearance brought about by a reaction between their unique genetics and the high levels of radiation on the Chapter Planet of Nocturne. This terrifying appearance is entirely superficial, but has intimidated more than one rebellion into submission without a shot.

Each of the Salamanders' seven line companies is recruited exclusively from one of the seven settlements on Nocturne. This inevitably leads to a certain amount of rivalry between the companies, but serves to bind the Salamanders' fighting units even closer in brotherhood and determination.

Skills of the forge and artisanship are highly favoured on Nocturne, and each Salamander is expected to refine and maintain his own armour and weaponry. This compensates for the Salamanders' relatively low fighting strength and slow recruitment rate, as each battle brother has access to far superior wargear than a Space Marine in another Chapter might.

Company Banner
Salamanders 2nd Company

"Into the fires of battle!
Unto the anvil of war!"

Battle-cry of the Salamanders

Nocturne-pattern
master-crafted flamer

HAWK LORDS
The Hawk Lords eschew Drop Pods in favour of Thunderhawk gunships for low-altitude insertion. They are the undisputed masters of such tactics, and it is not unknown for Thunderhawk pilots of other Chapters to hone their skills on temporary service as part of a Hawk Lords' Talon Wing.

DEATH SPECTRES
Stationed beyond the bounds of the Imperium, the Death Spectres maintain constant vigil to ensure that the supernatural inhabitants of the Ghoul Stars never again threaten the galaxy.

DARK HUNTERS
Founded in the dark days of the Occlusiad, the Dark Hunters have a reputation for being particularly grim and resolute warriors. They are one of the seven Chapters charged with the elimination of the Chaos Renegades faction known as 'The Punishers'.

HOWLING GRIFFONS
Few Chapters have won as much renown as the Howling Griffons. They fought in the Badab War, the Vengeance Crusade, the overthrowing of the mad Regent of Amar, and thousands of other major engagements. The current location of the Howling Griffons is unknown.

EXORCISTS

The Exorcists maintain two additional Scout Companies for a total of twelve companies in all. Without such a high influx of neophytes, the Exorcists would cease to exist, for their training methods are highly unconventional. The Exorcists are currently serving with distinction in the Battle for Armageddon.

IRON KNIGHTS

The Iron Knights are crusaders in the proud tradition of Rogal Dorn. They are one of the twelve Space Marine Chapters that send a champion to the centennial Feast of Blades, and are the only Chapter to have won the contest on two consecutive occasions.

INVADERS

Currently under-strength after an all-out assault on Eldar Craftworld Idharae, the Invaders Chapter is reported as operating in a support role to the Novamarines on the doomed planet of Skyfall.

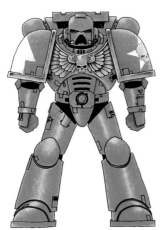

IRON HANDS

The Iron Hands abhor weak flesh, and make extensive bio-mechanical modifications to their physical forms in order to purge their failings. The Iron Hands make no secret of their ties to the Adeptus Mechanicus, a relationship viewed unfavourably by other Space Marines.

THE IMPERIAL FISTS

Rogal Dorn, the Imperial Fists' Primarch, was a tenacious and steadfast warrior whose final moments were of courage and supreme sacrifice. Though many millennia have passed since Dorn's death, his example still drives the Imperial Fists onwards to fresh victories. Indeed, if the Imperial Fists have a fault it is that they continue to strive when others would have yielded the battle. In the past, such stubbornness has rescued many a victory from the ashes of defeat, but only at a steep cost in lives.

The Imperial Fists and their successors have been instrumental in holding the Imperium together through the very bleakest of times. Several Chapters have been formed from the gene-seed of the Imperial Fists, each as famously stubborn as its progenitor. These Chapters, the Crimson Fists and Black Templars amongst them, form a tightly knit brotherhood of Space Marines, united by blood and the honour of their shared Primarch. It is unsurprising, therefore, that the Imperial Fists are judged second only to the Ultramarines as paragons of the Adeptus Astartes, and held as exemplars of everything that a Space Marine is heir to.

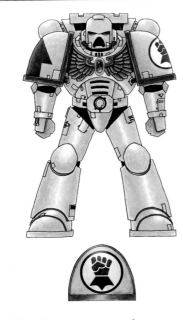

"The Emperor commands us. Dorn guides us. Honour shields us.

Fear our name, for it is vengeance."

From the teachings of Rhetoricus

The Fist of Dorn
Imperial Fists honoured artefact

KNIGHTS OF THE RAVEN

The Knights of the Raven Chapter is currently engaged in hit-and-run attacks on Hive Fleet Kraken. This arduous deployment is penance for coming to blows with Brother Marines from the Aurora Chapter – a conflict ended only by the intervention Marneus Calgar.

FIRE LORDS

The Fire Lords precede assaults with a barrage of incendiary missiles, and hurl themselves at the charred foe before the flames have burnt themselves out.

SABLE SWORDS

Founded in the latter years of M41, the Sable Swords have swiftly proven themselves the equal of more established Chapters with a series of decisive victories over the upstart Tau Empire.

DOOM LEGION

The Doom Legion is responsible for maintenance and garrison of the Faithful's Deliverance, the pre-Heresy star fortress that overlooks the notorious Elusian Maze asteroid fields. Few other Space Marine Chapters can boast spacebound firepower of this magnitude.

WHITE SCARS

White Scars are the masters of reconnaissance and adherents of the hit-and-run attack. They are hunters and raiders without peer, using ultra-rapid deployment to ensure that the foe's first sight of them is also his last. Such were the teachings of the Primarch Jaghatai Khan, and in the millennia since his disappearance these doctrines have been honed and refined in countless battles. Most Space Marine tanks are too slow for such methods of battle, so the White Scars' artificers have become adept at modifying the motive units of Predators, Vindicators and even Land Raiders to ensure that White Scars bikers and recon elements are never left without fire support. As the Great Khan once taught, speed is worthless if the blow it delivers is robbed of strength.

Though the White Scars embrace any opportunity to make war in the Emperor's name, they most of all welcome any opportunity to test their skills against other foes of their ilk, such as Ork Kults of Speed or Saim-Hann Wild Riders. The White Scars believe that to confront and defeat such enemies is the ultimate test of worth. Such victories are celebrated with gusto and enshrined in memory forever.

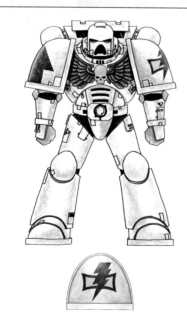

"If you can see us, we are dangerous indeed. But that is as nothing to the peril you face if you cannot see us, and all you can hear is our laughter."

White Scars proverb

White Scars biker helmets with tribal markings

CRIMSON FISTS

The Crimson Fists are a Chapter on the edge of extinction, their fortress-monastery destroyed and their numbers all but obliterated when Waaagh! Snagrod descended on the Loki sector. Yet the Crimson Fists fight on, bearing the blows of a cruel fate with a stoicism that has become legend across the Imperium. Even amongst the elite ranks of the Space Marines, the remaining Crimson Fists are held as warriors without peer, forged in the fire of the most terrible and hopeless battles.

As one would expect of successors to the Imperial Fists, the Crimson Fists are steadfast and stubborn warriors, reluctant to yield so long as victory is possible. Nonetheless, the Chapter's brush with annihilation has tempered this ardour with grim reality.

The Crimson Fists' future now lies with a handful of Space Marines, their lives to be expended for greater rewards than the salving of personal pride. Now the Battle Brothers of the Crimson Fists fight for more than the Emperor, more than honour and renown. They fight so that their Chapter may survive, and one day regain its former glories.

"We have been wounded sorely. Yet still we stand, with fire in our eyes and valour in our hearts. Let them think us beaten. We shall teach them otherwise."

Pedro Kantor
Crimson Fists Chapter Master

Crimson Fists Chapter Banner

Powerfist showing heraldry of Captain Cortez

BRAZEN CLAWS

After the destruction of their Chapter planet by daemonic forces, the Brazen Claws embarked on a crusade into the Eye of Terror. There have been few sightings since their departure, but Lord Castellan Creed of Cadia insists that the Brazen Claws are still active in the Imperium's defence.

IRON LORDS

It is by the efforts of the Iron Lords that the Barghesi are confined to the Grendl stars and, more importantly, that Hive Fleet Kraken is stymied from harvesting the Barghesi's destructive biological potential.

RELICTORS

The Inquisition has become suspicious that the Relictors are developing an unhealthy fascination with tainted artefacts. As a result, they have requested that other Space Marine Chapters keep a close watch upon the Relictors' activities lest they turn Renegade.

THE MENTORS

Shrouded in mystery, the Mentors are untrusting of other Chapters, and prefer to work alone and unobserved by all save their foes. Imperial records indicate that the Mentors are currently engaged against the Eldar of Biel-tan Craftworld and the Orks of the Charadon system.

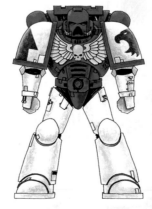

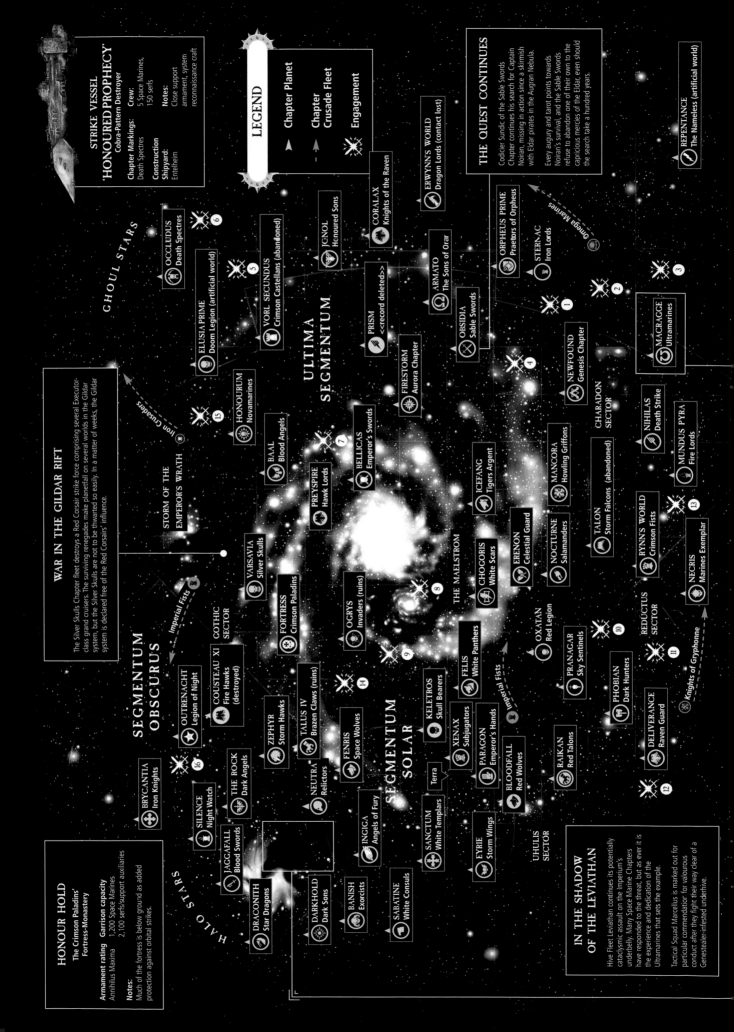

STRIKE VESSEL 'HONOURED PROPHECY'
Cobra-Pattern Destroyer

Chapter Markings: Death Spectres
Construction Shipyard: Entelheim
Crew: 5 Space Marines, 150 serfs
Notes: Close support armament, system reconnaissance craft.

LEGEND

△ Chapter Planet
↑ Chapter Crusade Fleet
✴ Engagement

THE QUEST CONTINUES

Codicier Surdic of the Sable Swords Chapter continues his search for Captain Noirian, missing in action since a skirmish with Eldar pirates in the Augran Nebula.

Every augury and tarot points towards Noirian's survival, and the Sable Swords refuse to abandon one of their own to the capricious mercies of the Eldar, even should the search take a hundred years.

WAR IN THE GILDAR RIFT

The Silver Skulls Chapter fleet destroys a Red Corsair strike force comprising several Executor-class grand cruisers. The surviving renegades make planetfall on several worlds in the Gildar system, but the Silver Skulls are not to be thwarted so easily. In a matter of weeks, the Gildar system is declared free of the Red Corsairs' influence.

HONOUR HOLD
The Crimson Paladins' Fortress-Monastery

Armament rating: Annihilus Maxima
Garrison capacity: 1,200 Space Marines, 2,100 serfs/support auxiliaries

Notes: Much of the fortress is below ground as added protection against orbital strikes.

IN THE SHADOW OF THE LEVIATHAN

Hive Fleet Leviathan continues its potentially cataclysmic assault on the Imperium's underbelly. Many Space Marine Chapters have responded to the threat, but as ever it is the experience and dedication of the Ultramarines that sets the example.

Tactical Squad Marcellus is marked out for particular commendation for valourous conduct after they fight their way clear of a Genestealer-infested underhive.

NOTABLE ONGOING ENGAGEMENTS 998.M41

1. Combined force from the Ultramarines and Genesis Chapters engage the growing might of Waaagh! Irontoof.

2. Multi-Chapter force deployed in response to Tau expansion.

3. Ultramarines 5th Company conducting operations against Eldar pirates in and around the Drasanac Nebula.

4. Three Companies of Sable Swords conducting Exterminatus against the Necron-held world of Eldritch.

5. Doom Legion 4th Company ordered to quell rebellion on Neo Khartoum. Civilian casualties exceeding projections.

6. Death Spectres deployed at Chapter strength in opposition to Hive Fleet Jormungandr. Further reinforcements en route.

7. Contact lost with Hawk Lords 7th Company. Hostile action by xenos forces suspected.

8. White Panthers Chapter crush systematic rebellion in the Dynathi cluster. Chapter Master Jorus Shadowmaw killed in action.

9. Imperial Fists 2nd Company engaged with outlying elements of Waaagh! Dethzarka. 6th and 9th Companies despatched in support.

10. Salamanders 5th Company conducting search-and-destroy actions against several suspected Tomb Worlds in the Heracles sub-sector.

11. Hive Fleet Leviathan containment operations. Two dozen Chapters engaged to a greater or lesser degree. Captain Aajz Solari of the Raven Guard in overall command.

12. Waaagh! Skullkrak continues to rage through Targus and other nearby systems. Captain Kayvaan Shrike of the Raven Guard believed to remain operative in this area, despite the lack of recent contact.

13. Under-strength Crimson Fists' Companies assist in the ongoing battles against the Arch Arsonist of Charadon.

14. Two Companies from the Angels of Fury rout Word Bearers warband.

15. Novamarines task force Septus under attack from Chaos Renegades believed to be in the employ of Huron Blackheart.

16. The ongoing War for Armageddon. Upwards of twelve Chapters still engaged in battles against Ork warbands. Current projections indicate operations will extend well into .M42 or beyond.

17. Daemon Warpship 'Accursed Eternity' sighted in the Balanor system. Containment Fleet Kappa moving to investigate.

18. Containment Fleet Sanctus engaging substantial Black Legion assault force. Casualties heavy, but victory is imminent.

19. Imperial Fists Star Fort 'Endeavour of Will' under attack by an Iron Warriors warband. Enemy commander is believed to be the infamous Warsmith Shen'tu (ref. a435-34 Siege of Malodrax).

20. White Consuls report banishment of Greater Daemon tentatively identified as the Fateweaver.

ULTRAMAR

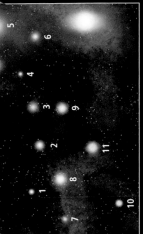

1. Tarentus	Agri World
2. Quintarn	Agri World
3. Konor	Adeptus Mechanicus Research World
4. Calth	Cavern World
5. Espandor	Cardinal World
6. Iax	Garden World
7. Masali	Agri World
8. Talassar	Ocean World
9. Macragge	Chapter Planet
10. Talasa Prime	Inquisition Fortress
11. Parmenio	Training World

MACRAGGE

Adeptus Astartes Chapter Planet

Home of the Ultramarines Chapter, Ultramar is an empire of beautiful and highly developed civilised worlds that stand as an indomitable bulwark against the encroaching darkness of the Eastern Fringe.

IN DEFENCE OF MANKIND

"Let them bestride the galaxy like the gods of old, sheltering Mankind from destruction at the hands of an uncaring universe."

From the teachings of Roboute Guilliman as laid down in the Apocrypha of Skaros

The Space Marines are Mankind's most mobile fighting force. As a result, it would be impossible to accurately catalogue even a small percentage of their actions. This map therefore shows only the most notable Space Marine campaigns and fortresses at 998.M41.

EYE OF TERROR CONTAINMENT

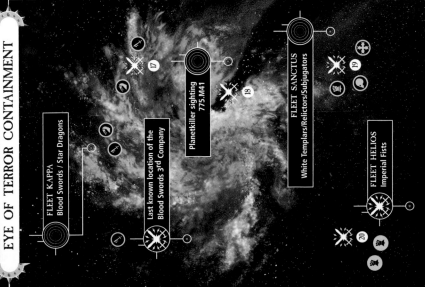

FLEET KAPPA
Blood Swords / Star Dragons

Last known location of the Blood Swords 3rd Company

Planetkiller sighting
775.M41

FLEET SANCTUS
White Templars/Relictors/Subjugators

FLEET HELIOS
Imperial Fists

STAR FORT GARRISON ALLOCATION 998.M41

- Imperial Fists
- Exorcists
- Silver Skulls
- Star Dragons
- Dark Sons
- Relictors
- White Templars
- Subjugators
- Blood Swords

"We shall never rest while a single renegade draws breath. Let them fear our names."

Captain Leitz
Exorcists Chapter

BATTLES OF THE ULTRAMARINES

They are the guardians of the eastern fringe, the defenders of Ultramar.

Ultramar held against all manner of invaders – some so strange as to defy the comprehension of the common man. The Ultramarines have tested their might against Ork Waaaghs! and renegade uprisings, Tau incursions and Necron raids, but the measure of their heroism is shown truest in battles where they have defended the galaxy itself in the face of threats from beyond known space. So did the Sons of Ultramar prove in the 35th Millennium in battle against the Star-Striders of Crioth, and in retaliation for the Heavenfall Massacres. But of all these terrible wars and heroic struggles, there is one conflict that stands above all others – the onset of Tyranid Hive Fleet Behemoth, and the Battle for Macragge.

THE BATTLE FOR MACRAGGE

Upon learning the threat posed to Ultramar by Hive Fleet Behemoth, Marneus Calgar at once drew his plans. Deeming Macragge to be the system most immediately threatened, Calgar ordered its formidable defences to be further improved. A dozen warships already hung in orbit, and each day more arrived from the Warp. Massively beweaponed strike cruisers cast shadows over civilian vessels and Imperial Navy destroyers, and were themselves dwarfed by the brooding presence of the Ultramarines' Battle Barges. Between this mighty fleet of warships and the planet's no less formidable orbital defence stations, Macragge was anything but defenceless.

Scant weeks later, the outrider vessels of the Tyranid fleet attacked Macragge. The alien bio-vessels swept aside attacks by Ultramarines Strike Cruisers and swarmed over the planet below. Soon many thousands of spore-birthed beasts scurried and rampaged across Macragge. Deeming that the Tyranid threat was too massive to be opposed piecemeal, Calgar combined his ground forces into three mighty armies. The primary and secondary taskforces, composed largely of 1st Company veterans and Ultramar Planetary Defence Forces, bolstered Macragge's polar fortresses against the Tyranid onslaught. Meanwhile, Calgar's taskforce, the largest of the three, performed a series of rearguard actions, attempting to slow the Tyranid advance and eliminate Hive control organisms.

Calgar achieved great success in the early days of the campaign, buying time with blood for his Battle-Brothers to the north and south. However, the Tyranids kept coming. In a final climactic battle on Cold Steel Ridge, the Ultramarines rearguard were brutalised by the Tyranid horde and Calgar himself gravely wounded. Knowing that to remain planetside was to doom his followers to wasteful death, Calgar withdrew to the orbiting Battle Barge *Octavius*. Refusing all but the most vital medical attention, the Master of Macragge took command of the fleet, and sought a way to save his world from certain destruction.

Hours later, the main Tyranid fleet arrived at Macragge. With no sign of reinforcements, Calgar led his fleet in a series of daring attacks, striking at isolated vessels as they spread out to invade Macragge in force. Caught between the blistering firepower of Macragge's polar fortresses and the vengeful hammer blows of Calgar's fleet, Tyranid vessels were destroyed by the score, but many more yet remained. As battle raged, the Tyranids unleashed thousands of spores above the vital polar fortresses – if the fortresses were taken, Macragge's guns would be silenced, and the world left defenceless. So it was that the Tyranids landed in even greater numbers than before, and the fortresses soon found themselves sorely beset. Their gruesome cargo delivered, the battered Hive Ships retreated from orbit. Trusting to his Ultramarines to keep the fortresses secure, Calgar relentlessly pursued the Tyranid fleet, determined that it would not bring ruin to other worlds.

Never before or since has the valour of the Ultramarines been tested as it was in the defence of the polar fortresses. The veteran Space Marines of the 1st Company led the lightly armed auxilia in a tenacious defence of the fortresses, holding every wall and trench until the last possible moment before it was overrun by the Tyranid swarm. Slowly the troops withdrew ever deeper into the fortress, while making the Tyranids pay for every single yard of ground they advanced. The Titans of Legio Praetor stalked the ice fields and drove smoking furrows through the onrushing Tyranid hordes with shells and plasma. The ferocity of the swarms was unbelievable. At the northern fortress they overran the walls by using the steaming piles of their own dead for cover. Titans were dragged down and ripped apart by sheer weight of numbers. The defenders' gun barrels glowed red hot and jammed in spite of the arctic cold, ammunition began to run low though the fortress contained stockpiles for months of siege.

Yet still the defenders fought on. Lumbering scythe-armed Carnifexes tore into the defenders' bastions like living battering rams, smashing their way through metal and rockcrete walls with equal fury. The Ultramarines had to rely on heavy short-range firepower to bring down the foe, but for each Tyranid that fell, another three sprang forward to continue the fight. Lesser men were paralysed with terror as the Tyranids broke through the perimeter again and again, but the Ultramarines never despaired and never gave thought to defeat.

The War in Space
Calgar pursued the Tyranid fleet toward the ringed world of Circe at the edge of the Macragge system. The timely arrival of the Tempestus fleet from Bakka finally sealed the Tyranids' fate by catching them in a vice between the two fleets. Even now, the Imperial fleet was overmatched, for the Tyranids were too many. The battle would have been lost save for the heroic sacrifice of the *Dominus Astra*. Charging into the heart of the Hive Fleet, the huge Emperor-class battleship detonated its Warp drives, creating a vortex that dragged both it and the entire Tyranid fleet to oblivion.

With the Hive Fleet destroyed, Calgar's surviving ships came about and roared back to Macragge to try to save the beleaguered polar garrisons. The survivors of the Ultramarines 1st Company were believed still to be fighting amongst the defence laser silos of the northern citadel, but all contact with them had been lost after the Tyranids overran the surface outposts. Of the southern garrison, nothing was known. Calgar, feeling that the situation was becoming critical, sent the 3rd and 7th Ultramarines Companies ahead in their fast Strike Cruisers while his remaining damaged ships limped back to Macragge.

The Space Marines of the 3rd and 7th Companies deployed onto the poles by Drop Pod, their supporting units following up in Thunderhawk Gunships. Scenes of unbelievable carnage awaited them below. Piles of mangled Tyranid corpses and shattered wargear lay strewn across the ice. Vast steaming craters pocked the snows where Titan plasma reactors had gone critical. The stench of death lay everywhere. The 7th Company landed unopposed at the southern fortress and quickly linked up with the survivors of the garrison above ground. Together they pushed on to clear the subterranean passages that the Tyranids had overrun.

Battle for the Northern Fortress
In the north, the 3rd Company came under attack as soon as it landed. Hundreds of creatures emerged from dark tunnel mouths and shattered bunkers to assail the Space Marines. Only staunch fire laid down by the Company's Devastator squads kept the alien swarm at bay until Thunderhawk Gunships arrived to blast the Tyranids back into the darkness. Captain Fabian of the 3rd Company prudently awaited the arrival of the Company's three Dreadnoughts before proceeding into the fortress itself to search for survivors.

The dark, dank corridors beneath the northern fortress were already altered by the alien presence. Mucous dripped from the walls and ceilings and a pervasive musky stench filled the air. Alien screams and roars echoed and reverberated along the tunnels. The Space Marines pushed onward into corridors littered with Tyranid and Ultramarines dead, the darkness reluctantly receding before their suit lights. Chameleoid Lictors lay in ambush amongst the corpses, slashing into the advance squads in an orgy of destruction. Eventually the forward squads used flamers to burn their way along the passages and flush out their enemy. Even as fire consumed them, the creatures still leapt forward with claws outstretched to rend and slay.

The Fate of the 1st Company
Through darkness and terrors unimaginable, the 3rd Company finally reached the lower penitorium where the defenders had made their last stand. Tyranid bodies were piled six deep around the doors, and within the room a circle of Terminators lay where they had fought back to back. Each had given his life for his brothers. The Ultramarines 1st Company had been wiped out to the last man.

The Battle for Macragge remains a great source of both sorrow and pride for the Ultramarines. The names of its fallen are commemorated each year at the Feast of Days, their sacrifice remembered throughout Ultramar with honour and gratitude. But the cost had been great. The Ultramarines 1st Company was gone and the 3rd and 7th sorely diminished. It would be many long years before the Chapter could properly replace its losses, but replace them it would. The Ultramarines would endure.

THE BATTLE OF THE SEPULCHRE

The Battle for Macragge took a heavy toll on the Ultramarines, incurring wounds and losses that would take many long years to heal. Nonetheless, the sons of Guilliman did not rest idle in those years, and lent their might to many a battle. On Yundo, Tylannia, Archos and a hundred other worlds, the Ultramarines strove against the enemies of the Imperium, but they did not fight together as a Chapter for a long while, not until the Siege of Orar's Sepulchre.

Orar had been one of the Ultramarines' greatest heroes in the aftermath of the Horus Heresy, who strove to keep the eastern fringe secure against alien threats. After triumphs and victories uncounted, Orar finally fell in battle and was entombed on the world of Commrath, where his monument has stood as a reminder of sacrifice and victory ever since. So it was that when the Ultramarines received a distress call from Commrath's planetary governor, Calgar responded immediately with all the might at his command.

An Emissary Arrives

Some weeks before, an emissary from the alien Eldar had sought parley with the Governor of Commrath. Orar had been entombed with many relics of his campaigns, some of Imperial heritage and many others of unknown provenance. The alien had claimed ownership of one such relic, known to the Ultramarines and the people of Commrath as the Sceptre of Galaxian, and requested its return. Such a thing was impossible, of course, for the sanctity of Orar's tomb was not for the breaching at the whims of an alien, nor could the surrender of any holy item be countenanced. Accordingly, the Governor had refused, at which point the Eldar's requests became demands, and then threats. The Governor would not be swayed, and ordered the emissary slain for his impertinence, but was not so foolish as to ignore the Eldar's threats. He immediately placed the Planetary Defence Forces on alert, and sought aid from the Ultramarines.

The Eldar struck a month later. Bypassing Commrath's orbital defences, they materialised on the planet's surface through unknown means three hundred leagues to the west of Orar's Sepulchre. The Planetary Defence Forces saw success for a time, as whatever method the Eldar had employed to reach the planet's surface had denied them use of Titans and other super-heavy support. But little by little, Commrath's defenders were scattered, and the Eldar advanced.

Such was the situation when the Ultramarines arrived at Commrath. Receiving status reports from Planetary Defence units on the ground, Calgar deemed the Eldar to be on the verge of breaking through to the sepulchre and his reinforcing Commrath's defence units would serve little purpose. Whether or not the Ultramarines reinforced the defenders, the Eldar were sure to break through, and when they did the sepulchre would fall. Calgar's only hope therefore was to fortify Orar's Sepulchre as best he could, and hold it through strength of arms. So reconciled, Calgar ordered his Battle-Brothers to their Thunderhawks, and the Ultramarines descended on Commrath.

Though not intended for defence, Orar's Sepulchre was a formidable position nonetheless, covering many acres and standing on a great hill that overlooked scrubland plains and petrified forests. Its marbled stairs rose many hundreds of metres into the air, to the very summit of the hill, giving those inside a commanding view of any assailants. From the moment the Ultramarines landed, they strove to further reinforce the sepulchre. Statues were toppled to serve as barricades, crumbling walls shored up and fields of fire cleared of obstructions. Orar's Sepulchre was no fortress, but it would serve – or so Calgar hoped.

The Battle Begins

The Eldar arrived at Orar's Sepulchre to find it held against them, and they struck hard at the main gate. Aspect Warriors and Guardians darted forward as Falcon grav-tanks and artillery engines battered the defenders, yet the Eldar could not bring their heaviest weaponry to bear, for to do so would be to risk destroying the Galaxian Sceptre within. The Ultramarines sheltered from the Eldar firestorm in their crudely prepared defences, holding position behind weathered marble until the first assault wave was on the uppermost steps. On Calgar's command, the Ultramarines emerged from cover. Heedless of the shuriken and plasma that screamed all around them, the defenders scoured the invaders from their sight with bolter, missile and grenade.

Held at bay at the main gates, the Eldar attack wave now broke apart and sought gaps in Calgar's defences, only to find their own flanks assailed by roving bands of Ultramarines. Calgar had fought the Eldar many times, and knew that no fixed defence could long endure against their fluid and precise strikes. Accordingly, Calgar's battle plan had been to divide his Chapter. The main taskforce, under his direct command and comprising five full companies of Ultramarines, garrisoned Orar's Sepulchre and defended the Galaxian Sceptre therein. The remainder of the Chapter was further subdivided into a dozen mobile strikeforces consisting of between fifty and one hundred Space Marines who had lain concealed in the surrounding valley and now engaged the Eldar in hit-and-run attacks. Moment-to-moment command of each strikeforce lay with the captain or sergeant at its head, but it was Calgar, and Calgar alone, who directed the overall strategy. Yet he never once yielded his position at the gates to better command the wider battle. Even as Calgar's armoured gauntlets cast the foe from the steps of the sepulchre, his voice directed the Chapter with every iota of strategic and tactical experience his august mind possessed.

So deftly did Calgar direct the Ultramarines that the Eldar were opposed by equal force wherever they struck. Fire Prism grav-tanks seized vantage points on the scrubland north of the sepulchre, yet were assailed by fast-moving Tactical squads before they could fire so much as a shot on Calgar's position. To the west, bellowing guns of Predator battle tanks drove Warp Spiders scuttling into the dead forests and ambush at the hands of Ultramarines Scouts. Thunderhawk Gunships roared across the skies, cannon and missile searching for elusive and agile Eldar Nightwings. Bike squads of the 6th Company prowled hill and crag, percussive bursts of bolter fire hammering Eldar Vyper squadrons. A lesser man would have been unable to direct such spiralling chaos, but Calgar's will prevailed in every corner of the battle. A word here, and a strikeforce manoeuvred clear of an incoming Eldar assault wave. A command there, and

Ultramarines on the far side of the battlefield intercepted and crushed an isolated Eldar force. Never once did the strain show upon Calgar's face, not for a moment did he let up from his personal battle at the sepulchre's gate.

The battle for the sepulchre lasted all day and into the night. Shells and energy blasts gouged stone walls and statuary, sending shards tearing through Space Marine and Eldar alike, and great gouts of acrid mist roiling through the sepulchre. Through it all the Ultramarines stood firm, stalking through the smoke-clogged rubble like vengeful nightmares. The Eldar mustered every arcane science at their command, yet their impossible technology counted for little in the face of the Ultramarines' determination. Shuriken and plasma-bolt, fusion gun and wraithsword – these things could and did slay the Ultramarines but, whilst Calgar lived, not one of his Battle-Brothers contemplated defeat. Bound by ties of brotherhood and exhorted to greatness, the defenders fought on amongst shattered statues and broken walls, knowing that to do any less was to dishonour the noble history of the Ultramarines.

Many heroes made their mark that day, their names to live forever in the annals of Ultramar. Sergeant Caturi of the 3rd Company, who slew a dozen Aspect Warriors on the sepulchre's north wall, though his own body was rent and torn. Brother Cunion, who defended the unconscious Captain Agemman against all attackers until aid reached them. Honoured Brother Tiberan, who single-handedly stoppered a breach in the sepulchre's southern walls with the enemy dead, and whose blade carved a Wraithlord asunder. Through such acts did the Ultramarines deny their foes.

The Avatar Strikes

Ultimately, the battle ended where it had begun – at the front gate of the sepulchre. A fresh assault, greater than any that preceded it, swept onto the great marble stairs. This attack was led by a being not yet seen on that battlefield, a colossal figure wreathed in ashen smoke and roiling flame whose mighty blade smote all who stood before it – the Avatar of Khaine.

Each irresistible sweep of the Avatar's flaming sword sundered armour, flesh and bone, leaving naught but unmoving bodies. Terminators of the 1st Company set upon the Avatar with power fist and thunder hammer, but their blows did little more than stagger it. Heavy weapons of every kind were brought to bear on the Avatar's glowing molten form, yet their fury did little save to anger the creature further. Wherever the Avatar trod, the Eldar redoubled their efforts. Aspect Warriors and Guardians surged forwards in the Avatar's wake, its unearthly presence fuelling their determination.

Already hard-pressed, the Ultramarines' defence line buckled beneath this new onslaught, and Calgar knew that only desperate means could preserve victory. Bowling his opponents clear with one mighty sweep of his armoured gauntlets, Calgar moved to challenge the Avatar himself. Many Eldar stood between the Master of the Ultramarines and his target, but Calgar would not be stayed – those his gauntlets did not crush were smashed aside by the sheer bulk of his Terminator armour.

Calgar's Triumph

So it was that Calgar fell upon the Avatar before the other was aware of his presence, and smote the creature a dolorous and terrible blow. Bellowing with fury, the Avatar turned to face its new attacker. Its first strike missed the Chapter Master by a hair's breadth. The second tore a great wound from Calgar's armour. A third drove deep into his shoulder, cleaving the pauldron and driving the Chapter Master to one knee. But the fourth, intended as the coup de grâce to sever Calgar's head from his shoulders, slammed into the armoured palm of Calgar's left hand.

The armoured glove charred and warped as Calgar closed his grasp about the blade. No other gauntlet could have withstood that mighty blow nor the furious heat behind. But the fabled Gauntlets of Ultramar were of older and sterner make, crafted with skill and technology long lost to the race of Man. For a moment, mortal and god strove for control of the incandescent sword, and in that moment the Avatar was defenceless. Rising up, Calgar struck with all his strength, bringing his other gauntlet around in a mighty arc. The Avatar roared in pain and fury as the power fist punched clean through the molten ichor of its torso. With a final bellow, the Avatar exploded in a white-hot flash that showered cinders and molten metal all around.

His strength spent, Calgar sank to one knee. Ultramarines encircled their wounded Chapter Master to protect him from any Eldar who sought to exploit his weakness, but there was no need. With the fall of their war god, the Eldar lost all heart. Some fled without heed while others fell back in good order, but all retreated into the darkness. Silence prevailed where the din of battle had reigned so shortly before. The Battle for the Sepulchre was done.

All remaining Eldar forces assailing Commrath melted away within the next few hours, but Calgar knew that they would return for the Galaxian Sceptre. He also deemed that Commrath's fractured and ruined defences would not hold against a second assault. Indeed, save for the presence of the Ultramarines, the Galaxian Sceptre would have fallen into the hands of the Eldar. So it was that Calgar informed Commrath's Governor that the Galaxian Sceptre would be removed from Orar's Sepulchre to Macragge, where it could be properly defended.

ASSAULT ON BLACK REACH

By the time Captain Sicarius and the Ultramarines taskforce arrived on the hive world of Black Reach, Waaagh! Zanzag controlled most of the northern continent. Only three of the twelve major hive cities still held out. When the Strike Cruiser *Valin's Revenge* made orbit, the defences of Ghospora, the largest of the three towering hive cities still free, were faltering. Zanzag was a Warboss of uncommon mekaniacal skill and had perfected a design for supacharged shootaz that could punch through a Leman Russ' armour plating or even a Space Marine's power armour. With such weapons at their command, the brutal Ork invaders were annihilating Black Reach's defenders.

Wasting no time in contemplation, Sicarius ordered his Battle-Brothers to their Drop Pods and directed the *Valin's Revenge* to begin an orbital bombardment of Ghospora's attackers. The Drop Pod assault landed hard on the heels of the bombardment. In a brief but bloody battle, the Ultramarines cast the Orks from Ghospora's walls, forcing a bloodied and beaten Zanzag to retreat. Scarcely had the battlecries ceased than Sicarius was on the move again. Leaving a portion of his force to bolster Ghospora's defences, Sicarius took off in search of the leader of the Waaagh!

With Sicarius and the bulk of the Ultramarines now elsewhere, the Orks renewed their assault on Ghospora Hive. Unfortunately for the greenskins, Sicarius had foreseen the possibility and ordered the deployment of several Thunderfire cannon to strengthen the hive's defences. No sooner did the

assault get underway than a salvo of shells tore through the advancing Orks and drove them back to the shelter of the petrified forests surrounding Ghospora Hive.

Meanwhile, Sicarius' search for Zanzag continued. Thunderhawk and Land Speeder reconnaissance patrols identified several Ork encampments along the Blackwallow River. In the space of a week, Sicarius planned and led strikes against each, but although plenty of supacharged shootaz were in evidence, Zanzag was nowhere to be found. After the fourth ramshackle fort was reduced to rubble, Sicarius received an urgent request for assistance from the Black Reach Planetary Defence Forces defending Sulphora Hive. Torn between duties, Sicarius reluctantly abandoned his hunt for Zanzag's base of operations and headed south to Sulphora, leaving the search in the hands of two squads of Scouts under the command of Sergeant Telion.

Rather than searching the surrounding area, Telion instructed his Scouts to begin surveillance of the destroyed outpost. The Sergeant knew the Orks to be scavengers and felt sure they'd return to the site to recover any scraps of armour or weaponry that could be reused. By nightfall, Telion's Scouts were concealed around the perimeter of the ruined outpost, their eyes and ears alert for the merest sign of any approaching greenskins.

Two nights later, while Sicarius still fought in the shadow of Sulphora Hive, Telion's theory proved correct. Under the light of Black Reach's twin moons, a lumpen but serviceable

submersible rose from the cloying waters of the Blackwallow. Safely concealed in a cluster of petrified trees to the south, Telion and his Scouts watched as the Ork submersible disgorged a dozen Boyz and two score Gretchin onto the bank. As the greenskins spread out and combed the wreckage for whatever detritus that could still be put to use, one of the Scouts swam out to the moored submersible and planted a tracer beacon. Come the first sun of morning, the submersible had gone and Telion had the location of its base of operations – a vast natural cavern hidden beneath the Blackwallow waterfall, midway between Ghospora and Sulphora hives and within striking distance of both.

The Assault on Zanzag's Lair

On receiving Telion's news, Sicarius was hearty in his congratulations. Gathering what forces as could be spared from the defence of Sulphora, he boarded the Thunderhawk Gunship *Gladius* and headed north with as much speed as could be mustered. In the meantime, Telion's Scouts moved into position and busied themselves with the task of eliminating the base's sentries.

The first indication Zanzag's Boyz had that they were under attack was when the nose of the *Gladius* burst through the waterfall's spray. For a moment, the Gunship's roaring engines held it steady in the centre of the cavern, shoota-fire pattering harmlessly off its hull. Then, with an earsplitting screech, the *Gladius* unleashed a volley of hellstrike missiles into a cluster of Kans and Deffdreads at the rear of the chamber, tearing them apart in a series of fiery explosions that momentarily banished the chamber's gloom. The sound of hellstrike detonations were still rolling around the chamber when the Thunderhawk's ramp clanged down onto a crude metal walkway, and Cato Sicarius led his Ultramarines into battle.

Recovering from their shock, the Orks barrelled towards the invaders and joined battle with all the bestial fury of their kind. With a roar that echoed through the cavern, Tankbustas unleashed a volley of rokkits that forced the Thunderhawk Gunship to withdraw. At the rear of the chamber, Zanzag bellowed at nearby Boyz to unleash their supacharged shootaz at the oncoming Space Marines. But Sicarius had planned his attack well. The first wave of Space Marines were not from Sicarius' own company, but rather five Terminator veterans from the 1st Company. Zanzag's supacharged shootaz might be able to penetrate power armour, but against the inviolable Tactical Dreadnought armour they were near worthless. By the time Zanzag realised his mistake many of his Boyz were dead, their bodies heaped around the shattered stalagmites of the cavern floor. With the threat of the gunz greatly diminished, Sicarius ordered his power-armoured Battle-Brothers into the fray.

THUNDERHAWK GUNSHIPS

With hardened ceramite armour, a substantial transport capacity and a devastating weapons array, Thunderhawks are versatile craft indeed. Although initially designed to airlift Space Marines into a battlezone and then provide fire support, the Thunderhawk's role has broadened considerably over the millennia, with many Chapters using them as high-atmosphere reconnaissance craft, long range strike assets or even spacebound heavy fighters. In the hands of an experienced commander, a single Thunderhawk Gunship can double the effectiveness of a Space Marine strikeforce, particularly in warzones where manoeuvrability is key to victory.

Even dismayed and robbed of their advantageous weaponry, the Orks fought hard. Sicarius's foothold was tenuous, for the waters of the submersible pens lay to either side, and Zanzag sent wave after wave of Boyz forward in the hope of forcing the Space Marines into the inky depths. Nevertheless, the Ultramarines continued to advance, striding forward with bolters blazing. It took an hour's bloody fighting to secure the cavern, but finally the Orks fled into the network of caves behind.

Sicarius eventually won a bloody victory. Zanzag was dead, cut down by the Captain in the closing moments of the battle – but the cost had been high. One of the Terminators was dead, and a dozen of the Ultramarines 2nd Company would not see battle again. As the *Gladius* returned to redeploy the Ultramarines, Sicarius oversaw the placing of explosives to bring in the roof of the cavern to trap any surviving Orks within the tunnels. In the aftermath of the Ultramarines' evacuation, Sicarius also directed the Strike Cruiser *Valin's Revenge* to conduct a thorough bombardment of the site.

Within three days of the battle at the battle-scarred cavern, Sicarius led a series of strikes that broke the back of the Ork war machine. Though several Warbosses attempted to assume control in the weeks that followed, Waaagh! Zanzag was effectively ended with the death of its leader. Too many Boyz had perished before the walls of the Ghospora and Sulphora hives for the Orks to prevail through sheer numbers alone. Furthermore, with the loss of Zanzag's Orky-know-wots and supacharged shootaz, the greenskins no longer had the technology to compensate. Judging his work finished, Sicarius made ready to leave the world. As the Ultramarines' taskforce left Black Reach for fresh battles, the planet's inhabitants began the long process of reclaiming their world from the surviving greenskins.

THE DAMNOS INCIDENT

The Ultramarines arrived on Damnos to find a war in the balance. A year before, the tectonic disruptions that had crippled Damnos' geothermic fusion stations had also heralded a more potent menace. Beneath the arctic chill of Damnos' surface, a Necron tomb had awoken to malice. Within six months, Damnos' Planetary Defence Force was under attack from an enemy below their feet. Before the year was out, almost all of Damnos' vast manufactorum cities were in ruins, and the planetary capital of Kellenport under siege.

The Ultramarines Strike Cruiser *Valin's Revenge* and its taskforce arrived at Damnos just as the final assault on Kellenport began. Using wreckage strewn throughout the upper atmosphere for cover, Captain Sicarius ordered the *Valin's Revenge* into orbit above Kellenport to begin ground assault. The Necrons responded immediately. Far below, Necron Pylons shuddered into new firing positions and launched crackling energy bolts into the atmosphere, searching the skies for the debris-shielded Strike Cruiser. In the minutes that followed, the skill of the *Revenge's* helmsmen was tested as never before as they tried to anticipate the pattern of the incoming fire. For the most part they were successful, and the gauss streams wasted their energy on wreckage or else spiralled harmlessly into space. Thrice did the *Valin's Revenge* shudder under impact. The third shot pierced the straining void shields and dealt the cruiser a terrible blow amidships, forcing it to withdraw from orbit. But it mattered not – enough time had been bought. The 2nd Company's Drop Pods had cleared the ship and the assault was underway.

The Relief of Kellenport

Captain Sicarius had divided his force into three groups. The first, under the direction of Sicarius himself, struck the Necron onslaught at its very heart, scouring the soulless machine-warriors back from Kellenport's outer walls. The second, its command given to Chief Librarian Tigurius, hit home amidst the gauss siege cannon and Pylons whose flickering fire rained down upon those areas of Kellenport where the defenders still held out. The third wave, consisting entirely of unmanned Deathwind Drop Pods, slammed into the broken rubble outside the besieged capitolis administratum. The hatches slammed down and autosense targetters began unleashing volleys of missiles into the packed Necron ranks.

Through the combined fire of Deathwind Drop Pods and desperate defenders, the capitolis administratum building held firm, but lasting victory rested on the success of both Sicarius' and Tigurius' assaults. Of the two, it was Sicarius who faced the greatest struggle. Through bitter chance, his strike force had made planetfall in close proximity to a Necron command node – instantly, several nearby phalanxes rerouted to eliminate the Space Marines' threat. Gathering together his most experienced Battle-Brothers, Sicarius led the charge against the gleaming ochroid Necron Lord who directed the battle. A War Cell of Immortals moved to shield their master, but the Ultramarines would not be stayed. Bolter shells punched through metallic exoskeletons and plasma bolts seared through armour plates as the inheritors of Guilliman proved their mettle in the direst of adversity.

Sicarius himself fell in that battle, sorely wounded by a warscythe's cruel blow, but this small triumph was too little to save the Necrons from defeat. As Sicarius' Command squad stood resolute over the Captain's injured form, the hulking form of Venerable Brother Agrippan strode into the fray. Sorely pressed by the ferocity of Sicarius' assault, the remaining Immortals could not stand against the Dreadnought's fury. Smashing Necrons aside, Agrippan descended upon the golden Necron Lord and, in an explosion of swirling energy, smashed it asunder with one mighty blow of his power fist.

With their commander destroyed, the Necrons reverted to secondary protocols and began to retreat. With Sicarius incapacitated, Agrippan took command of the surviving Ultramarines and mercilessly harried the retreating Necrons. Many thousands of the machine warriors were destroyed in that pursuit. Later that day yet more Necrons perished in the viridian explosion that rocked the Thanatos foothills to the north, proving that Tigurius had succeeded in his part of the mission. With the Necrons driven back and the orbital defences cleared, *Valin's Revenge* returned to orbit once more, its Thunderhawks launched in support of planetside operations. Before the day was done, Sicarius' grievously wounded form was secure in the Strike Cruiser's apothecarium, and the 2nd Company's tanks and heavy equipment were planetside. But the battle for Damnos was not yet done…

The Evacuation Begins

Whilst Techmarines worked with civilian labourers to restore what they could of Kellenport's defences, Tigurius' strikeforce returned from the Thanatos foothills with ill news. Kellenport was an island of sanctuary in a land overrun by Necrons. Thunderhawk reconnaissance indicated that at least two-score phalanxes were massing for a fresh offensive, and that yet more Necrons were awakening far to the north. Such tidings meant certain doom for the defenders of Kellenport. Through injury and death, the Ultramarines could muster little more than half their initial strength. Kellenport's small number of surviving Guardsmen were bone-tired from the siege and, despite the efforts of the Techmarines, the city itself would not long endure another assault – as a bastion it was near worthless. Tigurius and Agrippan were forced to acknowledge that Damnos was lost. Their duty now was to evacuate as many of the planet's inhabitants as possible, and they drew their plans accordingly.

Under Tigurius' direction, efforts to fortify Kellenport were redoubled. All attempts to repair the outer defences were abandoned and that resource applied to the capitolis administratum and its adjacent spaceport. Arvus lighters and other landing craft were brought out from hardened silos beneath Kellenport and began to ferry terrified civilians to the *Valin's Revenge* and its frigate escorts. Meanwhile, Agrippan utilised the *Revenge's* Thunderhawks in a series of surgical strikes. The Thunderhawks *Gladius* and *Thunderstorm* secured a drop zone for heavy transporters to deploy Predators and other heavy units. These then destroyed crucial phase generators or command nodes, and withdrew before the Necrons could respond. Through Agrippan's strikes, the Necron advance was slowed, but within a week Kellenport was under siege once more.

The Final Battle

The Ultramarines defended Kellenport with fury the like of which legends are made. They fought upon those breached walls without fear and without doubt. When the walls could be defended no more, they battled for control of the streets, and when the streets could not be held, they fought for the ruins behind, determined to make the Necrons pay dearly for every inch of rubble. Kellenport's Guardsmen, stirred to greatness by those sons of Guilliman, found courage and resolve like never before, and hurled themselves into the fray like warriors whose moment of destiny had come. Yet even this bravery would have counted for nought without the leadership of Tigurius and Agrippan.

Wherever the day was darkest, there Tigurius was found, shattering the advancing Necrons with the fury of his mind or summoning psychic shields to cheat the machines of their prey. He was the light of valour personified, and the shadows on men's hearts dwindled and fled at his coming. If Tigurius' battle was of the mind and of the spirit, Agrippan's was one of indomitable force. Though his adamantium hide was rent and torn, the armoured behemoth strove against the foe with every lesson learned in five thousand years of war. For three hours, Agrippan held Kellenport's western gate alone and unaided, obliterating all who opposed him. When the first Monolith phased into the Courtyard of Thor, it was Agrippan who bore the brunt of its eldritch onslaught, and Agrippan who smote it into ruin.

Throughout it all, the evacuation continued. The Necrons had weaponry enough to spare for the skies above, and pilots were forced to bank and dive through a crossfire of gauss blasts to collect their human cargo. Many vessels were lost this way, slamming into the ground as their engines were shot from under them, or exploding in clouds of shrapnel amongst Damnos' sparse clouds. Even so, the evacuation continued apace. By the time Kellenport's defenders had been driven back to the defences around the spaceport, the only humans left alive were those who fought amid the ruins.

As the Thunderhawks *Gladius* and *Thunderstorm* came screaming down into the spaceport there were but sixty souls still fighting in Kellenport – forty Space Marines and twenty Guardsmen carrying their wounded with them as they defended an ever-shrinking perimeter. Yet still not one amongst them faltered, each man fell back through the smoke-laden air, comforted by the knowledge that the deeds of those who had fallen that day would live on. Agrippan was lost in those last few minutes, his mighty frame pinned between a dozen streams of heavy gauss cannon fire. Even in death the ancient warrior claimed a tally of the foe. As the Thunderhawks sped Tigurius and the last of the defenders to the safety of the *Valin's Revenge*, Agrippan's reactor went critical – the resulting explosion obliterated the spaceport and every Necron within it. Damnos had fallen, but the 2nd Company would fight again.

BATTLES OF THE ULTRAMARINES

Date Code	Event
745.M41	The Tyranids enter the galaxy and the Tyrannic Wars begin. Hive Fleet Behemoth descends upon the realm of Ultramar, laying waste to several planets. Only by the valour and determination of the Ultramarines is the threat of Behemoth ended, though the cost is high.
762.M41	Marneus Calgar leads the remnants of his Chapter against the Daemon-corrupted forge world of Thrax. Under the leadership of their Chapter Master, the Ultramarines banish countless thousands of Daemons and recover crucial data-records from the twisted manufactorum complexes. With the mission complete, Calgar issues the order for Exterminatus.
797.M41	The Siege of Zalathras. Marneus Calgar, Chapter Master of the Ultramarines, holds the gate alone against the greenskin horde for a night and a day.
799.M41	The Ultramarines begin to fortify the eastern bounds of their realm against the emergent forces of the upstart Tau Empire.
805.M41	Waaagh! Gutshredda rampages through the Forgoil system. Marneus Calgar leads three companies to the assistance of the Forgoil Planetary Defence Forces. In a little more than three weeks, the Ultramarines destroy the tellyporta ships and Stompa factories that provided Waaagh! Gutshredda with much of its momentum. In the final battle of the war, Calgar and his Terminator-armoured retinue board and destroy Gutshredda's flagship, *Da Supadestructa*.
815.M41	Contact is lost with Explorator Fleet 913. The Ultramarines send three companies to investigate, but find only empty vessels drifting in deep space.
841.M41	The Ultramarines' 1st Company's operational strength exceeds fifty percent for the first time since the Battle for Macragge.

Date Code	Event
849.M41	Brother Captain Cato Sicarius is appointed as High Suzerain of Ultramar.
855.M41	Assault on Black Reach. The Ultramarines 2nd Company defeats Waaagh! Zanzag.
861.M41	Chapter records indicate that the Ultramarines have finally replaced the losses incurred during the Battle for Macragge.
878.M41	Chaos pirates, led by the Daemon Prince M'kar the Reborn, claim several uninhabited worlds on the borders of Ultramar. In a decisive battle in the Halamar Rift, Captain Sicarius destroys much of the pirate fleet, although M'kar the Reborn escapes into the Warp.
888.M41	The Battle of the Sepulchre. Eldar from the Alaitoc and Iyanden Craftworlds assault the planet Commrath. For the first time since the Battle for Macragge, Marneus Calgar leads the entire Ultramarines Chapter to war. At the pivotal Battle for Orar's Sepulchre, Calgar defeats the Alaitoc Avatar in single combat, breaking the spirit of the surviving invaders.

Date Code	Event
900.M41	The Tau listening post on Morix Prime is eliminated by the Ultramarines 4th Company.
921.M41	Marneus Calgar is ambushed by Night Lords whilst en route to the Darkhold battlezone. The Chapter Master's crippled vessel makes planetfall on the sparsely settled world of Barathred. Several hundred Chaos Space Marines make landing shortly thereafter, but Calgar rallies the planet's feudal population to defeat them.
929.M41	The Trenor Uprising. Three dozen Scouts, under the expert direction of the famed Sergeant Telion, put down a rebellion on Trenor in less than a day.
935.M41	A daemonic horde under the direction of M'kar the Reborn seizes control of the star fort *Indomitable* in Calth's outer orbit. Under the command of Marneus Calgar, Terminators from the Ultramarines 1st Company board the star fort. M'kar is slain by the hand of Lord Macragge, who tears the upstart Daemon Prince limb from limb.
941.M41	Waaagh! Ghazghkull descends upon Armageddon. The Orks are defeated only by the extreme stubbornness of the defenders and the combined might of the Blood Angels, Ultramarines and Salamanders Chapters. Thought dead by his foes, Ghazghkull himself escapes into space.
963.M41	The Ultramarines clash with a Tau expeditionary fleet for control of the cursed planet of Malbede. When the conflict awakens the Necron Tombs hidden on Malbede, the Ultramarines and the Tau join forces to defeat the emerging Necrons. In the wake of the battle, Marneus Calgar initiates Exterminatus on Malbede, but allows the Tau to evacuate before the planet is destroyed.
974.M41	The Damnos Incident. The 2nd Company rescues survivors from the doomed world of Damnos.
989.M41	The Ultramarines 3rd Company liberate the Lagan system from the Tau Empire.
993.M41	The Ultramarines quash rebellion on the industrial world of Ichar IV, only to find themselves at the forefront of a desperate defence against Hive Fleet Kraken. Elsewhere, the Eldar Craftworld Iyanden is ravaged by other tendrils of the Kraken. Two Space Marine Chapters – the Scythes of the Emperor and the Lamentors – are all but wiped out and hundreds of Imperial worlds are lost to the Tyranids before the incursion is blunted.
509997.M41	Elements of the Ultramarines and Mortificators Space Marine Chapters make a stand against one spur of Hive Fleet Leviathan on the world of Tarsis Ultra. The defenders defeat this tendril with a biological plague, but the remainder of Hive Fleet Leviathan rampages on unabated.
010999.M41	The Taking of Bridge Two-Four. Uriel Ventris succeeds Captain Idaeus as commander of the Ultramarines 4th Company.
303999.M41	Captain Sicarius leads an army to halt the Tau expansion. A crusade drawn from thirty Chapters drives the Tau back from dozens of Imperial worlds, but is recalled before its work can be completed.
854999.M41	Ultramar comes under renewed assault from the forces of Chaos. M'kar the Reborn, clad in mortal flesh once again, leads the onslaught against Talassar. Other warlords attack Calth, Espandor and Tarentus. Marneus Calgar recalls all Ultramarines forces to defend Ultramar, dispatching a reinforced Battle Company to each threatened planet. Calgar himself accompanies the 2nd Company to defend Talassar, determined to slay M'kar a hundred times over if need be.

A BROTHERHOOD AT WAR

By their valour is the Imperium of man preserved.

The Ultramarines may be the most famous and respected of the Space Marine Chapters, but they do not stand alone. All across the galaxy, every Chapter fights its own battles against the darkness that seeks to claim Mankind. As the Ultramarines guard the eastern fringe, so do the Death Spectres, Crimson Templars, White Consuls and many other Chapters besides tread the very rim of known space, guarding against terrors from without. Elsewhere, the Silver Skulls, Brazen Claws, Dark Templars and several hundred others stand vigil over strategic sectors or contested zones within the Imperium itself.

Space Marine Chapters are not spread evenly throughout the galaxy. As both Mankind's best line of defence and its final hope, they are found wherever the need is greatest. So it is that a score of Chapters lie within striking distance of the Eye of Terror, void-crafted lair as it is to all manner of renegades and traitors. Conversely, in some parts of the Imperium it is possible to traverse hundreds of light years without even once encountering a Space Marine. This is not to suggest that there are areas of the galaxy that lie undefended – nothing could be further from the truth. As every Space Marine Chapter maintains a Warp-capable fleet, even the most far-flung outpost of Mankind can call upon the Adeptus Astartes should need arise.

As a result of their fortress monastery's location, many Space Marine Chapters develop understanding and skill that allows them to more easily defeat a particular foe. Such is true of the Raven Guard and their continual battles against the Ork menace in and around the Targus system, and of the seemingly endless series of conflicts between the Mentors and the Eldar of Biel Tann Craftworld. Such Chapters are often called upon for aid in campaigns far from their usual sphere of authority, as their specialist knowledge can mean the difference between victory and defeat. While these practices are not specifically encouraged by the Codex Astartes, the innate practicality of war always wins through.

While it is not unheard of for two or more Chapters to fight together in a campaign, neither is it particularly common. Indeed, some Chapters consider it a point of pride never to request aid from their more distant Battle-Brothers, as this might be construed as admission of ill-preparedness or weakness. Only a few respected Chapter Masters, of whom Marneus Calgar of the Ultramarines is one, can overcome such deeply ingrained traditions. To see several Space Marine Chapters fighting side-by-side is therefore one of the main indicators of a hard-fought campaign, whose consequences will surely stretch far beyond its battlezones and mar the destiny of Man.

THE GREY KNIGHTS

The Grey Knights were the first of the new Chapters to be created during the Second Founding. They are an exception amongst the Second Founding Chapters in that they have no antecedents, their gene-seed was engineered from sources unknown to all save their long-dead creators. The history of the Grey Knights' inception is not a matter of record and even their inclusion in the Second Founding is debatable. There are hints in the Adeptus Terra's vaults that the Chapter was actually created by the Emperor in secret, sometime during the Great Crusade.

Designated Chapter 666, the Grey Knights work in close co-operation with the Ordo Malleus, the militant arm of the Inquisition. As a consequence the Chapter stands apart from other Space Marines in many ways, and its organisation is wholly unique. While the Chapter maintains a fortress monastery on Saturn's moon of Titan, much of its strength is scattered across the trackless Imperium.

Guided by the finest Navigators of the Navis Nobilite and conveyed by the swiftest ships in the service of Mankind, the Grey Knights stand ready to meet the foul minions of Chaos wherever they may strike. With psychic power and Nemesis force weapon, so do the Grey Knights strive against the servants of the Dark Gods, meeting corruption with purity, malice with honour, and betrayal with the Emperor's justice.

THE HUNT FOR VOLDORIUS

At the centennial feast in celebration of his ascension, Honoured Kyublai, the Great Khan of the White Scars announced his intention to bring to justice one of the greatest foes ever to have opposed the Chapter. Kernax Voldorius was a Daemon Prince and warleader of the renegade Alpha Legion, and as vile a foe as any the White Scars had fought. Thousands of billions had died when Voldorius had unleashed the merciless horror of the Bloodtide some two thousand years earlier, and billions more had perished in the sacrilegious massacres on Kento, Loran and Blindhope. Now, the Great Khan declared, Bladespite's triumphal reign of terror would cease. Kor'sarro Khan, Captain of the 3rd Company and the Master of the Hunt, was despatched, charged to return with the Daemon Prince's head, or not at all.

It was a hunt to last more than a decade. Though Kor'sarro caught sight of his prey on the battlefields of Zoran and Kavell, and almost came within striking distance in the choked underhives of Modanna, chance always conspired to save Voldorius from his deserved fate. And so the trail led Kor'sarro Khan and his Company to Quintus, a desolate planet to the galactic south of Chogoris. Quintus had only recently been one of the Imperium's chief bulwarks against the brutal greenskin empires of the Jagal Stars, but that was before the coming of Kernax Voldorius. Through intimidation and false promises, the Daemon Prince's warband had infiltrated and corrupted Quintus' military. The White Scars found no mere warband, but a whole planet ready to stand against them, but Kor'sarro would not be so easily denied.

Leaving their Strike Cruiser in the outer system, the White Scars mounted their Thunderhawk Gunships. Following rigorously plotted stealth trajectories, the attack craft slipped through Quintus' defence grid and made landing amongst the blasted canyons south-west of the planetary capital of Mankarra. Kor'sarro expected to have a battle on his hands to secure the landing zone but he found no waiting enemies, but rather unexpected allies in the shape of Kayvaan Shrike and the Raven Guard 3rd Company.

Shrike had been on campaign in the Targus system when news of Quintus' fall had reached his ears. With the Targus battlezone swinging into the Imperium's favour, Shrike redeployed his company to Quintus and had been fighting a guerrilla war against the Night Lord invaders ever since. The piloting expertise that had allowed the White Scars to make planetfall unobserved by the rebels had not been skillful enough to go unnoticed by Shrike's forces, and the Raven Guard had mustered to meet the new arrivals.

An Alliance is Forged

As dropships deployed the White Scars' support vehicles, the two Captains held a council of war. Neither entirely trusted the other. The rivalry between the White Scars and the Raven Guard went back many thousands of years, but both Shrike and Kor'sarro knew that they had little choice but to set aside their inherited differences, weighty though they were. The Alpha Legion and their treacherous vassals were simply too numerous for one company to defeat without the other's aid, and so the Space Marines' battleplans had to be drawn accordingly.

The following morning before dawn, Shrike led his Company in a surprise assault against the traitors garrisoned in an orbital defence battery some leagues west of Mankarra. This was the method of war Shrike and his brothers had perfected against the forces of Waaagh! Skullkrak, and within moments of the assault's beginning, the traitor forces were in disarray. A good portion of the complex was already in Space Marine hands when Kernax Voldorius, seeing the danger, despatched half of his Alpha Legion and much of Mankarra's garrison as reinforcements. But Shrike had drawn his plans well. As the Raven Guard Captain led Assault squads into the heart of the complex, his remaining forces entrenched themselves on the perimeter.

So it was that Voldorius' tide of reinforcements crashed upon the bastions of the defence complex's outer fortifications as an ocean upon rocky shores. The lieutenant directing the assault was a canny foe, and held his deadliest troops back from the slaughter. Instead he sent wave after wave of cultists and traitors unto the guns of the Raven Guard, casually expending their worthless lives in search of a weakness to exploit. Such a weakness offered itself up when one of the bastions cracked asunder, broken by fire from *Ironsoul*, a Baneblade manned by traitorous crew. Seizing his opportunity, the lieutenant led his reserves forwards.

Over three hundred Chaos Space Marines flung themselves at that single point in the defences. The Raven Guard stood their ground, pouring bolter fire into the oncoming horde, but their numbers were thin and the enemy ferocious. Shrike emerged from the depths of the complex to lead a counter-attack and the enemy fell back wherever the Shadow Captain trod but, little by little, the Raven Guard began to give ground. The Alpha Legion lieutenant roared his praise to his terrible gods and drove his men forwards over the dead and dying. It was then that the White Scars struck.

Before Shrike had led the assault on the orbital defence complex, the White Scars had concealed themselves in the caves to the south. Now, with the bulk of the Chaos force strung out, the White Scars launched their attack. With a throaty roar of engines, Rhinos and bikes broke from the shadows and spurred towards the fray. The Ironsoul was the first to feel the White Scar's wrath. Though the Baneblade's commander bellowed at his crew, the massive tank could not turn swiftly enough to engage the new threat. Kor'sarro's vanguard, skilled bikers all, tore through the traitors that protected the Ironsoul's flanks. Never once slowing their breakneck charge, the White Scars bikers swarmed about the adamantium leviathan's flanks, targeting sponsons with melta-fire and vision slits with flamers. One by one, the Ironsoul's guns were silenced and the bikers spurred on towards the embattled Raven Guard, leaving only a crippled tank and slain rebels to their rear.

Dismayed by the unforeseen assault to their flank and the swift demise of the Ironsoul, the traitors fled. The Alpha Legion fought on to the last, but the White Scars were upon them. Squads of bikers swept through the ranks of Chaos Space Marine, blades and lances flashing. More White Scars disgorged from Rhinos, bolters coughing death at the foe. By the time Kayvaan Shrike led the Raven Guard over the defences and into the fray, the outcome of the battle was no longer in doubt.

The Taking of Mankarra

Shrike and Kor'sarro had no time for celebration. Voldorius and his followers still had control of Mankarra and, if given time, would be able to fortify it further. Leaving a small garrison in the orbital defence complex, the White Scars took to their Rhinos and the Raven Guard to their Thunderhawk Gunships.

Mankarra's defences remained a concern. Both Shrike's and Kor'sarro's companies had travelled light, and could only boast a single Vindicator between them, the *Thunderheart*. Fortunately, the efficiency of Voldorius' despotic rule did not extend to repair and maintenance. A salvo of hellstrike missiles from the Raven Guard's Thunderhawks and a brief close range pounding from the *Thunderheart* brought down a sizable segment of Mankarra's outer fortifications. Before the traitor garrison could react, the White Scars were loose in the city.

Not wishing to get caught in the brawl of a cityfight, the White Scars fought from their transports, debarking only to launch lightning assaults. Bikers hurtled through the streets and alleys, swarming wherever the defenders were unprepared. As the White Scars commanded the battle at street-level, Shrike's Thunderhawks deployed squad after squad of Raven Guard into the upper levels of manufactorums and basilicas. Beset from above and below, the defenders stood little chance. Many threw down their arms and begged for mercy, but there was none to be had in those blood-soaked streets.

At the end, only Voldorius and his personal bodyguard remained. Infused with the bloody joy of battle, the Daemon Prince fought on against the impossible odds. Many Battle-Brothers fell to Voldorius' wrath that day, but the vengeance of the Space Marines would not be denied and they pressed forwards to finish their foe.

Encircled, outnumbered and trapped in the shadow of the Cathedral of the Emperor's Wisdom, Kernax Voldorius finally met his end. The Daemon Prince did not easily fall, and his bodyguard of corrupt and twisted Chaos Space Marines fought without fear, yet the outcome was surely never in doubt. At the last even Voldorius' unholy strength could not prevail against the determination of his enemies. Pierced and pinned to a fallen statue of the Emperor by Shrike's Talons, Voldorius could not escape the vengeance of Kor'sarro's blade. With one terrible blow, the White Scars Captain clove the Daemon Prince's head from his shoulders, erasing his foul stain from existence.

A month later, with Quintus in the hands of an Imperial Guard army sent from Tallarn, Kor'sarro and Shrike exchanged their finals words and went their separate ways once again. Shrike returned to the Targus battlezone. Claiming Voldorius' head as gloried prize, Kor'sarro Khan returned to a hero's welcome in the great palace of the White Scars. Each Captain took with him the respect of the other and the glory of a hard battle won, and perhaps the beginnings of a brotherhood restored between Chapters that had for too long been rivals.

THE WORLD ENGINE

On the outskirts of the Danorra system lies the scarred and lifeless planet of Safehold. It was here that the Astral Knights Chapter made the ultimate sacrifice to halt the onslaught of the Necron World Engine, and it is here, in the dead heart of the Battle Barge *Tempestus*, that a shrine was raised in their memory. Seven hundred and seventy-two arbalstone statues stand silent vigil amongst the ruined flagship, one for each fallen Battle-Brother of the Astral Knights. Beyond the wreckage, a score of living guardians patrol the dusty landscape, their eyes ever alert for scavengers whose presence continues to mar the sacred site. These are Space Marines, Battle-Brothers from a dozen disparate Chapters standing as one out of respect to the fallen.

The World Engine's arrival in the Vidar sub-sector took the Imperium completely by surprise. Even now it is unknown if the World Engine was a Necron Tombworld mobilised by arcane technology, or merely a starship of planetary proportions constructed in the darkness between the stars. By the time the World Engine's gauss projectors had scoured all life from the agrarian worlds of Gaios Prime and Gaios Tertio, all speculation as to its origins was abandoned – only its demise mattered.

The entire Vidar sector fleet and no less than fifteen Space Marine task forces, including elements from the Ultramarines, Astral Knights, Invaders and Aurora Chapters, opposed the World Engine as it reaped a bloody harvest from planet after planet. Yet not even the mightiest of Mankind's weapons could break the World Engine's

shielding. A dozen sorties were launched, twelve attempts to overwhelm the World Engine with sheer valour and firepower, yet all the Imperial fleet had to show for its pains were a string of destroyed and crippled ships, and millions of casualties. Worse still, direct assaults seemed impossible. Drop Pods and boarding torpedoes could not penetrate the World Engine's shields, and teleport beams targeted onto its surface lost all coherency. After two full Terminator squads from the Invaders Chapter were lost in this manner, further attempts were forbidden.

A Desperate Gambit

Following the Galax Rift disaster, in which a good third of the Vidar sector fleet had been lost to no avail, Artor Amhrad, the Master of the Astral Knights Chapter, adopted a desperate strategy. Forgoing weaponry that had many times proved to be ineffective, Amhrad employed the Astral Knights' Battle Barge itself against the World Engine's shields. With its engines roaring at full power and its proud adamantium hull shuddering under the impact of incoming fire, the *Tempestus* forced its way through the World Engine's defence screens. With such momentum behind it, the *Tempestus* could not hope to avoid a collision with the surface of the World Engine, but such was not Amhrad's intent. The moment the Battle Barge pierced the shields, the Astral Knights had taken to their Drop Pods. The *Tempestus*' scored and ravaged form collided with the World Engine in a storm of metal and fire, but the Astral Knights were safely on the surface of the artificial world, continuing the fight with undimmed determination.

It is impossible to say how many Necrons dwelt within the armoured skin of the World Engine, but their numbers must have reckoned in the tens of thousands. A mere seven hundred souls, though they were Space Marines all, should have made little account against such odds, yet Amhrad and his Battle Brothers were determined that their sacrifice would not be in vain. Bereft of hope, the Astral Knights fought without fear, destroying every flux generator, weaponforge and command node in their path. For one hundred hours and more the Astral Knights wrought havoc. Yet each battle amid the cyclopean structures that choked the World Engine's surface took its toll in dead and wounded. Some perished buying time so that their Brothers might fall back and march to fresh battles. All died on their feet, spitting defiance at the soulless warriors who opposed them.

The Final Sacrifice

The Astral Knights' final assault consisted only of Amhrad and five others. Though wounded and weary, they fought their way through a vast tomb complex that housed many of the World Engine's command arrays. His followers dead or dying, Amhrad's final act was to detonate the melta bombs that tore the tomb apart. This last heroic act overwhelmed the World Engine's already overtaxed control nodes and brought not only the shields crashing down, but also silenced many of its weapon systems. The Astral Knights were gone, but by their sacrifice the World Engine was laid bare for the vengeance of Mankind. Seeing the foe defenceless, the Imperial fleet attacked with a vengeance, and tore the World Engine apart with repeated volleys of cyclonic torpedoes.

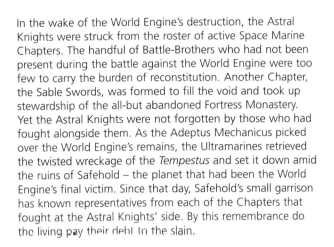

In the wake of the World Engine's destruction, the Astral Knights were struck from the roster of active Space Marine Chapters. The handful of Battle-Brothers who had not been present during the battle against the World Engine were too few to carry the burden of reconstitution. Another Chapter, the Sable Swords, was formed to fill the void and took up stewardship of the all-but abandoned Fortress Monastery. Yet the Astral Knights were not forgotten by those who had fought alongside them. As the Adeptus Mechanicus picked over the World Engine's remains, the Ultramarines retrieved the twisted wreckage of the *Tempestus* and set it down amid the ruins of Safehold – the planet that had been the World Engine's final victim. Since that day, Safehold's small garrison has known representatives from each of the Chapters that fought at the Astral Knights' side. By this remembrance do the living pay their debt to the slain.

THE PURGING OF CONTQUAL

The Iron Hands have ever been a wrathful and merciless Chapter, and many would-be usurpers and heretics have renewed their faith in the glory of the Emperor under the threat of the Iron Hands' fearsome retribution. Nowhere was this seen more plainly than during the reclamation of the Contqual sub-sector.

The citizens of Contqual had prospered and lived a decadent life, believing they had found an earthly paradise far removed from the turmoil and ugliness of the rest of the universe. Such moral weakness was to be their downfall. As best as can be determined, the corruption of Contqual began in late 812.M41 when the High Governor succumbed to the false promises of the Chaos God Slaanesh. Thereafter the taint spread quickly through Contqual society, feeding off the desires and weaknesses of those in positions of power. Within a month, the entire sub-sector writhed with the corrupting essence of Chaos.

The task of cleansing Contqual fell to the Iron Hands, whose hatred of Chaos in all its forms burned bright enough to eclipse all others. They stormed into the sub-sector, taking several planets before any form of resistance could be assembled. Entire populations were ruthlessly cut down to a man, slaughtered while their pleas for mercy went unheard. The death of every heretic and traitor only strengthened the Imperium, and the Iron Hands had no mercy for those who would let such corruption overtake their world.

The pivotal battle came on the hive world of Shardenus, where a tear had appeared in the fabric of real space, opening a direct and hungry link to the Warp. Daemons poured through the rift to be welcomed and embraced by the twisted inhabitants of the planet. All this the Iron Hands saw when they made planetfall, and it served only to feed and enflame their righteous wrath. Untold thousands of traitors assailed the invaders, but the Iron Hands merely cursed their names and fought on. Daemons whispered sweet words of corruption, but their honeyed temptations found no purchase. The Iron Hands never slowed and never yielded, meeting each fresh battle with redoubled determination. In a desperate battle, the Warp rift was closed through the combined will of the Chapter Librarians. With the Daemons banished, Shardenus was swiftly scoured of all taint.

After the fall of Shardenus, the rest of the sub-sector was quickly forced into submission. One by one, worlds turned on their perverted overlords and begged for clemency from the vengeful Space Marines, but the Iron Hands were without pity for such callow folk. In a year of bloodshed, the Iron Hands executed one in every three citizens of Contqual. The message was clear – to court damnation was to invite only destruction. Not one of the survivors doubted that the Iron Hands stood ready to mete out punishment once more, should need arise.

Space Marine Battle Barges are primarily configured for close support of planetary landings. A considerable amount of hull space is given over to launch bays for intra-system craft, boarding torpedoes and Drop Pods. Even so, most Battle Barges can bring an obscene amount of firepower to bear – almost as much as the Grand Cruisers of the Imperial Navy.

The most venerable Battle Barges, notably the Storm of Wrath and Spear of Vengeance of the Imperial Fists Chapter, date back to the days of the Great Crusade are as much shrines as weapons of war.

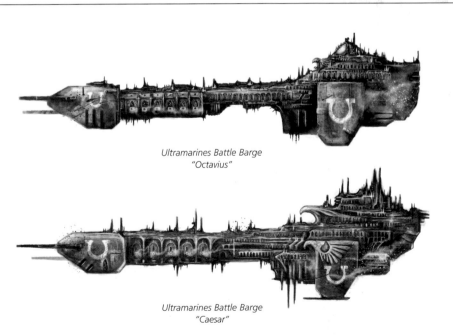

Ultramarines Battle Barge "Octavius"

Ultramarines Battle Barge "Caesar"

BATTLE FOR TRAITOR'S GORGE

Many know the tragedy of the Crimson Fists, of how the mighty Chapter was brought low by Waaagh! Snagrod and the most damnable fortune. Even more widespread is the legend of the Crimson Fists' heroic struggle to survive, to rebuild their brotherhood from the ashes of war. One tale is not so widely told, and known only to Chapter Master Pedro Kantor and his closest Battle-Brothers.

The tale begins a half-year after the reclamation of Rynn's World from Waaagh! Snagrod. Although the planet was officially designated as secure, Orks were ever difficult to eradicate. Several greenskin warbands were known to be lurking in the Jaden Mountains, conducting raids that the weary and wartorn populace of Rynn's World could ill-afford.

As the Crimson Fists' surviving Techmarines salvaged and repaired what little had survived the Waaagh! Meanwhile, Kantor dedicated himself to cleansing the Jaden mountains of the beasts that lurked within. It was a difficult campaign, for the Orks defended every crag and cavern, and Kantor had neither the men nor the equipment he would have wished for such a task. Nonetheless, the Crimson Fists forged on, slaying greenskins wherever they could be found. Under such a threat, it was perhaps only a matter of time before the Orks of the Jaden Mountains united. So it was that when Kantor's force came under attack in Traitor's Gorge, they found themselves assailed not only by the warband they had been hunting, but every Ork for leagues in every direction.

Though but two dozen in number, Kantor and his Crimson Fists fought as heroes born of legend, taking a grievous toll on an Ork horde that numbered hundreds. With Kantor at the forefront, the Space Marines battled their way clear of the ravine's treacherous confines and sought the high ground. There they planted their feet and fought shoulder to shoulder against the horde, but still the Orks kept coming.

With all the Crimson Fists' Thunderhawk Gunships lost in battle or under heavy repair, Kantor knew that both evacuation and reinforcement were impossible, and the Orks showed no sign of giving up the battle. Three of Kantor's Battle-Brothers had been slain in the escape from the ravine, and only the Chapter Master remained unwounded. In return, the Crimson Fists slicked the dirt of Traitor's Gorge red with the blood of slain greenskins, and fought from behind barricades of lumpen Orkish dead, but Kantor knew that the odds were stacked against him.

Aid Unlooked For

Without warning, the greenskin tide began to slacken. Seeking the reason, Kantor's keen eye saw ghostly figures on Widow's Spire to the west and Darkridge to the east, high above and behind the encircling Orks. Graceful were these newcomers, darting from cover to cover and paying no heed to the treacherous footing as their longrifles brought precise death to the Ork horde. Who his fresh allies were, Kantor could not immediately tell, for their forms shimmered as insubstantial as mist in the morning sunlight, but nor did he care. All that mattered was that this intervention gave his Battle-Brothers the chance that they needed to counter-attack and turn the battle's tide.

Giving a mighty shout, the Crimson Fists charged over their rampart of dead greenskins and set upon the Orks with new vigour. Caught between the re-doubled rage of the Crimson Fists and fresh attackers on the slopes, the Orks were thrust back. The greenskins fled down Traitor's Gorge, leaving more than ten score dead and twice as many wounded behind them. As Kantor's men walked amongst the carnage, ending the lives of those Orks too foolhardy or injured to flee, a robed figure detached itself from the shadows clustered on Widow's Spire and strode swiftly to Kantor's side. Coldly contemptuous of any threat posed by the watchful Space Marines, it cut through the Chapter Master's wary greeting.

"The surviving beasts cower in the shadows below, ensnared in a web of our devising. Pursue them into the darkness and a great victory shall be yours."
"And should I choose not to do so?" Kantor asked, for he could not bring himself to place his trust in the elaborately-helmed alien that stood before him.
"Then they will escape and grow ever stronger in the darkness. In fifty years a shadow of their making will arise to envelop this area of space which, unopposed, shall be the doom of your people and mine. Catastrophe will reign, and you shall lament your inaction this day."
"Will you aid us in the gorge as you did here?" Kantor demanded, but the figure shook its head.
"Be not so swift to embrace us as allies. Auspicious fate dictated that we should fight side-by-side this day but, fate is a fickle creature. At our next encounter, it will be my fists that bear the stain of your blood."

And with that, the alien turned and was gone, and the shadows that lurked amongst the scree of Widow's Spire and Darkridge were gone also. Kantor weighed the words and actions he had borne witness to and led his men into Traitor's Gorge. There in the darkness great victory was indeed his, forever ending the Ork threat in the Jaden Mountains. Returning to the lowlands, Kantor continued the rebuilding of his Chapter, and in time raised the Crimson Fists out of ruin to once more stand alongside the greatest champions of Mankind. But in all the years of triumph that followed, the robed figure's words would dwell heavily on Kantor until, at the last, they met again.

THE RETURN TO ARMAGEDDON

When Waaagh! Ghazghkull descended upon Armageddon in 998.M41, many were the Space Marine Chapters that responded. Black Templars, White Scars, Exorcists, Scythebearers, Iron Champions, Storm Lords – the list goes on, their raiment every colour under the Emperor's sun. Yet of all those Chapters that fought in the shadow of Armageddon's smoke-wreathed factories and hives, the populace remember none with the same gratitude as they do the Salamanders.

The Salamanders had been instrumental in Ghazghkull's defeat in the Second War for Armageddon, but victory had cost them sorely. Perhaps then it was vengeance that drove the Chapter to make such a generous contribution to the Third War. Whatever the reason, almost the entire Salamanders Chapter was present in the crucial early months of the war. Under the eye of their bold Chapter Master Tu'shan, they fought with determination on the most terrible battlefields. When the storm of war grew quiet and the Ork attacks slowed, the Salamanders did not sit idle, but instead launched several devastating counter-attacks against the rock-forts landed by the Orks along the Hemlock River. Preferring the close-quarter fighting within the maze of crudely carved tunnels within the Roks to the long-range duels in the desert, the Salamanders made their mark. By the start of the Season of Fire, at least nine Roks had been destroyed by the Salamanders' attacks, killing untold thousands of greenskins.

The glory of such battles was one shared with many other Chapters, and alone it does not explain the fierce loyalty that the Salamanders engendered in the people of Armageddon. The truth of the matter remains that while some Chapters fought for the Emperor, and others for renown and glory, Tu'shan and his Salamanders fought each battle for the people of Armageddon.

On more than one occasion, Tu'shan threw his Brother-Marines into the most hopeless of battles to rescue embattled civilian enclaves and settlements that other Imperial commanders had been prepared to sacrifice for the sake of the wider war. Indeed it is even rumoured that Master Tu'shan himself came to blows with Captain Vinyar of the Marines Malevolent after it became known that the latter's men had shelled a refugee camp simply because there were Orks within the perimeter. This act alone won Tu'shan and his Chapter much reknown, although relations between the Salamanders and the Marines Malevolent have since never been quite the same.

The majority of the Salamanders departed Armageddon following the Season of Fire, but the Chapter's work was not done. The two companies that remained did so to protect the major population centres from marauding Ork warbands that would never quite be eradicated. The Chapter's Techmarines have been instrumental in repairing and rebuilding the infrastructure required to maintain such a vast amount of people, and it is certain that they have saved many thousands of lives with these vital but often overlooked duties. Armageddon will not soon forget the efforts the Salamanders undertook in their name. The legend that the sons of Vulkan have left behind will surely shine all the brighter with every passing year.

THE DARK FOUNDING

Not all the foundings of Space Marine Chapters are recorded in exact detail. However, the Adeptus Terra maintains a bank of original gene-seed from every single Chapter ever created since the Horus Heresy. There is one notable exception: the Thirteenth Founding, also known as the Dark Founding.

No-one knows how many Chapters were created by the Dark Founding or what became of them. Perhaps the secret lies in some deep vault in the record office of the Adeptus Terra. Maybe the Space Marines of the Dark Founding are still out there, somewhere, waiting to return to the world that created them.

THE ZEIST CAMPAIGN

In the dying embers of 997.M41, the Tau Empire began to expand with vigour. Imperial logisticiers projected that unless action was taken, the Tau would double their holdings within fifty years, and captured Imperial worlds would provide the raw material for exponential growth. By 999.M41 System Lords all across the Ultima Segmentum were screaming out for reinforcements, but the onset of Hive Fleet Leviathan, as well as heightened Chaos Renegade activity around the Maelstrom meant that there were few to send. Inexorably, the boundaries of the Tau domain continued to expand.

Such dire events had not gone unnoticed on Macragge. Having fought at their side against encroaching elements of Hive Fleet Kraken, Marneus Calgar had a grudging respect for the Tau, but could not allow the annexation of Imperial space to continue. To this end, he despatched Captain Sicarius and the 2nd Company to the Zeist sector where they would draw a line in space and halt the Tau advance. Word was also sent to all nearby Chapters, asking for aid in the coming campaign.

The Ultramarines arrived at Zeist to find the sector secure. Faced with a highly mobile opponent, the sector's military commanders had entrenched their forces on a handful of vital worlds, leaving many planets at the mercy of the Tau. Sicarius immediately went on the offensive. His first act was to rout the Tau from the heavily embattled forge world of Praetonis V, and use the momentum to drive the invaders from the sector. Further successes followed by the score as Sicarius fought the Tau at their own game, striking with speed and precision at lightly defended targets and using the resulting confusion to destabilise more keenly defended worlds. The Tau expansion slowed, and then stopped completely. With the Tau onslaught blunted and most of the invaded worlds liberated, Sicarius' task was almost complete – only the staging post on Augura remained.

By the time Sicarius' force struck Augura it had swollen to nearly Chapter strength. Few Chapter Masters could contemplate refusing a request from Lord Macragge, and throughout the campaign fresh squads and companies had arrived to place themselves under Sicarius' command. Tactical squads arrived from the Night Watch, the Halo Dragons, Silver Skulls, Sable Swords, Crimson Fists and more besides. The Iron Lords sent Devastator squads, the Aurora Chapter a Predator spearhead and the Eagle Warriors a score of Terminator-armoured veterans. Most significant of all was the arrival of no less than three companies of the Knights of the Raven, sent to fulfil a debt incurred some twelve centuries earlier. So it was that when the Drop Pods fell on Augura, no less than a dozen company banners were hoisted aloft to challenge the upstart Tau.

On Augura's killing fields, the assembled Space Marines put aside all rivalries of Chapter and status to fight as brothers against a deserving foe. For all their technology, their battlesuits and their weaponry, the Tau could not hope to prevail against such an assemblage of might – it is doubtful that any foe could have. Augura's fortresses were smashed asunder, its shipyards and weapons factories destroyed. The Tau expansion was ended and their remaining expansion forces retreated to secure territory in dismay.

Sicarius was fully-prepared to carry the assault deeper into the Tau Empire, and reclaim those worlds captured at the very start of the campaign, but it was not to be. The Imperial Tarot was predicting dire times ahead for the Imperium and the might of the Adeptus Astartes was needed elsewhere. Reluctantly surrendering the defence of the Tau border to local governors, Sicarius dispersed his armies and returned to Macragge to rearm and replace his losses.

The greatest battle of the age was brewing, and in the name of Guilliman and the Emperor, the Ultramarines 2nd Company would do their part.

FAMOUS BATTLES

Date Code	Event
749.M41	The 812th Feast of Blades. All twelve competing Chapters are in attendance. The Iron Knights' champion Hervald Strom wins the competition.
750.M41	In their search for the possessed cruiser *Shadeblight*, Night Lords Chaos Space Marines wreak havoc throughout the Ango sub-sector. The Night Lords are initially opposed only by Space Marines from the Red Wolves Chapter. Though they stand alone, the Red Wolves manage to deny the Night Lords their prize.
754.M41	The Salamanders 2nd Company scour all traces of Genestealer infestation from the moon of Ymgarl.
772.M41	Forgefather He'stan Vulkan of the Salamanders recovers the Gauntlet of the Forge after defeating the warband of Eldar pirate lord Iath Bloodweaver.
777.M41	A sizable Black Legion warband exits the Eye of Terror. Cadian Imperial Guard forces slow the onslaught, but it takes a determined counter-attack from the Imperial Fists to throw the Chaos Space Marines into the Warp.
812.M41	The Purging of Contqual. The Iron Hands Chapter drive the taint of Chaos from a dozen planets in the Contqual sub-sector.
819.M41	A perceived slight causes the Mortifactors and Crimson Fists to come to blows. Only a personal intercession by Marneus Calgar ends the dispute before it escalates to open war. The matter is kept from the attention of the Adeptus Terra.
845.M41	The Blood Swords Chapter conduct the purging of the Inando system. More than one hundred billion Imperial citizens are slain in the resulting Exterminatus actions.
849.M41	The 813th Feast of Blades. Despite suffering heavy wounds in the Vinculus Crusade, Hervald Strom emerges triumphant once more. Never before has one Chapter, let alone one champion, prevailed in two successive assemblages.
852.M41	The Invaders Chapter launch a direct assault on the Craftworld Idharae. Though the Space Marines suffer horrific casualties, they leave the Craftworld a ruined and desolate hulk.
857.M41	The Chapter Fleet of the Silver Skulls blockades the dead worlds of the Lazar system for three years. Nothing gets into or out of the system while the blockade remains in place, and no explanation is ever provided by the Silver Skulls themselves.
862.M41	Waaagh! Skullkrak invades the Targus system. Kayvaan Shrike and the Raven Guard 3rd Company are amongst the forces that respond.
865.M41	The Purging of Modanna. Kor'sarro Khan drives Kernax Voldorius from his foremost stronghold.
871.M41	The Liberation of Quintus. With the aid of the Raven Guard 3rd Company, Kor'sarro Khan finally slays Kernax Voldorius in the streets of Mankarra.
895.M41	Craftworld Alaitoc launches a devastating attack on the Invaders' Chapter Planet. With the Invaders still under strength following their assault on Idharae they are quickly overcome. Though three companies escape the disaster, the fortress-monastery is lost. The Invaders are thereafter a spacebound Chapter.
926.M41	The Necron Worldengine is revealed as the architect of the destruction in the Vidar sub-sector. It is destroyed on the edge of the Doranno system, thanks chiefly to the noble sacrifice of the Astral Knights Chapter.
934.M41	The Toran VI Massacres. The Crimson Fists defeat the warband of Chaos Lord Sathash the Golden.
949.M41	The 814th Feast of Blades. The ravages of war dictate that only eight of the twelve participating Chapters are in attendance, but the tradition is still observed. Supremacy is tied between the Imperial Fists and Crimson Fists Chapters.
951.M41	Rapid strikes by the Howling Griffons brings the Amar secession to a swift and bloody end.
954.M41	The Fall of Rogue's Spire. Waaagh! Dethrekka descends upon the sparsely defended planet of Rogue's Spire. Only the courageous fighting retreat conducted by the Sable Swords Chapter allows the Explorator and Mechanicus research teams to escape the greenskins.
960.M41	The Red Corsairs and their allies assault the Marines Errant fortress monastery and plunder the loyalist Chapter's supplies of gene-seed.
964.M41	Darnath Lysander, lost hero of the Imperial Fists, escapes from the Iron Warriors stronghold of Malodrax. Returning finally to his Chapter, he spends much of the next year undergoing tests to verify his identity and purity.
966.M41	Lysander leads the Imperial Fists to Malodrax and scours the Iron Warriors from the planet.
970.M41	The Emperor's Swords Chapter is wiped out to the last man when a Necron Tomb stirs to life in the caverns of their Chapter Planet, Bellicas.
989.M41	Waaagh! Snagrod rampages across the Loki sector, culminating with a devastating assault on Rynn's World. The Crimson Fists Chapter is left battered and bloodied, but determined to rebuild.
990.M41	The Fire Lords Chapter descends on Bellicas, exterminating the Necron menace and avenging the destruction of the Emperor's Swords.
995.M41	The tendrils of Hive Fleet Jormungandr begin to brush against the north-eastern boundaries of the Imperium. The Death Spectres and Honoured Sons Chapters lead the counterattack.
757998.M41	Warlord Ghazghkull returns to Armageddon at the head of a new, even greater, Waaagh! More than twenty Space Marine Chapters, including the White Scars, Salamanders, Doom Eagles and Exorcists, commit forces to the battlezone.
980999.M41	A Chaos Space Marine fleet, under the command of Huron Blackheart, emerges from the Maelstrom and swiftly brings the Chogoris, Kaelas and Sessec systems under siege. The White Scars withdraw from Armageddon to meet the threat.
990999.M41	Imperial worlds in the galactic south are caught in the crossfire between Saim Hann Eldar and the Orks of Octavius. The Raven Guard, White Scars and Salamanders Chapters unite to defend the embattled planets from the aliens.

FORCES OF THE SPACE MARINES

This section of the book details the forces used by the Space Marines – their weapons, their units, and some famous special characters that you can choose, such as Marneus Calgar of the Ultramarines or Kor'sarro Khan of the White Scars. Each entry describes the unit and gives the specific rules you will need use them in your games. As such, the army list given later refers to the page numbers of these entries, so you can easily check back as you pick a force.

The Forces of the Space Marines section is sub-divided into two parts. The first part describes all of the troops and vehicles fielded by the Space Marines, including the special characters, while the second part details the Space Marines armoury of weapons and equipment.

EQUIPMENT

The army list at the back of the book shows all the standard and optional wargear available to a particular model. You will find that some items of equipment are unique to particular characters or units, while others are used by more than one unit. When an item is unique, it is detailed in the following entry for its owner, and where an item is not unique, it is detailed in the wargear section.

A good example is the Spear of Vulkan, a potent weapon wielded by He'stan, Forgefather of the Salamanders Chapter. As such, its rules are detailed in He'stan's entry. He'stan also carries a bolt pistol. This is a common Space Marine weapon, and so its rules are to be found in the wargear section.

SPACE MARINES SPECIAL RULES

The models in the Space Marines army use a number of special rules that are common to more than one unit, as specified in the individual entries that follow. Given here are either the details of those rules or a reference to where you can find them.

AND THEY SHALL KNOW NO FEAR

Space Marines automatically pass tests to regroup, and can take such tests even if the squad has been reduced to less than half strength by casualties, though all other criteria apply. Usually troops that regroup cannot move normally and always count as moving whether they do or not, but these restrictions do not apply to models subject to this special rule. If Space Marines are caught by a sweeping advance, they are not destroyed and will instead continue to fight normally. If this happens then the unit is subject to the No Retreat! rule in this round of close combat and might therefore suffer additional casualties.

Units which include Servitors are still subject to this rule, providing that the unit contains at least one Space Marine.

COMBAT TACTICS

Roboute Guilliman favoured a balanced approach to battle, pulling together units with different roles to form an army far more effective than the sum of its parts. If Guilliman was conservative in his selection of military assets, he was calculating in their disposal. Not for him the futile stand against unconquerable odds, or a bloody victory to no purpose. Guilliman knew when to stand, when to withdraw and when to strike with every weapon at his command.

Though many thousands of years old, Guilliman's tenets of warfare remain as potent today as they did when the Horus Heresy raged across the galaxy. His fluid and flexible battle stance is still employed by the vast majority of Space Marine Chapters today.

A non-fearless Space Marine unit with this special rule can choose to automatically fail any Morale check it is called upon to take.

INDEPENDENT CHARACTER

See *Characters*, in the Warhammer 40,000 rulebook.

COMBAT SQUADS

A number of ten-man units in the Space Marines army have the option of breaking down into two five-man units, called combat squads. This option is clearly specified in the unit's entry. For example, a ten-man Sternguard Veterans squad can either fight as a ten-man unit or break down into two five-man combat squads.

The units that can be split into combat squads are:

- Vanguard Veteran squads
- Sternguard Veteran squads
- Scout squads
- Scout Bike squads
- Tactical squads
- Assault squads
- Terminator squads
- Assault Terminator squads
- Bike squads
- Devastator squads

The decision to split the unit into combat squads, as well as which models go into each combat squad, must be made when the unit is deployed. Both combat squads can be deployed in separate locations. The one exception to this is a unit that arrives by Drop Pod. The player can choose to split such a unit into combat squads when it disembarks from the Drop Pod.

If you decide to split a unit into combat squads, then each combat squad is treated as a separate unit for all game purposes from that point.

INFILTRATE, FEEL NO PAIN, MOVE THROUGH COVER, SCOUT

All these rules are detailed in Universal Special Rules, in the Warhammer 40,000 rulebook.

CHAPTER MASTER

To be a Chapter Master is to be a god amongst men. His personal combat prowess is unmatched, for his body is that of a Space Marine, with all the might and endurance that a scion of the Emperor is heir to. Hundreds of years of battlefield experience as Scout, Brother Marine and Captain have taught him every facet of war, trained him in the tools of slaughter and honed his wits to the level of instinct.

These dark days of Mankind's survival have known many heroes, bold men whose names are honoured across the Imperium, and whose valorous deeds have become unyielding legend. Ranked high amongst such men are the Chapter Masters of the Space Marines. Even in the 41st Millennium, a time of war and warriors like no other, there are few amongst humanity's defenders that can claim such honour and renown as they, for in sheer scope of battles won and foes vanquished, the Masters of the Space Marines are without peer.

With the merest glance, a Chapter Master can appraise a warzone, can see every threat and opportunity presented by the shifting lines of battle and divine how victory can be assured. All this he does from the vanguard of his army, scouring the enemy with bolter and blade even as his mind and voice command the wider battle. A Chapter Master stands firm when other men falter, advances without fear when other men flee and retreats when only a fool would fight on. By his example does he inspire men to greater valour, not only the Space Marines at his command, but Imperial Guardsmen, hive militiamen and others besides. Such is the value of true heroism – the awakening of lesser men to great deeds.

If a Chapter Master's personal might is unmatched, then the wider power he wields is nothing short of epic. A Chapter Master is a peer of the Imperium, with authority to act as he wishes according to his own judgement and answerable only to others of his rank. In addition to the thousand Space Marines at his command, most Chapter Masters also hold dominion over star-spanning Strike Cruisers, Navigators, Astropaths, Armourers and Planetary Defence Forces. Indeed, most Chapter Masters rule entire worlds, systems or sub-sectors of space in the Emperor's name. Such places are zones of relative prosperity and stability in a galaxy riven by war, their formidable defences buttressed by the might of a Space Marine Chapter and the patronage of its Master.

> "My sword is at the Emperor's command. I answer to no other man, living or dead."
>
> Tu'shan
> Chapter Master of the Salamanders

	WS	BS	S	T	W	I	A	Ld	Sv
Chapter Master	6	5	4	4	3	5	3	10	3+

SPECIAL RULES
And They Shall Know No Fear, Combat Tactics, Independent Character.

Orbital Bombardment: A Chapter Master has the authority to call down a bombardment from a Strike Cruiser. This ability can be used once per game in his Shooting phase, providing that the Chapter Master did not move in the preceding Movement phase (though he may later assault if the controlling player wishes). Calling down an orbital bombardment otherwise counts as firing a ranged weapon and uses the following profile:

Range	Strength	AP	Type
Unlimited	10	1	Ordnance 1, Barrage

Note that if an arrow is rolled on the scatter dice an orbital bombardment will always scatter the full 2D6" – the Chapter Master's Ballistic Skill makes no difference.

WARGEAR
Iron Halo: An Iron Halo incorporates a powerful energy field that can turn aside even the most deadly attacks. It confers a 4+ invulnerable save.

HONOUR GUARD

For a Space Marine to have become one of the Chapter's Honour Guard is for him to have fulfilled many centuries of exceptionally courageous service. Every member of the Honour Guard is a living exemplar of the ideals for which Guilliman intended the Space Marines to be forever known.

Honour Guards are taciturn and spiritually solemn individuals in repose, but ferocious and unyielding warriors in battle. Each has received the very highest honours that his brother Marines can bestow, performing deeds the like of which lesser men can only dream. Indeed, it is said that each member of the Ultramarines Honour Guard has earnt more commendations and glories in a lifetime's service than a whole company of Space Marines from any other Chapter, and that each individual has slain more foes than an entire regiment of Imperial Guardsmen.

So steeped are the Honour Guard in the trade of battle and blood that their accumulated insights and understanding of warfare commonly outstrips even the experience of the Chapter's Captains. They rarely give unsolicited advice, for to do so is to risk undermining their commander's authority, yet such restraint serves only to lend gravitas to an Honour Guard's words. It is considered folly for even the Master of the Chapter – though he be a noble and peerless warrior of several centuries standing – to ignore the solemn counsel of his Honour Guard.

An Honour Guard's wargear is drawn from amongst the most ancient and venerated relics of the Chapter, for such men above all others have earnt the right to bear such a burden. So it is that the Honour Guard enter the fray clad in ornate suits of artificer armour and wielding weapons that have seen battle at the hands of a thousand great heroes. So is the perfect weapon wedded to the perfect warrior, creating a force that only the boldest or most terrifying foes can hope to stand against.

Most Space Marine Chapters have only a handful of Honour Guard, enough to form a distinct and capable fighting unit, but no more. A few of the older and larger Chapters can muster as many as two dozen Honour Guards, but it is a rare and terrible day when they all fight as one.

In battle, the Honour Guard commonly act as the Chapter Master's retinue, responsible for the safety of their commander and hoisting aloft the Chapter's battle standard. These are sacred tasks and the Honour Guard fight for both with stern fury, without ever succumbing to doubt or allowing rage to subvert their actions. Such courage and devotion has been the salvation of more than one Chapter Master's life and turned the tide of countless battles. Accordingly, when an Honour Guard is slain, his companions fight all the harder in order that his mortal shell can be recovered and laid to rest in the Chapter's Vault of Heroes.

	WS	BS	S	T	W	I	A	Ld	Sv
Chapter Champion	5	4	4	4	1	4	3	10	2+
Honour Guard	4	4	4	4	1	4	2	10	2+

SPECIAL RULES
And They Shall Know No Fear, Combat Tactics.

Honour or Death: The Chapter Champion must be ready to challenge any enemy leader to single combat, and all his training is bent to this goal. In an Assault, the Chapter Champion must direct all of his attacks against an enemy independent character if in base contact with one. He always re-rolls any failed rolls to hit and to wound that are directed against an enemy independent character.

WARGEAR
Chapter Banner: Any Space Marine unit within 12" of the Banner Bearer always re-rolls failed Morale and Pinning tests. In addition, all models in the same unit as the Chapter Banner have +1 Attack whilst the banner bearer is alive. While the Banner Bearer is still alive, the Honour Guard counts as scoring one extra wound in close combat for the purposes of calculating the assault result.

"A foe without honour is a foe already beaten."

Ancient Helveticus
Ultramarines Honour Guard

CAPTAIN

Each company in a Space Marine Chapter falls under the command of a Captain. Each Captain is a hardened veteran, a master strategist who has proven his prowess in battle as a member of the Chapter's 1st Company, or through distinguished service in his own Company prior to the death of his predecessor.

In addition to his Chapter rank, each Captain also bears one or more honorific titles associated with the command of a particular company or responsibility. Some, such as Master of the Watch and Master of the Recruits, are common titles in use across almost all Space Marines Chapters. Other titles are products of Chapter history and creed. The Captain of the White Scars 4th Company is traditionally the Master of the Hunt, whilst the Aurora Talons Chapter maintain no less than five Master Bombardiers in their command roster.

Space Marine Captains are masters of the battlefield, able to read its ebb and flow as ancient mariners would judge the changing of the sea. It is not enough for a Captain to simply be a skilled fighter in his own right – each Chapter boasts many such men amongst its roster – he must also have a superhuman grasp of strategy and tactics, as well as the wit to employ them in the ever-changing arena of warfare. Every squad in a Space Marine strike force is a weapon, and a Captain must be proficient in the wielding of each, whether singly or in combination.

It is often said that in terms of raw military might, each Space Marine is easily worth a dozen or so Imperial Guardsmen. Under the command of an experienced Captain, this value can swell tenfold. Such power is not wielded lightly or recklessly, but with precision guided by meditation. Every Space Marine lost in battle is a bitter blow to the Chapter and if lives must be expended, they must be expended for good and noble reasons.

A Space Marine Captain is not simply a master of warfare, he must also have the gift of oratory and diplomacy. Whilst most Imperial Commanders are more than happy to receive aid from the Space Marines, there are those whose hubris must be carefully negotiated in order to prevent a problematic battlezone's collapse into disaster through unnecessary infighting.

This is not to say a Space Marine Captain lacks for other methods of dealing with petty dissent – as Kayvaan Shrike of the Raven Guard ably proved by summarily executing the vacillating Lord Cardinal Dostok. That said, the subtler methods of persuasion and negotiation are often best employed in grim situations – punitive measures can be enacted when the crisis passes. A Space Marine does not bend his knee lightly, but the Emperor's cause transcends all personal feelings. The mission is all. Humanity shall be saved from its own failings, one world at a time if need be.

	WS	BS	S	T	W	I	A	Ld	Sv
Captain	6	5	4	4	3	5	3	10	3+

SPECIAL RULES
And They Shall Know No Fear, Combat Tactics, Independent Character.

WARGEAR
Iron Halo: See page 52 for details.

A Captain leads from the front. By his example shall his men know what it is to be of the Adeptus Astartes, and from his teachings shall they learn the trade of battle in the Emperor's name.

No ordinary man can a Captain be, for many are the paths to victory and he must be master of them all. His very being shall be an extension of the Emperor's work. With every strike of his sword, with every word of his speech, does he reaffirm the ideals of our honoured master. He will vanquish darkness and heresy with every thought, word and deed. So shall his coming be a sign of deliverance to the dutiful, and a herald of dismay to all traitors. No living man shall stay his wrath.

From the teachings of Roboute Guilliman as laid down in the Apocrypha of Skaros

COMMAND SQUAD

Command squads accompany high-ranking Space Marine officers on the field of battle. The exact nature and title of a Command squad's members can vary, depending on a Chapter's organisation and the personality of a company's Captain. The most common are Company Champion, Apothecary and Company Banner Bearer, and these can be found in almost all Command squads. Even so, some Chapters maintain other titles and positions in accordance with their traditions, such as the Foeseekers of the Omega Marines, the Prognosticars of the Silver Skulls, the Terrorblades of the Death Spectres and the Pyre Wardens of the Fire Lords.

Company Standard Bearers carry the battle flag of the company in which they serve. Each standard is an ancient relic, steeped in history and heavy with the glories of the Chapter. The company banner is the physical heart of the company on the battlefield, and every Space Marine, from the most inexperienced Scout to the hoariest veteran, fights all the harder in its august presence. The Standard Bearer is trusted never to let the standard out of his grip while he still draws breath – to do otherwise is to invite the most terrible and shameful dishonour.

The Apothecary is well-versed in the arts of battlefield aid as well as advanced surgery, cybernetics and bio-engineering. He must also be a warrior of untold might and unquenchable bravery, for his place is in the bloody heart of battle. If a comrade falls, the Apothecary can use his narthecium to tend the wounds, allowing his brother to return to battle even after suffering the most appalling of injuries. However, not all the wounded can be saved. Some weapons are terrible enough to mortally wound a Space Marine outright. The Apothecary can then only calm the spirits of the dying and prepare them for death. Once dead a Space Marine can live on through his gene-seed, the Apothecary using his reductor to remove the progenoid organs from the body. From the genetic imprint held within these precious organs, future generations of Space Marines are created, and the continuation of the Chapter is assured.

Company Champions are charged with defending the honour of their Company, their Chapter and the Emperor himself. They engage the warlords and champions of the foe in single combat, leaving the Captain free to conduct the wider battle, rather than engage in a series of personal combats. Company Champions have key roles in the rituals and ceremonies of the Chapter, representing their brothers in rites and mysteries as they do in war.

Service in a Command squad undoubtedly speeds promotion within the Chapter – most Captains fill their retinues with Space Marines in whom the bloody skills of combat are matched by a tactical and strategic brilliance. However, only the luckiest and most hardened warriors survive more than a few battles. Captains and their Command squads can invariably be found where the fighting is thickest. This being the case, a protégé who survives long enough to be nominated as the Captain's successor will have proven himself in the midst of the most gruelling of battles against the most terrible of foes.

	WS	BS	S	T	W	I	A	Ld	Sv
Company Champion	5	4	4	4	1	4	2	9	3+
Veteran	4	4	4	4	1	4	2	9	3+
Apothecary	4	4	4	4	1	4	2	9	3+

SPECIAL RULES
And They Shall Know No Fear, Combat Tactics.

WARGEAR
Narthecium: As long as the Apothecary is alive, all models in his squad have the feel no pain universal special rule.

Company Standard: Any Space Marine unit within 12" of the Standard Bearer always re-rolls failed Morale and Pinning Tests. In addition, while the standard bearer is still alive, the Command squad counts as scoring one extra wound in close combat for the purposes of calculating the assault result.

"Raise the flag high. Let those degenerates know who comes to claim their lives this day!"

Sergeant Adar Geronan
Imperial Fists 4th Company

LIBRARIAN

The Imperium of Man is eternally vigilant for the taint of mutation. The Chapters of the Adeptus Astartes are, if anything, even more careful to ensure that their gene-seed is not polluted. Apothecaries rigorously screen potential recruits for any sign of genetic deviation, but not all mutation is physical. Psychic talent is a mutation too, and is at once the most dangerous and the most useful. Detecting and developing nascent psykers is one of the many responsibilities of the Chapters' Librarium.

Few normal Space Marine recruits survive the rigorous training, enhancement and indoctrination. Amongst Librarians, the attrition is far worse. Not only must the recruit endure everything a normal recruit would, but he must be strong enough in spirit to withstand the moulding of his mind. A recruit must be taught how to hone and wield his powers, and how to protect himself from the perils of the Warp. A Librarian faces a thousand enemies before he even goes to war – to the creatures of the Warp he is a choice prize, with sorcerous aptitude and strong flesh to contain daemonic essence. Each day is a walk along a precipice where a false step can send a recruit tumbling into madness.

If a recruit survives the testing he joins the Librarius as Lexicanium, rising through the ranks to become Codicier, Epistolary or perhaps even Chief Librarian. He will use his abilities to pierce the Warp, provide the means for interstellar communication as well as to identify more of his own kind. He will judge others as he was himself once judged, scrutinising potential candidates and peers for frailty of mind or spirit. A moment's weakness can unleash untold evils, and vigil must be kept against any wavering of purpose.

Librarians' talents set them apart from their comrades – after all, they wield abilities that every Space Marine is normally expected to abhor – yet their presence is always welcomed on the field of battle. Most Librarian battle-disciplines focus on strengthening and enhancing his already formidable combat prowess. He can unleash powerful energy bolts, project force shields or increase his might to near godlike proportions. Even so, the most skilled Librarians can master more subtle gifts. Some can step outside the confines of linear time, sense the enemy's movements or redirect bullets with the power of their mind. In all of the Imperium there are few greater warrior-mystics, combining the prowess of the Adeptus Astartes with the steel discipline needed to contain and control their powers.

> "I can pulp your flesh and snap your bones in less than a second, and without so much as lifting a finger. What is the power of technology compared to that?"
>
> Vel'cona
> Chief Librarian of the Salamanders

	WS	BS	S	T	W	I	A	Ld	Sv
Librarian	5	4	4	4	2	4	2	10	3+

SPECIAL RULES

And They Shall Know No Fear, Combat Tactics, Independent Character.

Psyker: Librarians are Psykers, as described in the Warhammer 40,000 rulebook.

WARGEAR

Force weapon: See the Warhammer 40,000 rulebook.

Psychic hood: Psychic hoods are embedded with arcane constructions of psychically-attuned crystals that allow a Librarian to nullify an opposing psyker's power.

Declare that you'll use the psychic hood after an enemy model within 24" of the Librarian passes a Psychic test. If there are several Librarians in range, only one can attempt to nullify the psychic power – you must choose which.

Each player then rolls a D6 and adds their model's Leadership value to the score. If the Space Marine Librarian beats the opposing model's score then the psychic power is nullified and does not take effect that turn. If the opposing model's score is equal or higher, it can use its psychic power as normal. The psychic hood can be used once each time an enemy model uses a psychic power within range.

LIBRARIAN PSYCHIC POWERS

A Space Marine Librarian has two psychic powers (chosen when the army is picked). He can only use one power each player turn unless he has been upgraded to an Epistolary, in which case he can use up to two psychic powers each turn. All Space Marine Librarian psychic powers are used following the rules given in the main Warhammer 40,000 rulebook.

SMITE

Lethal bolts of lightning leap from the Librarian's fingertips, tearing his enemies apart in a barrage of psychic power.

This power is a psychic shooting attack and has the following profile.

Range	Strength	AP	Type
12"	4	2	Assault 4

FORCE DOME

Reaching out with his mind, the Librarian erects a barrier of shimmering force about himself and his companions.

This power is used at the start of the Librarian's Movement phase. The Librarian and any unit he is with receive a 5+ invulnerable save until the end of the following player turn.

MACHINE CURSE

The Librarian calls down a powerful curse upon the machine spirit of an enemy war engine.

This power is is a psychic shooting attack with a range of 24" that only affects vehicles. If the Machine Curse hits, the target vehicle automatically suffers a single glancing hit.

THE AVENGER

The Librarian draws on the ancient legends of his Chapter to create a destructive avatar of roiling flame. The psychic construct billows forward, leaving destruction in its wake.

This power is is a psychic shooting attack and has the following profile:

Range	Strength	AP	Type
Template	5	3	Assault 1

QUICKENING

Using his uncanny mind to project his physical being forwards into the timestream, the Librarian acts so swiftly as to defy the vision of his foes.

The power is used at the start of the Librarian's Assault phase. If successful, the Librarian has the fleet special rule and Initiative 10 for the duration of that Assault phase.

NULL ZONE

The Librarian turns the full force of his mind upon the foe, peeling away their layers of mystical protection and leaving them vulnerable to the weaponry of his brothers.

This power is used at the start of the Librarian's Shooting phase. All enemy units within 24" of the Librarian must re-roll successful invulnerable saves for the remainder of the player turn.

MIGHT OF THE ANCIENTS

The deadly powers of the Immaterium heighten the Librarian's strength to unimaginable levels, the better to vanquish the foes of the Emperor.

The power is used at the start of the Librarian's Assault phase. If successful, the Librarian has Strength 6 and rolls 2D6 for armour penetration for the remainder of that Assault phase.

THE GATE OF INFINITY

Focussing his Warp-sense, the Librarian creates a corridor of safe passage through the Immaterium, allowing him to cross great distances in but the blink of an eye.

This power is used at the beginning of the Librarian's Movement phase. The Librarian, and any unit he is with, are removed from the tabletop and immediately placed back together anywhere within 24" using the deep strike rules. If the Librarian travels alone, there is no risk, but if he takes a unit with him, there is a chance something will go wrong. If the deep strike attempt scatters and a double is rolled, one member of the unit, chosen by the controlling player, is claimed by the Warp and removed as a casualty (the survivors scatter normally).

VORTEX OF DOOM

The Librarian opens a tear between the material realm and the howling destruction of the Warp, unleashing devastating energies that utterly consume his foes.

This power is a psychic shooting attack and has the following profile:

Range	Strength	AP	Type
12"	10	1	Heavy 1, Blast

If when using this power the Librarian fails his Psychic test, place the Vortex of Doom blast marker on the Librarian – in this case the template will not scatter.

CHAPLAIN

Chaplains are the spiritual leaders of the Chapter. They administer the rites, preserve the rituals and perform the ancient ceremonies of Initiation, Vindication and Redemption that are as important to a Space Marine Chapter as its roll of honour and skill at arms.

Chaplains are daunting figures even for other Space Marines to behold. Their power armour is jet black and adorned with icons of battle and tokens of ritual and mystery; their skull helms are death masks that evoke the stern visage of the immortal Emperor. Every aspect of a Chaplain's garb serves to remind all who gaze upon him of mortality's impermanence and thus the importance of preserving the immortal soul. Beneath this stern cladding is a man no less grim of aspect and manner. Chaplains are notoriously strict individuals. They are responsible for the spiritual wellbeing of their Battle-Brothers and renowned for their sense of duty. Through tenet and catechism they armour their brother Marines against heresy and false pride, instilling the wisdom of the Emperor in those who are his most trusted servants.

A Chapter's Chaplains are the keepers of the Reclusiam, the fortress-monastery's central shrine where prayer and worship is conducted. The Reclusiam is a place of great spiritual reverance, where battle standards hang from hallowed walls and the very stones echo with remembrance. Here are kept the Chapter's most holy relics: fragments of armour, banners from times of legend, and the raiments of ancient heroes who long ago passed beyond mortal service. But the Chaplains teach that the presence of a formal chapel is not necessary to honour the Emperor, that the maelstrom of battle is the only true place of worship for a Space Marine and the slaughter of foes the truest offering.

Space Marine Chaplains care nothing for the ravings of the Ecclesiarchy and ignore the dictates of the Imperial Cult in favour of their own ancient traditions. The first Space Marine Chapters were founded centuries before the development of the Imperial Cult and the dominion of the Adeptus Ministorum. Whereas the Adeptus Ministorum has gradually extended its influence over the many thousands of individual cults that once existed throughout the galaxy, it has never been able to influence the Space Marine cults which remain as stubbornly individualistic today as they ever were.

When war calls, a Chaplain fights wherever the conflict is fiercest, leading from the front and rejoicing in the slaughter of the enemy as one doing righteous work. He chants the liturgies of battle with every breath, punctuating his praise with strikes from his Crozius Arcanum – the skull-headed staff that is both badge of office and chosen weapon of war. By his example and his piety, the Chaplain exhorts his Brother-Marines to the pinnacle of dedication, so that they might conquer with valour that which would resist all else.

	WS	BS	S	T	W	I	A	Ld	Sv
Chaplain	5	4	4	4	2	4	2	10	3+

SPECIAL RULES
Combat Tactics, Independent Character.

Honour of the Chapter: A Chaplain utterly embodies the honour of the Chapter. He, and all members of a squad he has joined, are fearless, as described in the Warhammer 40,000 rulebook.

Liturgies of Battle: On a player turn in which he assaults, a Chaplain and all members of any squad he has joined can re-roll failed rolls to hit.

WARGEAR
Rosarius: A Rosarius is a gorget or amulet worn by Chaplains. It protects the Chaplain from physical and spiritual harm. A Rosarius confers a 4+ invulnerable save.

Crozius Arcanum: The Crozius Arcanum is a Space Marine Chaplain's rod of office. It is a power weapon.

"If your life is given in service to the Emperor, your death shall not be in vain."

Hauis Argento
Chaplain to the Crimson Fists 2nd Company

TACTICAL SQUAD

Tactical squads are the backbone of the Space Marine army. They are called upon to fulfil the full range of battlefield roles; they hold ground, provide fire support or charge into the bloody melee of close combat, as the ever-changing theatre of battle dictates.

For a Space Marine to be assigned to a Tactical squad he must have proven himself beyond doubt in all aspects of war. So it is that a Space Marine must complete several campaigns in both Assault and Devastator squads before he can earn a permanent position in one of the Chapter's Tactical squads. This progression must be earned in blood and can last for years, or even decades, depending on the skills of the Space Marine in question. Not all Space Marines make the transition. Some demonstrate a talent or obsession for a particular aspect of battle that, while immensely valuable in its own way, would prove a liability in the adaptive role of the Tactical squad. Other Battle-Brothers simply lack the mental flexibility to embrace the fluidity of the Tactical squad's role.

As befits its varied battlefield role, a Tactical squad takes to the field with a wide variety of weaponry. In addition to the standard Space Marine armament of bolt pistol and grenades, most Tactical Space Marines carry a bolter – the furious weapon of vengeance made famous on untold millions of blood-soaked battlefields.

This formidable anti-infantry firepower is complemented by a heavy weapon, such as a missile launcher, lascannon or heavy bolter, and a special issue weapon, such as a flamer or meltagun. As these armaments are chosen to match the requirements of each deployment, and weaponry duties are rotated between all members of the squad save the sergeant, so all Tactical Space Marines must be trained and capable with every weapon their squad can be called upon to field.

Of all Space Marine combat units it is the Tactical squad that makes the greatest use of the Chapter's transport pool, often performing surgical strikes or seizing strategic points with the aid of fast-moving Razorbacks or Rhinos. Some Chapters – most notably the Angels of Fury, the Raven Guard and the Legion of Night – have even forged their combat doctrines around such tactics.

Each Tactical squad is led by a grizzled Sergeant who has survived and thrived through several decades, or even centuries, of hard and brutal campaigning. It is essential that a Tactical squad be led by a canny and daring individual capable of reading the battle for opportunity, and it is quite common for Tactical squad Sergeants to be seconded from the elite 1st Company. So is it ensured that the mainstay of the Chapter's battle forces are led by the most experienced of its warriors.

	WS	BS	S	T	W	I	A	Ld	Sv
Space Marine Sergeant	4	4	4	4	1	4	2	9	3+
Space Marine	4	4	4	4	1	4	1	8	3+

SPECIAL RULES
And They Shall Know No Fear, Combat Squads Combat Tactics.

Of the Tactical Space Marine, bedrock of his Chapter and paragon to his brothers, I shall tell thee.

He shall be steeped in the lore of battle and schooled in all manner of weapon and strategy. With combat blade, boltgun and grenade he shall assail the foe.
But these are mere tools: a Tactical Space Marine's true weapons are his courage, his wits and his dedication to his brothers.

He will bring his foe to battle in a manner and time of his choosing, never himself caught unready or ill-prepared for the task at hand. In defence he shall be stalwart as the mountain, a bulwark stood firm against the enemies of Man. In attack he shall strike with the wrath of the Immortal Emperor, felling the foe without mercy, remorse or fear.

From the teachings of Roboute Guilliman
as laid down in the Apocrypha of Skaros

ASSAULT SQUAD

Assault squads excel at close-quarter fighting. Equipped with jump packs and armed with bolt pistols and chainswords, they scream across the battlefield like avenging angels, charging into the foe with little heed for personal danger. A Space Marine is commonly assigned to an Assault squad after exemplary service amongst the Devastators. By this time he has garnered battle experience amidst the fires of war and can be counted on to hold his ground before the foe. Now he must temper himself in the most brutal arena of war, and prove his worth in the melee of close combat, eye to eye with the foe and close enough to smell his blood.

The Codex Astartes dictates that Assault squads should be unleashed in the first wave of an attack, to strike hard and fast at weak points in the foe's formation. Opposing infantry are shredded with chainsword and bolt pistol, enemy tanks with krak grenades and meltabombs. Such is the way of the Space Marines – to deliver an irresistible and overwhelming blow to a single point, to crush the enemy without mercy before moving on to the next target. Such tactics are far from subtle but effective nonetheless – a foe who perceives this to be the extent of an Assault squads' capability is woefully mistaken.

The jump pack is easily as dangerous as any weapon the Assault Marine carries. With a jump pack comes mobility, allowing the Assault squad to traverse all manner of terrain swiftly and without hindrance, or even perform controlled low-altitude descents from Thunderhawk Gunships. So it is that the Assault squad can be a weapon of subtlety in the hands of a capable commander. It can dive without warning on an enemy warlord who believes himself secure amongst his own lines, operate as a highly mobile counterpunch unit or perform vital reconnaissance in warzones unsuitable for the deployment of Scouts. In certain circumstances, Assault squads are even used as bait, luring an unwary enemy force onto a prepared defensive position, or redirecting them away to buy time for further preparation or evacuation.

Assault squads draw the bloodiest, and most dangerous of all battle assignments. Often operating far ahead of the rest of the army, Assault Marines are in constant danger of being outflanked, cut off, or simply overwhelmed by the enemy. To guard against this, the commanding sergeant of an Assault squad has a direct uplink to myriad datastreams and tactical overlays – the command and control relays through which the Space Marines coordinate their deployments and battles. Even if he is knee deep in corpses and fighting for his life, an Assault squad sergeant must be aware not only of his current situation, but also any imminent or potential developments that will leave his squad stranded and beset in a sea of bloodthirsty foes. Should this occur, only raw might and iron resolve will allow the Assault Marines to hack their way clear of the foe and claim victory.

	WS	BS	S	T	W	I	A	Ld	Sv
Space Marine Sergeant	4	4	4	4	1	4	2	9	3+
Space Marine	4	4	4	4	1	4	1	8	3+

SPECIAL RULES
And They Shall Know No Fear, Combat Squads, Combat Tactics.

And of the Assault Marine so do I decree:

He shall descend upon the perfidious foe as an Angel of Judgement from on high. Let the jump pack be his wings, and the roar of its engines a hymn of retribution.

Let the chainsword be his sceptre of decree, its harsh voice singing joyfully with each and every blow. With it shall the Assault Marine bring bloody retribution to the heretic, the traitor and all alien aggressors who trespass on the Emperor's domain.

So will the Assault Marine be the hunter of warlords and the slayer of kings. His armour shall run slick with the life-blood of the vanquished, and all shall honour his name.

From the teachings of Roboute Guilliman as laid down in the Apocrypha of Skaros

DEVASTATOR SQUAD

Devastators are the most heavily armed of all Space Marine squads, trained to assail the enemy from great distance and with overwhelming firepower. As primarily long-range support, Devastators are capable of providing the Tactical and Assault squads with covering fire, visiting swift and brutal counter-battery fire, or engaging enemy vehicles and other heavily armoured targets.

Unlike most other Space Marine squads, Devastators operate from a largely static footing, abandoning fixed positions only to advance, fall back or occupy a position with more commanding arcs of fire. This is not to say that Devastators cannot be flexible upon the field of battle, indeed, each squad has its own assigned Rhino transport for such redeployments. However, it remains true that Devastator squads most completely define a Space Marine task force's reach and depth, for they promise destruction with greater range and measure than any of their Battle-Brothers.

Most Devastator squads are composed of Space Marines who have recently completed their tours of service in the Chapter's Scout squads. Though they will have taken part in dozens – or perhaps even hundreds – of deployments as neophyte Space Marines, service in a Devastator squad will not only be their first experience of fighting in power armour, but also mark their first engagements as part of the main Space Marine task force.

When first promoted into a Devastator squad, a Space Marine is issued with the bolter and grenades with which he will grow ever more skilled throughout his service. His primary functions are to provide close-fire support, call out targets and generally act as backup for the more experienced Brother-Marines who carry the squad's heavy weapons. Only when the neophyte has proved himself a steady and dependable warrior, able to hold true aim and steady nerve in the black heart of battle, is he entrusted a heavy weapon from the Chapter's arsenal. Devastator squads commonly carry four heavy weapons into battle. These can range from the commonplace heavy bolter and missile launcher, to the more exotic multimelta and plasma cannon. A Devastator squad's preferred weapons loadout varies from squad to squad and Chapter to Chapter, although all its members must be fully trained and capable with each tool of war they can be called upon to employ.

Most Space Marine Chapters equip their Devastators with a mix of weaponry, as favoured by the Codex Astartes. This allows them to better deal with any emergent threats. A single Devastator squad is able to excel at several battlefield roles by the simple expedient of splitting into an anti-tank and an anti-infantry combat squad. Even so, a few Space Marines Chapters have refined the role of their Devastator squads to suit a recurrent foe or engagement type. For example, the Crimson Fists, their tactics understandibly skewed by near-annihilation at the hands of Waaagh! Snagrod, tend to favour the hail of anti-personnel fire proffered by four heavy bolters. Whereas the Salamanders and Imperial Fists deploy their Devastators with multimeltas and lascannon to crack the formidable armour of enemy tanks and fortifications.

	WS	BS	S	T	W	I	A	Ld	Sv
Space Marine Sergeant	4	4	4	4	1	4	2	9	3+
Space Marine	4	4	4	4	1	4	1	8	3+

SPECIAL RULES
And They Shall Know No Fear, Combat Squads, Combat Tactics.

A Devastator's reach shall be without limit and his touch without mercy. Fire shall roar from his fingertips, but it shall consume him not. Thunder will roar when he calls, yet it will swallow him not.

Let the Devastator squad be thy blazing wrath, bringing the light of the Emperor's justice to the darkest corners of the battlefield. Wherever he stands, that shall be his fortress of righteousness. He shall hold in his gift the fate of all who pass before his unblinking gaze.

All shall fear him, and he shall fear no one.

From the teachings of Roboute Guilliman as laid down in the Apocrypha of Skaros

VANGUARD VETERAN SQUAD

Of all the fighting formations that make up a Space Marine Chapter, it is the 1st Company which is most feared. For a Space Marine to join the 1st Company is for him to have won renown on battlefields uncounted and to have earned the respect of his Battle-Brothers through deeds of blood and fire. Most such Veterans have served as sergeants elsewhere – sometimes for centuries – before being accepted into the First Company, but a notable few are elevated after performing insane acts of heroism.

Every member of the 1st Company is proficient in all manner of weaponry and stands as a living exemplar of the ideals and purpose of the Chapter. With such status comes the right to select weapons of choice from the Chapter's armoury and, as a result, Veterans squads are much less rigid in composition and doctrine than other Space Marine formations. They are often assembled and equipped to deal with specific theatre requirements, such as embarking upon seek-and-destroy missions to slay an Ork Warboss and his bodyguard, or cripple an inbound wave of Eldar Aspect Warriors before they can reach the battlefield.

A Vanguard Veteran squad is formed from those members of the 1st Company that completely immerse themselves in the art of close-quarter combat. Most have completed lengthy service rotations in the Chapters' Assault squads, their skills tested and honed in the crucible of bloody mêlée on a thousand worlds.

It is said that were a Vanguard Veteran armed only with his fists and his wits, he could still storm an enemy bastion and emerge victorious, and that with the bolt pistol and chainsword of his bloody trade the same Veteran would prove superior to thrice that figure of foes. Alas for the enemies of Mankind, with the vaunted weaponry of the Chapter's armoury at their disposal it is rare for Vanguard Veterans to take to the fray with such basic armament.

Power swords, plasma pistols and power fists are all common sights in Vanguard Veteran squads, and thunder hammers, lightning claws and rarer weaponry are also employed as the engagement requires. These weapons are not employed lightly, for they are without exception ancient and revered heirlooms. A Vanguard Veteran who returns from the field of battle without his armament is subject to the Chapter's gruelling rites of penitence. It is of little surprise therefore that a disarmed Veteran will fight all the harder, not merely to survive, but to reclaim his weapon and his honour along with it.

Whilst they can be deployed at the forefront of an assault, most Chapters employ their Vanguard Veterans as rapid-response forces, using jump pack or Rhino transport to apply crucial pressure to an already over-taxed enemy defence, or to reinforce overmatched allies. To use speed itself as a weapon, to strike the foe wherever he least expects it this was the way of war for jump troops in the days of the Space Marine Legions and it still serves well today. Such duty is arduous and never-ending. Often referred to as a Captain's 'Iron Fist', Vanguard Veterans are constantly in motion. As soon as one foe is annihilated, fresh orders dispatch the Vanguard Veterans to another corner of the battlefield, there to apply murderous skill in the Emperor's name.

	WS	BS	S	T	W	I	A	Ld	Sv
Space Marine Sergeant	4	4	4	4	1	4	2	9	3+
Veteran	4	4	4	4	1	4	2	9	3+

SPECIAL RULES
And They Shall Know No Fear, Combat Squads, Combat Tactics.

Heroic Intervention: Vanguard Veterans are famed for arriving at a time and place where their onslaught can make the most difference to a battle. If a jump pack equipped Vanguard Veteran squad arrives from deep strike, the player can elect for the squad to perform a Heroic Intervention – before the deep strike scatter dice are rolled. If he declares a Heroic Intervention, the Vanguard Veteran squad cannot shoot (or run) that turn but can assault (provided they are close enough). This ability cannot be used if an independent character has joined the Vanguard Veteran squad.

"We go where we wilt. We slay who we wilt. Let the Emperor judge the righteousness of our deeds."

Sergeant D'Kestrel
Raven Guard 1st Company

STERNGUARD VETERAN SQUAD

Sternguard Veterans deploy wherever the battleline is most vulnerable, facing down the most impossible odds with icy calm and precise bursts of bolter fire. They are the very image of what every Space Marine aspires to become, and the pinnacle of any Chapter's fighting force.

In contrast to the Battle-Brothers of the Vanguard squads, Sternguard Veterans draw upon the armoury's ranged weaponry. The squad's sergeant will sometimes wield a specialised mêlée weapon, but this is the extent to which a Vanguard squad will employ such tools. Better and more efficient to slay the foe at range, they argue, than to get bogged down in a close-quarters battle. Most Vanguard Veterans carry boltguns with meticulously crafted sights and modified scopes. Heavier weapons are also available, such as the missile launcher and lascannon, but these are normally eschewed for the more portable boltgun. Any potential shortfall in firepower is compensated for by the range of specialist boltgun ammunition a Sternguard Veteran can carry into battle, including unstable flux core vengeance rounds for heavily armoured targets, propellant-rich kraken bolts for extended-range engagements and the acidic fury of hellfire rounds for bringing down even the angriest greenskin or Tyranid bio-monstrosity.

In most Chapters there is a rivalry of sorts between the Vanguard and Sternguard halves of the 1st Company. These factions compete endlessly for honours and hazardous combat duties – the glories and shames of their adherents celebrated and atoned for by all. Despite the rivalry, Vanguard and Sternguard Veterans remain Battle-Brothers above all else, and fight unto death for one another.

	WS	BS	S	T	W	I	A	Ld	Sv
Space Marine Sergeant	4	4	4	4	1	4	2	9	3+
Veteran	4	4	4	4	1	4	2	9	3+

SPECIAL RULES
And They Shall Know No Fear, Combat Squads, Combat Tactics.

WARGEAR
Special Issue Ammunition: Each boltgun-armed model in a Sternguard Veteran squad automatically comes with several special ammunition types. Each time a Sternguard Veteran squad fires, the controlling player can choose which type of ammunition is being used. Each special ammunition type replaces the boltgun profile (including boltguns that are part of a combi-weapon) with the one shown here. All models in the squad must use the same ammunition type during that shooting phase.

"The deeds of one bold warrior can alter the course of a battle. I have four such men under my command, and our every deed changes the shape of the galaxy."

Sergeant Daegon Incursa
The Invaders 1st Company

Dragonfire Bolts: These hollow shells explode with a gout of superheated gas that makes a mockery of cover.

Range	Strength	AP	Type
24"	4	5	Rapid Fire, Ignores Cover*

*Ignores Cover: Cover saves cannot be taken against Dragonfire bolts.

Hellfire Rounds: See page 100.

Kraken Bolts: The adamantine core and improved propellant of these bolts can penetrate the thickest hide – even at extreme range.

Range	Strength	AP	Type
30"	4	4	Rapid Fire

Vengeance Rounds: Originally designed to breach the power armour of Traitor Marines, vengeance rounds employ unstable flux core technology that makes them hazardous to use, but incredibly effective against armoured targets.

Range	Strength	AP	Type
18"	4	3	Rapid Fire, Gets Hot!

TERMINATOR SQUAD

	WS	BS	S	T	W	I	A	Ld	Sv
Terminator Sergeant	4	4	4	4	1	4	2	9	2+
Terminator	4	4	4	4	1	4	2	9	2+

SPECIAL RULES
And They Shall Know No Fear, Combat Squads, Combat Tactics.

WARGEAR
Chainfist: A chainfist is a power fist fitted with a chainblade attachment designed to carve its way through armoured bulkheads or armour plating. Originally designed for boarding actions, the whirring adamantite blades of a chainfist have long since proven their worth when engaging armoured targets of all kinds.

A chainfist is treated exactly as a power fist, but rolls 2D6 for its armour penetration value.

Cyclone Missile Launcher: The cyclone is a specially designed missile launcher system, used by Space Marines in Terminator armour to provide heavy fire support. Essentially a rack of missiles fitted onto the shoulders of a Terminator, the cyclone missile launcher enables the Terminator to engage both heavily armoured vehicles and lightly armoured infantry.

A Terminator can fire his cyclone missile launcher in addition to his storm bolter. Each time a cyclone missile launcher fires, the controlling player can choose which type of missile is being used.

Krak Range	Strength	AP	Type
48"	8	3	Heavy 2

Frag Range	Strength	AP	Type
48"	4	6	Heavy 2, Blast

All Space Marine Chapters maintain a number of suits of the revered and rightly feared Tactical Dreadnought armour, or Terminator armour as it is more commonly known. Terminator suits are the pinnacle of armoured protection available to a Space Marine. Each is all but impervious to small arms fire and can even withstand the merciless onslaught of tank-busting krak missiles.

Terminator armour is incredibly rare. Space Marines hold it a great honour to be permitted to wear such a suit in battle, and it is only to members of the Chapter's elite 1st Company that this honour is granted. Once trained in the use of Terminator armour, a Space Marine is counted first among his brothers and is expected to conduct the most difficult of missions and to perform beyond even the lofty standards of the Adeptus Astartes. Boarding Tyranid-infested space hulks, launching teleport attacks, Titan assaults and combat actions in extremely hostile environments, such as deep space or volcanic marshland; these are the missions undertaken by Space Marine Terminators.

Truly are Terminators amongst the greatest heroes of Mankind, bold warriors in whom the indefatigable heroism of a Space Marine is combined with the terrible weaponry and indomitable mass of Tactical Dreadnought armour. No foe is safe from a Terminator assault, not a horde of Orcs, adamantium fortress or colossal Chaos Titan. Terminators are invincible, they are unstoppable and they never yield.

The left shoulder pad of a suit of Terminator armour carries the large solid stone icon known as the Crux Terminatus. This doubles as a tactical symbol and as a revered honour badge.

Each Crux is reputed to have bound within its core a tiny fragment of the battle armour worn by the Emperor during his epic duel with Horus the Arch-Traitor ten thousand years ago.

The design of this ancient badge can vary considerably, even within a single unit or Chapter. Sergeants' and Officers' Crux tend to be more elaborate and finely detailed than those worn by normal Battle-Brothers, but all are venerated equally. To lose even a single Crux in battle is to betray the Emperor's trust and bring great shame down on the entire Chapter.

DREADNOUGHT

When a Space Marine suffers grievous harm, the like of which even his superhuman physique cannot endure, his ravaged body is borne from the battlefield with great reverence. Most such men die swiftly of their wounds, or receive the Emperor's Mercy from one of the Chapter's Apothecaries. Their lifeless forms are cremated, interred or sent to journey the infinite void, according to the traditions of the Chapter.

However, the mightiest fallen, those within whom the spark of life and honour still burns bright though their body be rent and torn, are preserved from final rest. For such a man the eternal battle is not yet done. His skills, his wisdom and his fighting spirit must continue to serve, even if they do so in another form. The hero's crippled body is installed in the cyborganic web of an armoured sarcophagus, his dimmed senses bound to electro-fibre implants. So does he cast off a frail mortal frame for something greater and more difficile. So does he become a Dreadnought.

Many an assault commences with a wave of Dreadnoughts to first drive a wedge through the enemy's defences. A Dreadnought is a truly massive fighting machine, weighing several tons and standing two or three times the height of a man. As the Dreadnought strides purposefully into battle, incoming fire spatters like rain off his towering adamantium and ceramite hull. Fiery death roars from his weapons and his great metal arms churn through all who are foolish enough to stand before him. Actual weapon loadout varies from Dreadnought to Dreadnought and the needs of the mission. The close support pattern of assault cannon and powerfist is by far the most common Dreadnought configuration, although the tank-hunting lascannon or bunker-breaching multi-melta and seismic hammer combination are equally fearsome. Needless to say, the hero that guides the armoured hulk is more than proficient in all the many powerful weapons of death employed by the Space Marines.

A Dreadnought's raw power is made all the more deadly because it is wielded with all the grim resolve of the mortally wounded veteran bound in its core, and directed by centuries – or even millennia – of experience. The memories of these venerable "Old Ones" can extend back thousands of years to the founding of their Chapter and its earliest history. Thus they are revered by other Space Marines, not just as potent warriors, but also as ageless forebears and as a living embodiment of battles fought long ago. Dreadnoughts are not seen merely as formidable weapons of war, but as keepers of tradition and custodians of knowledge whose advice is sought by initiate and Chapter Master alike. It is not unknown for Dreadnoughts to serve as members of the Chapter Council, lending wisdom to strategy as they do fury to the battlefield.

Suits of Dreadnought armour are amongst the most prized of a Chapter's relics. Should a Dreadnought fall in battle, his brothers will fight with righteous anger to retrieve the shell so that they may lay its occupant to rest with honour and reclaim the suit to house another dying hero who will become an Old One to future generations.

				Armour				
	WS	BS	S	F	S	R	I	A
Venerable Dreadnought	5	5	6	12	12	10	4	2
Dreadnought	4	4	6	12	12	10	4	2
Ironclad Dreadnought	4	4	6	13	13	10	4	2(3)

SPECIAL RULES

Venerable: If a Venerable Dreadnought suffers a glancing or penetrating hit, you can ask your opponent to re-roll the result rolled on the Vehicle Damage chart. You must accept the result of the second roll, even if it is worse than the first.

Move Through Cover (Ironclad Dreadnought only).

WARGEAR

Dreadnought Close Combat Weapon: See the Warhammer 40,000 rule book for details.

Seismic Hammer: A blow from a seismic hammer causes catastrophic shockwaves to tear through the target. A seismic hammer is treated as a Dreadnought close combat weapon that adds +1 to rolls on the vehicle damage chart.

Ironclad Assault Launchers: See page 103 for details.

SCOUT SQUAD

When first accepted into a Space Marine Chapter, a new recruit joins the ranks of the 10th Company as a Space Marine Scout. He is placed under the tutelage of a sergeant who will lead him on the field of battle and oversee his training and educate him in what it truly means to be one of the Adeptus Astartes.

A Space Marine Scout has much to learn. Not only must he become accustomed to the many biologically engineered enhancements which are at work on his body, but he must learn the litany of battle which will fortify and strengthen him. Through a gruelling training regime that lasts for many months, the recruit will learn how to use the battlegear on which his life depends, and he will get his first real chance to fight the enemies of Mankind.

Throughout his entire tenure as a Space Marine Scout, the recruit is watched over and taught by his sergeant, his actions guided and judged as he strikes the foe at the weakest point with bolter, shotgun and blade. As his training progresses, the Scout will grow proficient with many other weapons of death, such as the heavy bolter, sniper rifle, missile launcher and melta bomb. Acting as part of an infiltration force, a Scout will become skilled at every aspect of war. He will learn that to be a Space Marine is to be death incarnate, no matter the terrain, the nature of the foe, or the weapons that dominate the battlefield.

More lightly armed and armoured than more experienced Battle-Brothers, Space Marine Scouts chiefly fight as skirmishers. Their duties are to infiltrate enemy positions ahead of the rest of their Chapter, relying on stealth – rather than brute force – to accomplish their mission objectives.

Operating behind enemy lines, Scouts set ambushes for the unwary, destroy ammunition dumps and vehicle pools, spy out the enemy's movements and gather what information they can about their opponent's plans. Sometimes Scouts will pounce unseen within an unsuspecting enemy camp, capturing a commander for interrogation or sabotaging equipment and supplies. Striking in silence, the Scouts' goal is to accomplish their mission and vanish before the enemy has the chance to retaliate in force.

Scout squads are often detailed to conduct boarding actions against Tyranid Hive Ships or perform seek-and-destroy missions against the Hive Mind creatures that direct Tyranid invasions. As standard heavy bolter shells have often proven ineffective against the larger Tyranid bio-monstrosities, most Chapters now issue their Scouts with specialised Hellfire ammunition – heavy ceramic shells containing a virulent mutagenic acid that ruptures and burns its way through cellular tissue. Such weaponry can bring down even a rampaging Carnifex, and is no less deadly when turned upon more mundane foes.

	WS	BS	S	T	W	I	A	Ld	Sv
Scout Sergeant	4	4	4	4	1	4	2	9	4+
Scout	3	3	4	4	1	4	1	8	4+

SPECIAL RULES
And They Shall Know No Fear, Combat Squads, Combat Tactics, Infiltrate, Move Through Cover, Scouts.

WARGEAR
Hellfire Shells: A heavy bolter in a Scout squad can fire a single hellfire shell instead of firing normally:

Range	Strength	AP	Type
36"	X	-	Heavy 1, Blast Poisoned (2+)

Shotgun: Shotguns are sturdy and versatile weapons often carried by Space Marine Scouts.

Range	Strength	AP	Type
12"	4	-	Assault 2

Sniper Rifle: Sniper rifles boast powerful telescopic sights that enable the firer to target weak points and distant foes with unerring accuracy.

Range	Strength	AP	Type
36"	X	6	Heavy 1, Sniper

Camo Cloaks: See page 100.

SCOUT BIKE SQUAD

During the final stages of a Space Marine Scout's training, he is attached to a Scout Bike squadron. Scout Bikers are employed as fast-moving reconnaissance and disruption units. They operate on a far longer leash than other Scouts, often operating as a seperate and distinct adjunct to the main Space Marine strike force, answerable to none save their commanding sergeants.

While Scout Bikers continue to perform the hit-and-run tactics they perfected in earlier years of service, their repertoire of combat skills is broadened by hard-won experience and further augmented by supplies of special-issue equipment. While the enemy concentrates on the main Space Marine attack, the Scout Bikers ride rampant behind his lines, calling down orbital bombardments and reserve deployments with pinpoint accuracy.

	WS	BS	S	T	W	I	A	Ld	Sv
Scout Biker Sergeant	4	4	4	4(5)	1	4	2	9	4+
Scout Biker	3	3	4	4(5)	1	4	1	8	4+

SPECIAL RULES
And They Shall Know No Fear, Combat Squads, Combat Tactics, Infiltrate, Scouts.

WARGEAR
Cluster Mines: When operating behind enemy lines, Scout Bikers carry cluster mines – explosive devices crammed with tiny anti-personnel bomblets and triggered by tripwires or pressure sensors. They are deployed in defensible positions to deny their use to all but the bravest or most foolhardy foes.

Each Scout Bike squad equipped with cluster mines can booby-trap one piece of area terrain before the game begins. Note that a Scout Bike squad that splits into combat squads is still counted as a single squad for the purposes of cluster mines. At the start of the game, after terrain is placed, declare that your Scout Bikers have placed booby-traps and secretly write down the piece(s) of area terrain that have been booby-trapped in this fashion. Each terrain piece can only be booby-trapped once.

Cluster mines are automatically triggered the first time a unit (friendly or enemy) moves into the booby-trapped terrain. When triggered, the cluster mines inflict 2D6 hits on the unfortunate unit once it has finished its move. These are treated as shooting hits and use the following profile:

Range	Strength	AP	Type
n/a	4	-	No cover saves

If a vehicle triggers the cluster mines, the hits are always resolved against rear armour, to represent the munitions striking at its weaker under-armour. Once the effect of the cluster mines has been resolved, they are assumed to have been expended and have no further effect.

Shotgun: See page 66.

Locator Beacon: Scout bikers often carry a locator beacon, a signalling package containing a teleport homer, broad-spectrum communicators and geo-positional tracking. When activated, the locator beacon uploads detailed positional information to the Astartes Tactical Grid, allowing precision reinforcement by reserve forces.

If a unit wishes to arrive on the battlefield via deep strike and chooses to do so within 6" of a model carrying a locator beacon, then it won't scatter. Note that the locator beacon must already be on the table at the start of the turn for it to be used.

Astartes Grenade Launcher: Scout Bikers can employ grenade launchers. These are loaded with frag and krak grenades and outfitted with adaptive targeting systems to compensate for the high speeds at which the bikers commonly travel. Each time a grenade launcher fires, the controlling player chooses which type of ammo is used.

Frag Grenade

Range	Strength	AP	Type
24"	3	6	Rapid Fire, Blast

Krak Grenade

Range	Strength	AP	Type
24"	6	4	Rapid Fire

BIKE SQUAD

Space Marine Bike squads carry out fast-moving assault missions, often operating on intelligence gathered by infiltrating Scout squads or Land Speeder reconnaissance flights. Bike squads attack at incredible speeds, using surprise and unstoppable momentum to punch holes in the enemy formation, accelerating away as the enemy recovers his wits only to circle back and attack once again from an unexpected direction. Bike squad tactical strikes are often likened to thunderbolts – by the time a foe has heard their approach, the damage has already been done.

For a Space Marine biker to operate at full potency, the superhuman rider and his mechanical steed must function flawlessly as one. To this end, the Codex Astartes dictates that all of a Chapter's Assault Marines, Scouts and the entire 6th Company should master the art of mounted warfare as part of their training regimen.

A few Chapters take this further, with every Space Marine required to maintain his mounted training, even though he may have long passed into the 1st Company, or perhaps even into the exalted ranks of the Chapter Council. Few Chapters exemplify this better than the White Scars, who proudly employ Bike Squads as the main body of any strike force. Other Chapters are less enamoured of a Bike Squad's tactical value, preferring to send assault forces into battle in Rhinos or Razorbacks.

The Space Marine bike itself is a robust construction. It needs to be, for it must be powerful enough to propel a fully armoured Space Marine at dizzying speeds, and yet responsive enough to perform a full range of death-defying combat manoeuvres. Even at low speeds the combined impact mass of bike and rider is no small thing to encounter. Indeed, many experienced Space Marine bikers can boast of riding through rockcrete walls at full pelt, suffering neither harm nor impediment. The effect such an impact can have on living tissue is perhaps best left to the imagination.

For the heaviest assault missions it is common for a bike squad's firepower to be further augmented through the attachment of an Attack Bike. Each Attack Bike is a highly formidable mobile firebase, with the twin bolters of the bike itself augmented by a multimelta or heavy bolter mounted on a sturdy sidecar.

So potent is the striking power of the Attack Bike that many Chapters field them in entire squads, employing them as fast-moving fire-support units to complement Scouts, Assault Marines or other bike squads. Few Space Marine Chapters have enough Attack Bikes to field them in large numbers. On those rare occasions when Attack Bikes are deployed en masse, as they were by the fabled White Scars Chapter during the third war for Armageddon, they prove to be a nigh-unstoppable foe.

	WS	BS	S	T	W	I	A	Ld	Sv
Biker Sergeant	4	4	4	4(5)	1	4	2	9	3+
Space Marine Biker	4	4	4	4(5)	1	4	1	8	3+
Attack Bike	4	4	4	4(5)	2	4	2	8	3+

SPECIAL RULES
And They Shall Know No Fear, Combat Tactics.

Combat Squads: A Bike squad chosen at full strength (for a total of eight bikes and one Attack Bike) can split into two combat squads as described on page 51. Note that if this is done the Attack Bike counts as two models, giving one combat squad of five bikes, and one of three bikes and an Attack Bike.

Use your Bike squads as a blade, striking the enemy and turning aside his counter-blows in equal measure. But in all things beware that speed is nothing without direction, just as even the mightiest weapon is worthless without careful aim.

A biker's stance should always be resolute and dauntless, but never immobile or rigid. Speed is his advantage, and surprise his deadliest weapon. In fluidity he will find success, and in success shall he find renown.

From the teachings of Roboute Guilliman
as laid down in the Apocrypha of Skaros

DROP POD

The Space Marines are known as the Angels of Death, and the title is never more appropriate than when they attack using Drop Pods. Drop Pod assaults are the ultimate weapon of terror and surprise, aimed right at the heart of the foe. Scarcely have the smouldering hulls come to rest when their hatches blow clear, and the occupants disembark to wreak havoc on wrong-footed enemies. Such is the velocity of approach there is little a foe can do to intercept Drop Pods once launched. All he can do is wait for their arrival and cling to the misguided hope that his warriors can somehow withstand the righteous onslaught of the Adeptus Astartes.

Drop Pods resemble a ship's life pod in look and function, and are fired from low orbit from an orbiting vessel with colossal force, using a ring of powerful retro burners to direct their approach to the target drop zone. Inside each Drop Pod, a squad of Space Marines or a Dreadnought is carried in exceedingly spartan conditions, protected from the incandescent rage of atmospheric re-entry only by the Drop Pod's ceramite armour plating. During the descent it is common for the Space Marines to give voice to hymns of vengeance, steeling their hearts against the terrors of orbital assault and preparing themselves for death or glory in the battle that lies ahead.

Most Drop Pod assaults comprise only a handful of craft. However, it is not unknown for entire Chapters, such as the Invaders or the Black Consuls, to commence their campaigns with a massed Drop Pod landing. Such an assault is a thing of terrible beauty, with a hundred or more Drop Pods descending upon the foe like screaming harbingers of woe.

| | Type | BS | Armour | | |
			F	S	R
Drop Pod	Open-topped	4	12	12	12

TRANSPORT

The Drop Pod has a transport capacity of 12 models. It can transport a single Dreadnought or Thunderfire Cannon.

Once the Drop Pod has landed, the hatches are blown and all passengers must immediately disembark, as normal. Once passengers have disembarked, no models can embark on the Drop Pod for the remainder of the game.

Fire Points and Access Points: Once deployed the Drop Pod is no longer a sealed environment and is therefore counted as being open-topped.

> "We are coming. Look to the skies for your salvation."
>
> Captain Kayvaan Shrike to Commissar Lent prior to the Blindhope planetstrike

SPECIAL RULES

Drop Pod Assault: Drop Pods always enter play using the deep strike rules from the Mission Special Rules section of the Warhammer 40,000 rulebook. At the beginning of your first turn, you must choose half of your Drop Pods (rounding up) to make a 'Drop Pod Assault'. Units making a Drop Pod Assault arrive on the player's first turn. The arrival of the remaining Drop Pods is rolled for as normal. A unit that Deep Strikes via Drop Pod may not assault in the turn it arrives.

Inertial Guidance System: Should a Drop Pod scatter on top of impassable terrain or another model (friend or foe!) then reduce the scatter distance by the minimum required in order to avoid the obstacle.

Immobile: A Drop Pod cannot move once it has entered the battle, and counts in all respects as a vehicle that has suffered an Immobilised damage result (which cannot be repaired in any way).

WARGEAR

Deathwind Launcher: Some Drop Pods are upgraded to carry a deathwind launcher in place of a storm bolter:

Range	Strength	AP	Type
12"	5	-	Heavy 1, Large Blast

MASTER OF THE FORGE

The Master of the Forge is the Chapter's most senior Techmarine, charged with the maintenance of the Chapter's fleet of armoured fighting vehicles, such as Rhinos, Land Raiders and Predators. His knowledge of the arcane sciences has been refined over centuries of service, and rivals that of the senior Tech-priests of Mars. Indeed, a Master of the Forge's skill has been honed to a point where he can recognise a machine spirit's ailment with but a glance and the cause of its intemperance from the merest whisper of its tortured mantra of function.

Such uncanny, and perhaps unnatural, skill conspires to make the Master of the Forge something of an outcast in most Chapters. Though he is part of the Chapter Council, the Master of the Forge is an outsider to all save his subordinate Techmarines, whose company is shunned in all matters save those that pertain to his beloved mechanicals.

This isolation serves only to lead a Master of the Forge further down the path of eccentricity. Surrounded by tongueless machines and witless Servitors, his own voice becomes atrophied. On such rare occasions as a Master of the Forge does speak, it is in clipped and monotonous tones, coldly and discomfortingly precise in detail and delivery.

Not all Space Marine Chapters treat with their Master of the Forge in this way. Some, such as the Mentors, the Praetors of Orpheus and the Astral Knights, embrace the dwindling technologies of Mankind without superstition and, in the case of the Iron Hands, with gusto.

In these Chapters, the Master of the Forge is a personage honoured no less than the Chapter Master himself. Such cases are few. Indeed, for one Chapter to embrace the vision and purpose of a Master of the Forge is to invite suspicion from many of its more conventional brothers.

In addition to his responsibilities to the armoury, a Master of the Forge is also tasked with the conservation of any arcane mechanical relics to which his Chapter is heir. The oldest and most famous Chapters have many such technological wonders locked within their vaults. Most are so bewilderingly complex that no living man could hope to divine their secrets. Others are forged of secrets so ancient that only an artisan of a Master's knowledge could hope to maintain them without causing harm to himself and anyone else in proximity. If the need is great, a Master of the Forge will take up such a weapon and unleash the fury of Mankind's lost technological might upon the foe.

	WS	BS	S	T	W	I	A	Ld	Sv
Master of the Forge	4	5	4	4	2	4	2	10	2+

SPECIAL RULES
And They Shall Know No Fear, Combat Tactics, Independent Character.

Blessing of the Omnissiah, Bolster Defences:
See opposite page.

WARGEAR
Servo-arm, Servo-harness: See opposite page.

Conversion Beamer: Incredibly rare pre-Heresy artefacts, conversion beam projectors fire a beam that induces a controlled subatomic reaction in the target, converting its mass into energy. The further away the target, the more deadly the blast, as the beam has time to grow in power.

A shot from a conversion beamer has a different profile depending on how far the target is from the firer. When firing the conversion beamer, measure the distance to the target and place the blast template. Once the final location of a conversion beamer's template has been placed (after scatter) measure to the centre of the blast marker and consult the chart below to determine the effect.

Range	Strength	AP	Type
up to 18"	6	-	Heavy 1, Blast
18" to 42"	8	4	Heavy 1, Blast
42" to 72"	10	1	Heavy 1, Blast
over 72"	Miss!	n/a	n/a

TECHMARINE

Ancient pacts sworn between the Adeptus Mechanicus and the Adeptus Astartes allow the Space Marines to send those warriors with an affinity for technology to Mars to train and begin the long, arduous journey of becoming a priest of the Machine God. Without the passing on of such ancient lore, the Space Marines would be unable to make war.

Aspiring Techmarines train for many years on Mars, steeping themselves in rites of activation and hymnals of maintenance; how to call forth a machine spirit or placate its wrath. Techmarines return to their Chapter as aloof and mysterious figures steeped in superstitious awe. From that point forth they are men of dual loyalties, pledged by blood to their Chapter, but bound in mind and spirit to the mysteries of the Mechanicus Omnissiah. This dichotomy ensures that a Techmarine is never again truly trusted by his brothers and is kept at arms length from the Chapter's secrets and rituals.

Despite this suspicion, Techmarines are held in great esteem by their Battle-Brothers who recognise and acknowledge the Techmarines' expertise in the mysterious sciences. A Space Marine Chapter would be of little consequence without its many technological tools, and its ancient weapons must be kept in a constant state of readiness – without the Techmarines this would be impossible. Despite their arcane calling, they are warriors first and foremost. Should a vehicle or artefact of technology be lost, the Techmarines will fight for its retrieval as stridently as their brethren would fight to recover a fallen comrade; perhaps, as some suggest, harder.

	WS	BS	S	T	W	I	A	Ld	Sv
Techmarine	4	4	4	4	1	4	1	8	2+

SPECIAL RULES
Independent Character, Combat Tactics, And They Shall Know No Fear.

Blessing of the Omnissiah: If a Techmarine is in base contact with a damaged vehicle during the Shooting phase, he can attempt to repair it instead of firing. Roll a D6 and add the the following modifiers:

Each Servitor with a servo-arm in the unit	+1
The Techmarine has a servo-harness	+1

If the result is 5 or more, then either a Weapon Destroyed result or Immobilised result (owning player's choice) will be repaired. If a Weapon Destroyed result is repaired, that weapon can be fired in the following Shooting phase. The Techmarine cannot repair if gone to ground or falling back.

> "Thus do we invoke the Machine God.
> Thus do we make whole that which was sundered."
>
> From the Hymn of Reforging

Bolster Defences: Techmarines can increase the effectiveness of cover, reinforcing crumbling walls and re-welding badly-damaged spars. Each Techmarine can bolster a single ruin before the game begins. When you deploy, nominate one ruin in your deployment area for your Techmarine to bolster. The ruin's cover save is increased by one for the duration of the game. For example, a normal ruin (4+ save) so reinforced would offer a 3+ cover save. A ruin can only be bolstered once.

WARGEAR
Servo-arm: Techmarines and Servitors are equipped with powerful servo-arms that can be used for battlefield repairs or even put to use as a weapon. Each Servo-arm grants the model a single extra close combat attack, made seperately at Initiative 1 and Strength 8, ignoring Armour Saves.

Servo-harness: A servo-harness gives the Techmarine an extra servo-arm (giving him two servo-arm attacks), a plasma cutter (fired in the Shooting phase as a twin-linked plasma pistol, but cannot be used in close combat) and a flamer. In the shooting phase the Techmarine can fire both harness-mounted weapons, or one harness mount and another gun.

SERVITOR

Though essential to the maintenance of a Chapter's mechanical devices, Servitors rarely enjoy anything save indifference from the Space Marines they serve. In most Chapters, the Servitors are ignored by all but the Techmarines, treated as would any other machine or piece of equipment. In others they are treated with revulsion, considered necessary but abhorrences that pervert the spirit and the flesh of man.

Conversely, in a very few Space Marine Chapters, generally those with strong ties to the Adeptus Mechanicus, Servitors are regarded as having achieved spiritual union with the Omnissiah. In such Chapters, Servitors are biomechanoid shrines, revered almost as greatly as other artefacts, their words sifted and analysed for hints of prophecy and guidance from the Machine God. Those Space Marines who follow these arcane practices believe that in so doing they are brought closer to the Omnissiah. To other Chapters, such behaviour is thought distasteful to the point of heresy and regarded with hostility and suspicion. What the Servitors think of all this – if indeed they even notice – no one knows.

	WS	BS	S	T	W	I	A	Ld	Sv
Servitor	3	3	3	3	1	3	1	8	4+

SPECIAL RULES

Mindlock: The altered and fragmented brain of a Servitor functions poorly unless constantly supervised.

A unit of Servitors must test for mindlock at the start of each friendly turn. Roll a D6 for each unit of Servitors. If the result is a 4, 5 or 6 the test is passed and the unit can function normally for the remainder of the turn. If the result is a 1, 2 or 3, the Servitors have succumbed to mindlock – the unit (and any characters) may not move, shoot or assault that turn (though they will fight normally in close combat if already engaged). If a Techmarine or Master of the Forge is part of the Servitor unit at the start of the turn, the mindlock test is passed automatically.

Servitors are mono-task adapted slaves that exist solely to assist a Chapter's Techmarines in their laborious duties. Each is an arcane combination of man and machine, without personality or reason, sporting an array of mechanical modifications ranging from huge metal claws and infra-red sensors to bionic exoskeletons and flux-torsion drills, all the better to aid a Techmarine in his repair and maintenance of a Chapter's armoury. Some Servitors are even bonded to heavy weapons so that they may act as battlefield bodyguards to their master.

The creation mysteries for Servitors vary from Chapter to Chapter. Some are grown from human gene-cells in artificial nutrient. Others are failed neophytes, civilian criminals or fugitives from Chapter law who have been mind-wiped and lobotomised so that their flesh may serve anew.

Although physically strong and robust, Servitors are feeble-minded and can only function at the command of the bio-programs that Techmarines insert into their brains. They feel little pain, less fear and have no intuition whatsoever. Without a Techmarine's constant supervision, Servitors are erratic at best – most go into a state of mindlock, babbling incoherent nonsense as their ravaged brains try to assert some form of awareness. Nonetheless, a Space Marine Chapter relies heavily on its Servitors to maintain its weapons of war. Hundreds of biomechanoid slaves toil ceaselessly deep within the walls of every Chapter Monastery, preparing and maintaining weapons of war.

> As a commander your tools and devices shall be myriad, yet the wise man knows that battles are won by flesh, not the machine. Flesh can learn, whilst the machine must be forever instructed. Flesh knows loyalty to its brothers and veneration of its Emperor, whilst the machine knows not these things.
>
> Whenever the day is darkest and victory in doubt, look not to the machine for aid, but to your Battle-Brothers. The machine can only bring you victory if you tell it how such a thing can be done. Your brothers will walk through fire, they will stride through the most terrible carnage at a single word from your lips, and they will bring you victory simply because you ask it of them.
>
> From the teachings of Roboute Guilliman
> as laid down in the Apocrypha of Skaros

THUNDERFIRE CANNON

Space Marines taskforces strike hard and fast, and a unit that cannot maintain a rapid advance swiftly becomes a liability. For this reason, most Space Marine support guns are mounted on vehicles that can keep pace with the rest of the army, as can be seen with the Vindicator and Whirlwind. Designed for static defence, the Thunderfire Cannon is the one exception to the rule. Mounted on ponderous but rugged tracks, each Thunderfire Cannon is a quad-barrelled gun capable of a punishing rate of fire.

The Techmarine manning a Thunderfire Cannon can set its shells to detonate in a variety of different ways, depending on the tactical situation. Surface detonations are employed against numerous enemies in comparatively clear terrain, whilst airburst shells are used to scour a foe from cover. The most devastating barrage, however, is one programmed to burrow deep into the ground before detonating. Though the force of the blast is greatly reduced, the resulting shockwave is often sufficient to knock the foe sprawling, making them easy prey for other weaponry.

Thunderfire Cannons are primarily employed in mountainous or broken terrain, where the more traditional mobile artillery units, such as Whirlwinds, cannot operate. Though a Thunderfire Cannon can move under its own power, they are normally deployed from Thunderhawk Gunships or other fast-moving transport craft. Thunderfire Cannons are also invaluable in defensive deployments and evacuations, where their high rate of anti-personnel fire and disruptive subterranean shelling can wreak bloody havoc amongst the attacking forces.

	WS	BS	S	T	W	I	A	Ld	Sv
Techmarine	4	4	4	4	1	4	1	8	2+

Each Thunderfire Cannon is crewed by a single Techmarine (see page 71 for special rules). Note that the Techmarine does not benefit from the Independent Character and Blessing of the Omnissiah special rules unless his Thunderfire Cannon has been destroyed.

"I have travelled far and seen much. Yet nothing warms my heart so much as the sight of a gun so massive that its fury makes the very world tremble."

Attributed to Captain Darnath Lysander
Imperial Fists 1st Company

WARGEAR
Servo-harness: See page 71.

Thunderfire Cannon: The Thunderfire Cannon is a colossal multi-barrelled weapon. Each Thunderfire Cannon shell can be fused for surface detonation, airburst or subterranean blast. Declare which type of fusing you wish to use before the Thunderfire Cannon fires.

Surface Detonation
Range	Strength	AP	Type
60"	6	5	Heavy 4, Blast

Airburst
Range	Strength	AP	Type
60"	5	6	Heavy 4, Blast, Ignores Cover*

Subterranean Blast
Range	Strength	AP	Type
60"	4	-	Heavy 4, Blast, Tremor**

*Ignores Cover: Cover saves cannot be taken against wounds caused by an airburst salvo.

**Tremor: Any unit hit by a subterranean blast will move as if in difficult terrain in its following Movement phase. If the unit is actually moving through difficult terrain, it rolls one less dice than normal to determine its maximum move. A vehicle hit by a Tremor shell must take a dangerous terrain test if it moves in the following Movement phase. This even applies to skimmers, whose delicate grav-engines are pummelled by shockwaves.

LAND SPEEDER

The Land Speeders fielded by the Space Marines are an evolution of a Standard Template Construct (STC) pattern discovered in the wake of the Horus Heresy. Utilising ancient technology, the Land Speeder uses a repulsion plate to skim a planet's gravitational field, simulating the effect of flight, and enabling it to perform low-altitude manoeuvres that more conventional atmosphere-capable craft would find nigh-impossible.

Early Land Speeder designs were relatively unarmoured, but over the millennia the design has been modified with light adamantium plating. This alteration was made not for the sake of the crew – power armour provides a greater degree of protection than even the heaviest armour on a Land Speeder – but to better protect the delicate control units, without which a Land Speeder is merely a large chunk of welded metal swiftly approaching terminal velocity.

All of a Chapter's Space Marines are trained to fight as Land Speeder squadrons as part of their service in an Assault squad, but the craft are most commonly piloted by those Battle Brothers who embrace the speed of which a Land Speeder is capable. Most Land Speeder pilots are regarded as being not a little reckless by their Battle Brothers. Indeed, no wholly sane man, however courageous, would willingly embrace the repertoire of dizzying low-level combat manoeuvres of which the craft is capable. Land Speeder pilots think nothing of skimming close to rock spires, jinking through forests or performing abrupt nose-dives and barrel rolls to avoid incoming fire. Considering the mental and physical strain of such bewildering manoeuvres, the fact that few Land Speeders are lost to pilot error can be solely attributed to the superhuman reactions and stamina of the Space Marines who crew them.

With their versatile weapons loadout, Land Speeders can be tasked to a variety of battlefield objectives. These can range from lightly armed reconnaissance and scout deployments, to tank hunting or other seek and destroy missions.

The gravitational drive of a Land Speeder does not allow it to function at high-altitudes, but it can be used to perform a controlled descent from the upper atmosphere. This allows a Land Speeder to deploy from overflying Thunderhawk Gunships and assail the foe without warning.

Though they are often ordered to support other units, Land Speeders can be (and are) deployed en masse in many engagements. Some Space Marine Chapters routinely field their entire fleet of Land Speeders as a fast moving and nigh unstoppable assault wave, blasting a hole in the enemy battleline that Rhino-mounted Tactical squads can exploit, before peeling off and engaging another target with a similarly devastating effect.

	Type	BS	Armour F	S	R
Land Speeder	Fast, Skimmer	4	10	10	10

SPECIAL RULES
Deep Strike.

WARGEAR
Typhoon Missile Launcher: The typhoon missile launcher is equipped with frag and krak missiles. Declare which type of missile you wish to use each time the typhoon missile launcher fires.

Frag Missiles

Range	Strength	AP	Type
48"	4	6	Heavy 2, Blast

Krak Missiles

Range	Strength	AP	Type
48"	8	3	Heavy 2

"Victory often rests on the correct weaponry being in the right place and at the right time. Even the most destructive weapons of war are worthless if absent from the battle."

Artor Amhrad (deceased)
Chapter Master of the Astral Knights

LAND SPEEDER STORM

The Land Speeder Storm is a significant modification of the original design, trading the traditional heavy armament for a modest transport capacity. The resulting craft is the equal of its parent in matters of speed and manoeuvrability, but can also carry a small Scout squad without any loss of performance. Furthermore, a Land Speeder Storm's baffled engines and sophisticated spy array afford it a stealthy profile best suited to the Scouts' mission of clandestine hit and run attacks. As a result, each can be used as a mobile firebase, assault transport or stealth insertion craft as the combat objectives dictate.

To further enhance the Land Speeder Storm's effectiveness in strike missions, many Chapters replace a Land Speeder's standard underslung heavy bolter armament with a cerberus launcher. This tri-barrelled weapon fires a disorienting volley of frag, stun and blind rockets into enemy positions, allowing the Scouts to move in and mop up any survivors.

When combined with the rapier speed of the Land Speeder Storm, the cerberus launcher allows Scouts to launch rapid and daring assaults at an otherwise impenetrable defence line with impunity. So did the mad Regent of Amar discover one morning when he awoke to discover that his outer bastions were in the hands of the Howling Griffons, and that his own artillery positions, now crewed by Space Marine Scouts, were lobbing shells into the inner palace. This assault, conducted with a stealth and precision that would have been impossible for a conventional Drop Pod or Rhino onslaught to achieve, was the turning point in crushing the Amar secession, and guaranteed that the Land Speeder Storm would see ongoing use.

| | Type | BS | Armour | | |
			F	S	R
Land Speeder Storm	Fast, skimmer, open-topped	3	10	10	10

TRANSPORT
The Land Speeder Storm has a transport capacity of five models. It can only carry Scouts.

Fire Points and Access Points: The Land Speeder Storm is open-topped.

SPECIAL RULES
Deep Strike, Scouts.

WARGEAR
Cerberus Launcher: The cerberus launcher is used to stun enemy units prior to an assault by Scouts.

If a Scout unit charges into combat on the same turn as it disembarks from the Land Speeder, any enemy units that the Scouts assault have their Leadership reduced by 2 for the duration of that assault phase.

Jamming Beacon: Land Speeder Storms carry transmitters that broadcast powerful electro-magnetic and etheric interference. The resultant disruption denies enemy reserves crucial locational and navigational information, causing them to enter the fray a considerable distance from their intended entry point.

Teleport homers, Chaos Icons and similar wargear items that prevent deep strike scatter do not function within 6" of a Land Speeder Storm. In addition, enemies wishing to deep strike onto the board within 6" of a Land Speeder Storm scatter 4D6" rather than 2D6".

"Forget all your preconceptions of war, of battle-lines clashing in the churned ground. Your mission is to attack before the foe even realises that the war has begun, to strike hard at those vital weaknesses that all armies possess, but that no commander will admit to.

Under my tutelage you will learn how to seek out such fragilities and smite them with every weapon at your disposal. Master these duties and I will have nothing more to teach, and you will truly be a Space Marine."

Sergeant Torias Telion
Ultramarines 10th Company

RHINO

Rhino armoured troop carriers are the mainstay of every Space Marine Chapters' vehicle pool. With an optimal balance of armour, transport capacity and manoeuvrability, the Rhino allows the Space Marines to swiftly redeploy, rush squads into positions of strategic advantage or conduct surgical strikes on the enemy line.

As with much of the technology employed by the Imperium, the Standard Template Construct for the Rhino dates back to the earliest days of colonisation. It has changed little in the intervening millennia, for one of the Rhino design's great triumphs is its ease of assembly and simple adaptation to alternate construction methods and fuel systems. In the past, much of the Imperium's war machine relied on the Rhino, but now the knowledge of its construction and maintenance has faded. Only the Space Marines and a handful of other Imperial organisations can boast Rhinos in numbers sufficient to their needs.

The core triumph of the Rhino's design is its durability and ease of repair. Indeed, most Rhinos contain rudimentary self-repair systems that can restore motive and drive systems even after damage so severe that many similar vehicles would be utterly irreparable. Such catastrophic damage is rare, for the Rhino's design is incredibly rugged. Given time and facilities, a skilled Techmarine can nurse even a badly battered wreck to life, reconsecrating it in the eyes of the

Omnissiah and renewing it to the righteous wars of the Chapter. As a result, many Rhinos have remained in service for thousands of years. Over that time almost every component and armour plate will have been replaced or been subject to significant repair, but the honoured name and designation of the Rhino lives on.

Nocturne's Hammer is the oldest Rhino in existence and belongs to the Salamanders Chapter. It is said that this august vehicle once carried the legendary Primarch Vulkan into battle at the Siege of Devlin's Fastness, sallying out through the gates of the Imperial fortress into the midst of the encircling Word Bearers. *Nocturne's Hammer* has seen over eight thousand years of action and now has a place in the Salamander's reliquary. It is a great honour for a Techmarine to minister to the *Hammer's* scarred hide, and its needs are observed with devotion. At the dawn of each new century, the Chapter's Techmarines gather in the reliquary and the Master of the Forge strikes the rune of activation upon the Hammer's engine. It is said that doom shall befall the Salamanders should the engine fail to catch first time.

> "Versatile, enduring and uncomplaining – truly is the Rhino a fit steed for a Space Marine."
>
> Captain Emil Verigan
> Night Watch 5th Company

| | Type | BS | Armour | | |
			F	S	R
Rhino	Tank	4	11	11	10

TRANSPORT

The Rhino has a transport capacity of ten models. It cannot carry models in Terminator armour.

Fire Points: Two models can fire from the Rhino's top hatch.

Access Points: Rhinos have one access point on each side of the hull and one at the rear.

SPECIAL RULES

Repair: Rhinos are exceptionally resilient vehicles and can often be repaired by their crew in the heat of battle. If a Rhino is immobilised for any reason, then in subsequent turns the crew can attempt a temporary repair instead of the vehicle shooting. Roll a D6 in the Shooting phase, and on a 6 the vehicle is no longer Immobilised.

> As you are a knight in service of the Emperor, so is the Rhino your steed. Honour it, respect it, see that its needs are met, and it shall serve you well through all the battles you must face.
>
> From the teachings of Roboute Guilliman
> as laid down in the Apocrypha of Skaros

RAZORBACK

The vast armouries of the Space Marines contain many types of fighting vehicles. Some have been used for thousands of years whilst others, like the Razorback, have only recently been rediscovered. The Razorback is a heavily armed variant of the Rhino troop transport that sacrifices a portion of its transport capacity for turret-mounted armament, normally a twin-linked lascannon or heavy bolter.

Standard battle doctrine dictates that Razorbacks should be deployed as fire support vehicles, accompanying Rhinos or infantry squads into the thick of battle. As Rhinos have little in the way of firepower, even a single Razorback assigned as escort can dramatically increase the effectiveness of a strike. Impressed by its versatility, several Chapters have begun to field the Razorback in other roles, employing them as mobile command centres and heavy reconnaissance screens.

Despite the Razorback's proven effectiveness, some Space Marine Chapters regard it with distrust, claiming that it is 'new' technology and still not sufficiently proven in battle. While this has a certain inherent logic – the Razorback has been in use for a mere four thousand years, whilst the Rhino and Predator predate the Horus Heresy – the fact that most Chapters have embraced the Razorback as a keystone of their operational doctrines serves to highlight this suspicious attitude as misguided. Some time in the future the Razorback may replace the Rhino as the mainstay transport of the Space Marines. However, to do so will require the Razorback to prove its worth to the staunch traditionalists, which in turn will require the Razorback to prove its worth in the never-ending battle for Mankind's survival.

| | Type | BS | Armour | | |
			F	S	R
Razorback	Tank	4	11	11	10

TRANSPORT

The Razorback has a transport capacity of six models. It cannot carry models in Terminator armour.

Fire Points: None.

Access Points: Razorbacks have one access point on each side of the hull and one at the rear.

"I believe in three tenets of battle – firepower, firepower and more firepower. Should the Omnissiah have wished otherwise, he would not have provided me with such a mighty tool as the Razorback. I long for the day in which my entire Chapter can ride to war in transports such as these, vehicles whose rage can be given voice through their sanctified armament."

Kardan Stronos
Chapter Master of the Iron Hands

Razorbacks are known to sport the broadest range of weaponry of any Space Marine vehicle. This is perhaps due to their recent incorporation into the Space Marine armoury. As the Razorback is less established than such legendary tanks as the Rhino and the Predator, there are inevitably fewer taboos to be broken through reinterpreting the design.

The oldest pattern of Razorback is the Mark 1 or "Stronos" – a dedicated heavy infantry slayer that combines the firepower of twin-linked plasma guns and a single lascannon. Details of the dire events that married so powerful an armament to so lightly armoured a vehicle can now only be speculated upon, as all records from that time have been lost or sealed.

Despite its early successes, the Mark 1 is now an increasingly rare sight through the Imperium. Some records suggest that this could be due to an insurmountable design flaw, namely that the Razorback's hull simply could not bear the strain of the immense power its armament required. Regardless, the Mark 1 remains an honoured ancestor to the patterns that came after and it is treated with due reverence by those Chapters fortunate enough to still maintain one.

PREDATOR

The Predator is the main battle tank of the Space Marines. Broadly based upon the Rhino STC, the Predator sacrifices transport capacity for improved frontal armour and heavy turret-mounted armament. The result is a well-armed and mobile tank, equally capable of holding ground or spearheading armoured assaults into the most heavily defended of enemy territory.

The efficiency and durability of the Predator design are attested to by its long and proud history. Indeed, the records of the Adeptus Mechanicus indicate that the Predator was instrumental in establishing mankind's dominance of the galaxy as far back as the Dark Age of Technology. Here its formidable firepower and reinforced armour were decisive in curbing the menace posed by all manner of alien races, the bestial Orks and enigmatic Eldar foremost amongst them. Each Predator's service is therefore in the continuation of one of the proudest military traditions of the Imperium, a tradition that has endured unblemished through the dark days of the Horus Heresy, the Scouring and the Occlusiad. It is small wonder that the Predator has become a byword for armoured might, and its unique appearance became as much a symbol of the Imperium as the aquila upon its indomitable adamantium hull.

The Predator is a highly versatile vehicle, capable of receiving a number of weapon load-outs. There are two classes of Predator currently in use by the majority of Space Marine Chapters. The Destructor pattern is equipped with a turret-mounted autocannon, perfect for the suppression of light vehicles or troop formations, whilst the twin-linked lascannon of the Annihilator pattern is deadly to enemy armour. The firepower of both Predator types can be further augmented by sponson-mounted heavy bolters or lascannon, so ensuring that a Predator need never find itself without the correct weapon for the task at hand.

Most Chapters employ a balance of Predator types, although some heavily favour one model. The Subjugators are perhaps the most extreme example of this. Their Predator fleet is comprised entirely of Annihilators, requiring the bulk of Subjugator anti-infantry support duties to be allocated to Whirlwinds and Land Raider Crusaders.

Though a Space Marine Chapter will occasionally field its full fleet of twenty or so Predators as an armoured task force, the Predator's chief function is to provide fire support for the Chapter's infantry. In reinforcement of this designation, each freshly forged Predator is assigned a name that reflects its role as a protector of the Chapter's brethren.

Indeed, a Predator's name may endure in the collective memory of a Space Marine Chapter – long after its crew are forgotten by all but the recorders of a Chapter's histories. In part this is unsurprising, for a single Predator may serve its Chapter nobly for many thousands of years under the guidance of a score of crews, who themselves ascribe a noble personality to their armoured steed. *Heart of Defiance*, *Orar's Sentinel* and *Blade of Honour* all hold revered positions in the battle sagas of the Ultramarines and their destruction is mourned as greatly as the passing of the Chapter's greatest flesh and blood heroes.

| | Type | BS | Armour | | |
			F	S	R
Predator	Tank	4	13	11	10

Make the Predator's virtues your own. Let your resolve become as impervious as the Predator's armoured hull, and let your rage strike with the righteous fury of its guns. As it crushes the foe beneath its remorseless advance, so shall you smite the traitor and the alien without hesitation or regret.

Know that to take the field alongside a Predator is to fight at the side of one of Mankind's most honoured guardians. To strive with less than your all beneath its iron gaze is to dishonour yourself and your Battle-Brothers before one of Mankind's greatest heroes.

From the teachings of Roboute Guilliman as laid down in the Apocrypha of Skaros

WHIRLWIND

The Space Marines' role as a highly mobile strike force means that they can rarely afford to be slowed down by static artillery. However, the Codex Astartes does recognise the need for devastating support fire, particularly when engaging numerous hordes or highly mobile foes. It is vital that such enemies are broken or suppressed from a distance before they can take advantage of the Space Marines' lack of numbers. It is for this specialised mission that the Whirlwind was designed.

The Whirlwind is an adaptation of the Rhino design, a lightly armoured tank chassis armed with a multiple rocket launcher system capable of raining precision fire down upon enemy positions. Thanks to its target acquisition system, the Whirlwind is able to bombard hidden or entrenched targets with incredible accuracy, often from behind the safety of cover. The Whirlwind's normal payload consists of solid fuel frag missiles, launched in programmed salvos of paired rockets. The Whirlwind's sophisticated telemetry ensures that each barrage is delivered for maximum effect, resulting in a more formidable blast than that provided by conventional frag missiles.

The Whirlwind is also able to fire Castellan incendiary missiles. Here the fragmentation charge is exchanged for a volatile chemical warhead that throws out a blanket of searing flame on detonation. Even the most entrenched bulwarks offer no protection against a sustained barrage of Castellan missiles – if the defenders are not roasted alive by chemical fires, the acrid and acidic vapours swiftly eat them alive from the inside out.

The combination of manoeuvrability and overwhelming firepower offered by an experienced Whirlwind crew is an asset much prized by all Space Marine commanders. Whether delivering crippling bombardments onto enemy defences, providing supporting fire to spearhead advances or acting as a defensive firebase, a Whirlwind will always prove its worth a dozen times over or more. Few enemies do not dread an incoming Whirlwind barrage. Some warlords have been known to task large portions of their military might purely to the location and annihilation of Whirlwind batteries, only to find those self same forces ambushed in turn by a shrewd Space Marine commander who anticipated such a move. Some Chapters enhance this psychological impact still further by altering the Whirlwinds' payload so that the missile emits a terrible screeching wail as it hurtles through the sky. Sometimes the sound alone is sufficient to drive the foe from their fortifications, allowing the Space Marines to advance unopposed.

> "Victory does not always rest with the big guns:
> But, if we rest in front of them, we shall be lost."
>
> Commander Argentius of the Silver Skulls

	Type	BS	Armour F	S	R
Whirlwind	Tank	4	11	11	10

WARGEAR

Whirlwind Multiple Missile Launcher: Each Whirlwind in your army is equipped with the standard vengeance missiles and the incendiary Castellan missiles. Declare which type of missile you wish to use before the Whirlwind fires.

Vengeance Missiles

Range	Strength	AP	Type
12-48"	5	4	Ordnance 1, Barrage

Incendiary Castellan Missiles

Range	Strength	AP	Type
12-48"	4	5	Ordnance 1, Barrage, Ignores cover*

*Ignores Cover: Cover saves cannot be taken against wounds caused by incendiary missiles.

VINDICATOR

The Vindicator is a Rhino-based siege tank that boasts the most devastating weapon in the Space Marines' armoury – the demolisher cannon.

The notion of fitting a high-calibre cannon into the hull of a Rhino first evolved during the very early years of the Horus Heresy, during the fierce inner-city battles on Rothern I. Traitor formations had transformed the labyrinth of alleyways and rockcrete structures into formidable defensive positions, and the loyalist forces had to devise a way of delivering bunker-busting ordnance with precision amongst the cramped streets. Large-bore thunderer cannons were mounted onto remodelled and up-armoured Rhino chassis. Thus was born the Vindicator, undisputed victor of the Rothern I campaign, and evermore an essential part of any Space Marine Chapter's armoury.

In the millennia since the Heresy, the Vindicator has been called upon again and again to bring the Emperor's judgement to the foes of Mankind. The logic that led to the Vindicator's birth still holds as true at the end of the 41st Millennium as it did ten thousand years before. Amid the snarl of a hive world's streets or similar environments the Vindicator is unparalleled. Where other vehicles would quickly be outflanked, the Vindicator can simply obliterate obstacles that lie in its path and surge forwards over the broken rubble.

Overwhelming success has not preserved the Vindicator from alterations over the course of centuries. Indeed, there has been a steady stream of upgrades and technological tweaks to the vehicle pattern as time has passed. The most significant of these alterations has been the replacement of the bulky thunderer cannon with the much more compact, but no less potent, demolisher cannon. A legion of other alterations have been applied to armour plating, fire control and drive mechanisms, further refining what was essentially a battlefield jury-rig design into the siege workhorse that is the Vindicator at the close of the 41st Millennium.

While Vindicators remain the kings of urban warfare, their combat role has been greatly expanded since they entered widespread use. For the Space Marines, it matters not that the demolisher cannon is relatively short-ranged, as most of their armoured engagements are conducted at brutal close-quarters. Accordingly, it is a rare Space Marine tank assault that does not employ at least one Vindicator in the vanguard of the formation.

For larger engagements, a squadron of Vindicators flank the advance, unleashing their punishing firepower in support of the breaching Land Raiders. On smaller scales, a Vindicator may itself be the spearhead of the formation, punching a hole in the enemy fortification and allowing infantry to stream through in its wake.

| | Type | BS | Armour | | |
			F	S	R
Vindicator	Tank	4	13	11	10

WARGEAR

Demolisher Cannon: The demolisher cannon is the weapon of choice amongst the Imperium's armies when faced with dug-in enemy infantry in a dense environment such as a cityfight or siege. The terrific blast unleashed by the detonation of the huge demolisher shells is often sufficient to bring down buildings in which the enemy take cover, crushing them beneath tons of fallen masonry. The demolisher cannon has the following profile:

Range	Strength	AP	Type
24"	10	2	Ordnance 1

Siege Shield: Many Vindicators are equipped with an enormous bulldozer blade, allowing them to shoulder aside rubble and other battlefield detritus without risk.

A Vindicator with a siege shield automatically passes dangerous terrain tests.

"Let them hide in their fortress.
My crew can use the target practice."

Brother-Sergeant Chronus
The Spear of Macragge

LAND RAIDER

The Land Raider's heritage predates even the Imperium, yet it remains the single most destructive weapon in the Adeptus Astartes' arsenal. Protected by bonded ceramite and adamantium armour, the Land Raider is impervious to all bar the most destructive weaponry. Equally impressive are its armaments – four lascannon and twin-linked heavy bolters allow the Land Raider to deliver punishing support fire capable of decimating enemy infantry and tanks alike.

With transport capacity for a full squad of Space Marines, their field supplies, communications gear, munitions and medical facilities, the Land Raider is well suited for striking deep behind enemy lines and surviving for long periods in the field. This flexibility is further reinforced by a sealed hull and the complex environmental systems that allow it to operate in practically any theatre of battle. Indeed, the Land Raider is as fearsome in the airless atmospheres of dead moons as it is in the fume-choked environs of a manufactorum world. The Land Raider can also function without ill-effect under the extreme pressures of submarine environments, using its powerful tracks to traverse sea- and riverbeds and assail the foes from an unexpected angle. The Tau defenders of Morix Prime will not soon forget the sight of the Ultramarines' Land Raider *Pride of Argothia* emerging from the waters of Lake Pytha like some mythical leviathan, water cascading from the tank's hull as its engines drove it onward towards the aliens' lightly defended command post.

A Land Raider is a blessed artefact to the Techmarines that oversee its repair and maintenance. This is not least because a Land Raider's machine spirit is so much stronger than that of lesser tanks, a fact taken to mean that a substantial portion of the Omnissiah's essence resides within the Land Raider's impenetrable adamantium hull. Accordingly, should even a Land Raider's sponson be lost in battle, the rest of the Chapter will fight like men possessed for its retrieval, often calling in further reinforcements to ensure that the component is not lost. So it is that lives of men can be stilled in order to preserve the spirit of a machine, but the Space Marines honour such a sacrifice and go willingly into a battle of this kind.

Regardless of its value in matters of faith, the Land Raider's machine spirit is a weighty asset. The machine spirit allows the tank to function with a smaller number of crew than comparable vehicles, and is capable of taking control of engines, weaponry or other systems as the situation permits. Indeed, the Crimson Fists tell that the uncrewed Land Raider *Rynn's Might*, narrowly surviving the missile that levelled their Fortress Monastery, immediately thereafter fought a solo war against a rampaging Ork warband, killing the Warboss and many of his followers in a night of slaughter. *Rynn's Might* did not survive the encounter, but its example serves as a reminder that a Land Raider is not a machine to be taken lightly, whether it be served by crew or no.

	Type	BS	Armour		
			F	S	R
Land Raider	Tank	4	14	14	14

TRANSPORT

A Land Raider has a transport capacity of twelve models.

Fire Points: None.

Access Points: Land Raiders have one access point on each side of the hull and one at the front.

SPECIAL RULES

Power of the Machine Spirit: The interface between a Land Raider's machine spirit and its fire control mechanisms allow the crew to target with incredible accuracy.

A Land Raider can fire one more weapon than would normally be permitted. In addition, this weapon can be fired at a different target unit to any other weapons, subject to the normal rules for Shooting.

Therefore, a Land Raider that has moved at combat speed can fire two weapons, and a Land Raider that has either moved at cruising speed, or has suffered a 'Crew Stunned' or 'Crew Shaken' result can fire a single weapon.

Assault Vehicle: Models disembarking from any access point on a Land Raider can launch an assault on the turn they do so.

LAND RAIDER CRUSADER

The Crusader variant of the Land Raider was developed by the Black Templars Chapter during the Jerulas Crusade. The fortifications upon which the Jerullian hive cities were founded, though ancient, were nonetheless a formidable obstacle to the Black Templars' wrath. Before such a weapon even the fortresses of Jerulas could not stand, and soon the Black Templars were victorious and the Land Raider Crusader hailed an unmistakable success. Thus was born the Land Raider Crusader.

As news of the Crusaders' success spread, other Space Marine Chapters requested information regarding their remodelling of the Land Raider. In 763.M39, due in no small part to the favourable stance taken by the Ultramarines, the Crusader design was sanctioned by the Adeptus Mechanicus. In truth, many Chapters had been utilising the Crusader for some years already, but the blessing of Mars ensured the design's survival. With the support of the forge worlds, the Crusader began appearing ever more frequently on the battlezones of the Imperium and has since become the mainstay of many a Chapters' combat strategy.

A linebreaker without peer, the Crusader can smash through enemy formations and fortifications alike, disgorging Space Marine assault troops into the heart of the enemy position. Numerous short-ranged and swift-firing weapons allow the Crusader to weaken the enemy before the assault is launched, and provide a torrent of fire to support its cargo once in combat. Although the removal of the twin-linked lascannon reduces the Crusader's overall tank-hunting capability, most are equipped with a pintle-mounted multimelta to compensate. Reclamation of the space normally given over to the lascannon power generators provides a transport capacity far in excess of any other Imperial vehicle of comparable size.

Land Raider Crusaders are employed even more aggressively than other Land Raiders. Most crews use their vehicles as adamantium battering rams, relying on the Land Raider's mass to crash through walls, shoulder aside tanks and pulverise enemy troops. Nowhere was this seen more clearly than at the relief of Sanguina, when five Crusaders of the Invaders Chapter ploughed straight through the encircling wall and spurred forwards into the heart of the city, crushing everything in their path. Two score wrecked Ork Trukks and countless mangled greenskins later, the Crusaders arrived before the governor's palace just as the Ork Warboss launched his final assault. Caught between the guns of the defenders to the front and the massed firepower of Crusaders and freshly deployed Tactical squads to the rear, the Ork horde was shredded within minutes. Although it took no less than five Space Marines and twenty of the planetary garrison to finally bring Warboss Dakkamek himself down, the Waaagh! was ended before it had truly begun.

| | Type | BS | Armour | | |
			F	S	R
Land Raider	Tank	4	14	14	14

TRANSPORT
A Land Raider Crusader has a transport capacity of sixteen models.

Fire Points: None.

Access Points: A Land Raider Crusader has one access point on each side of the hull and one at its front.

SPECIAL RULES
Power of the Machine Spirit, Assault Vehicle: See page 81.

WARGEAR
Hurricane Bolters: Each hurricane bolter consists of three twin-linked bolters, fired as a single weapon.

Frag Assault Launchers: The hulls of Land Raider Crusaders and Land Raider Redeemers are studded with explosive charges designed to hurl shrapnel at the enemy as the troops inside charge out. Any unit charging into close combat on the same turn as it disembarks from a Crusader or Redeemer counts as having frag grenades.

LAND RAIDER REDEEMER

An assault fought amongst the rubble-strewn and treacherous environs of a ruined city is the most gruelling kind of battle. Under such conditions, the worst-equipped and most ill-led of troops can hold back the galaxy's finest warriors for months. Combatants lurk in the maze of shattered buildings, taking shelter amongst tumbled rockcrete and using a thousand vantage points to snipe at the enemy. For the Space Marines, whose whole ethos is of a lightning war won before the defender realises that he is fighting, such a situation is intolerable – the foe must be driven from his stronghold, and swiftly. In such battles, only fire will purge the enemy from his nest. In such a battle was the Land Raider Redeemer created.

As the Crusader was a modification of the original Land Raider, so is the Redeemer an evolution of the Crusader design. The Redeemer retains the assault cannon and frag launchers of the Crusader, but eschews the hurricane bolter sponsons for colossal flame projectors that send a billowing tide of burning promethium into the thick of the foe. Combined with the Redeemer's sophisticated targeting systems, these flamestorm cannons are able to purge even a well-defended bunker complex in seconds.

The Redeemer saw its debut amidst the ruined cities of Grissen, a once-prosperous planet torn apart by a civil war that had lasted for millennia. Due to a clerical error in the Imperium's labyrinthine bureaucracy, Grissen had gone unnoticed until a mid-level functionary discovered that the planetary tithes were now some eight thousand years overdue. An Imperial Guard regiment was immediately raised to bring the Emperor's law back to Grissen. When that regiment found itself overwhelmed by the sheer ferocity of the fighters they found planetside, a task force from the Fire Lords Chapter, under the command of Captain Jaric Phoros, joined the fray.

At first the Space Marines made little progress. The natives were so entrenched that even the most devastating orbital bombardments made scant impact on their positions. Nonetheless, the Imperial decree was that Grissen should be brought back into the fold, for it would prove an excellent recruiting ground for the Imperial Guard, and so Phoros held back from ordering exterminatus. Biting back his mounting frustration, Phoros directed his Techmarines to construct a weapon that would win the war. Within a week of the first Land Raider modifications the Fire Lords took Grissen's capital city. Within a month, the largest planetary faction was suing for peace and Grissen was part of the Imperium once more.

In the wake of the Grissen campaign, Phoros disseminated his new design's schematics. Having always been possessed of a sardonic frame of mind, he named the new pattern 'Prometheus' after a god from Terran legend who brought fire to men. He changed the official designation to Redeemer only upon learning that the name was already taken by a variant developed by the Salamanders. Nonetheless, the original Redeemer still serves in the Fire Lords' second company, the name *Prometheus* resplendent on its flanks and honoured in the Chapter's histories.

	Type	BS	Armour F	S	R
Land Raider	Tank	4	14	14	14

TRANSPORT
A Land Raider Redeemer has a transport capacity of twelve models.

Fire Points: None.

Access Points: A Land Raider Redeemer has one access point on each side of the hull and one at its front.

SPECIAL RULES
Power of the Machine Spirit, Assault Vehicle: See page 81.

WARGEAR
Frag Assault Launchers: See page 82.

Flamestorm Cannon: The flamestorm cannon has the following profile.

Range	Strength	AP	Type
Template	6	3	Heavy 1

MARNEUS AUGUSTUS CALGAR
CHAPTER MASTER OF THE ULTRAMARINES

Mankind boasts many heroes, men of purpose and dedication without whom the Imperium would crumble. Yet, even amongst their ranks there is a man whose nobility overshadows all others. His triumphs are without number and his deeds the stuff of legend. His name is Marneus Calgar, Master of the Ultramarines and Lord of Macragge.

To know the deeds behind the legend of Marneus Calgar, one would have to journey into the depths of Macragge's Chapter Fortress. At its heart lies a vault where records are kept of the labours performed by the greatest heroes of the Ultramarines. Thus far there are twenty-eight volumes dedicated to Marneus Calgar alone in this sanctum, a tally twice that of any other living Ultramarine and surpassed only by Roboute Guilliman himself.

Since rising to the rank of Chapter Master, Marneus Calgar has employed his flair for tactics and strategy in campaigns without number. Calgar does not throw his men uselessly at the foe, for he understands that while victories may begin with the general, it is the troops that carry the day. Calgar's men follow him not merely out of duty, but from the unshakeable loyalty that his presence inspires. Indeed, when Calgar was wounded during the campaign for Ichar IV, the surviving Ultramarines formed a wall of bodies around their lord, shielding his broken flesh with their own until aid arrived.

Though famous as a general, Lord Macragge is no stranger to personal valour. The tomes of Ultramar record how it was Calgar that led the breaching assault on the Hiveship designated Behemoth Primus – one of the first actions of its kind against the Tyranids. They also show it was Calgar who held the gate alone against the greenskin horde for a night and a day at the siege of Zalathras. And it was Calgar who recaptured the star fort Indomitable from the daemonic hordes of M'kar the Reborn. These entries have entire pages dedicated to them in the library sanctum, separated by far shorter passages that describe the fall of countless demagogues, pirates and traitors.

Calgar is a proud man, a trait that has earned him more than a fair share of enemies within the Imperium's internecine politics. Yet he also possesses a shrewd self-awareness that prevents that pride turning sour and leading him into arrogance. To the people of Ultramar, Calgar is the hero of heroes, the epitome of Mankind's will to endure and triumph. When Calgar travels Ultramar on tours of inspection he is met with adulating crowds that roar his name with a passion sadly lacking in other Imperial domains. The people of Ultramar believe to their very core that in Marneus Calgar they have a leader who will fight until the stars turn cold, not only for the immortal Emperor, but for Mankind itself.

	WS	BS	S	T	W	I	A	Ld	Sv
Marneus Calgar	6	5	4	4	4	5	4	10	3+

SPECIAL RULES
And They Shall Know No Fear, Combat Tactics, Eternal Warrior, Independent Character.

Orbital Bombardment: See page 52.

Titanic Might: Calgar can re-roll all failed attempts to wound with shooting and close combat attacks.

God of War: Marneus Calgar can choose whether to pass or fail any Morale check he is called upon to make. Whilst Calgar is on the table, all units with the Combat Tactics special rule can also choose whether to pass or fail any Morale check they are called upon to take.

WARGEAR
Gauntlets of Ultramar: These are a matched pair of power fists. They also contain a pair of integrated bolters that can be fired with the following profile:

Range	Str.	AP	Type
24"	4	2	Assault 2

Armour of Antilochus: Calgar may choose to wear this suit of Terminator armour, which includes a teleport homer.

CATO SICARIUS
CAPTAIN OF THE ULTRAMARINES 2nd COMPANY

Cato Sicarius is amongst the greatest heroes of the Ultramarines. His titles are many – Captain of the 2nd Company, Master of the Watch, Knight Champion of Macragge, Grand Duke of Talassar and High Suzerain of Ultramar. Each reflects but a fraction of a lifetime's diligent and exceptional service, not only to the Ultramarines Chapter, but to the realm of Ultramar itself.

Born into one of Talassar's ascendant houses, the young Sicarius began martial training as soon as he was old enough to grasp a sword, as is the way in Talassari nobility – a tutelage only reinforced by his later induction and training in the ways of the Ultramarines. Sicarius earned commendation after commendation and swiftly rose through the ranks. In the decades that followed he served with distinction as Sergeant and Company Champion before ultimately taking command of the Ultramarines 2nd Company – the finest fighting unit in this or any other Space Marine Chapter.

Only the most accomplished warrior could hope to command the Ultramarines 2nd Company, and Sicarius rose to the challenge as he had to every other that had been set in his path. All Space Marines make use of the lightning assault, but Sicarius refined such strategy to near-perfection, often committing his forces to battle with the briefest appraisal of the tactical situation.

In another man, such unstoppable haste might have seemed reckless, but Sicarius soon proved his ability to rapidly adapt to a chaotic warzone, swiftly marshalling his forces and seizing the advantage. Inevitably, Sicarius' assaults took a terrible toll of the foe's army and confidence in equal measure, and left them ripe for defeat. Indeed, even other Space Marines were awed by the speed at which Sicarius could react to a developing tactical situation.

As his tale of victories grew ever longer, Sicarius' name became a byword for victory, a legend forged in the bloody maelstrom of battle that would come to the ears of allies and foes far beyond the borders of Ultramar. So it is that at the close of the 41st Millennium, the 2nd Company draws the most dangerous missions, and Sicarius himself is widely believed to be the heir apparent to Marneus Calgar himself – something that cannot sit well with Agemman, Captain of the 1st Company and Regent of Ultramar.

> "Brothers! War calls you.
> Will you answer?"
>
> Captain Cato Sicarius
> Knight Champion of Macragge

	WS	BS	S	T	W	I	A	Ld	Sv
Cato Sicarius	6	5	4	4	3	5	3	10	2+

SPECIAL RULES
And They Shall Know No Fear, Combat Tactics, Independent Character.

Surprise Attack! An army that includes Sicarius can re-roll the dice when attempting to seize the initiative.

Rites of Battle: If Sicarius is on the table, all other Space Marine units can use his Leadership for any Morale or Pinning tests.

Battle-forged Heroes: Sicarius is accompanied by the finest warriors that the 2nd Company has to offer. One Tactical squad in an army that includes Sicarius can have one of the following special rules at no additional cost: **Counter-attack, Infiltrate, Scout** or **Tank Hunters**.

WARGEAR
Talassarian Tempest Blade: This is a power weapon. If Sicarius wishes, he can attempt a single 'coup de grâce' attack in lieu of his normal close combat attacks. If the coup de grâce hits, it is resolved at a Strength of 6 and causes Instant Death, regardless of the wounded model's Toughness.

Mantle of the Suzerain: This is a suit of artificer armour that bestows the **Feel No Pain** special rule on Sicarius.

VARRO TIGURIUS
ULTRAMARINES CHIEF LIBRARIAN

Tigurius has always stood apart from his Battle-Brothers. Even to the Company Captains of the Ultramarines he is a figure of mystery, possessed of knowledge that goes beyond the towering datastacks and myriad weighty scrolls of the Chapter arcanium.

In Tigurius' eyes, there is nothing more dangerous than incomplete knowledge nurtured in an unready mind. As such, it is not uncommon for Tigurius to meet question with question until he is satisfied that the enquirer has fully grasped the deeper meaning and consequences of the information bestowed. This practice has oft been a cause for tension between the Chief Librarian and the Chapter's Captains, for such forthright heroes seldom have time for the luxury of introspection.

Tigurius rewards those who persevere in their interrogations with insight that borders on prescience, spawned by uncanny hunches and honed through a lifetime's accumulation of knowledge. Little is hidden from the Chief Librarian's sight, and many amongst the Ultramarines believe him to be guided by the Emperor's hand. How else could one explain Tigurius' foretelling of so many incursions into Ultramar, and the insights that have allowed Lord Macragge to counter each invasion before it has truly began?

So ended Waaagh! Madbrakka, its ramshackle fleet blasted to atoms the instant it emerged from the Warp. Warmaster Niadar of the ruinous powers met with scarcely greater success. Only one of his ships made planetfall on the cavern world of Calth, and the weakened assault force fell swiftly to units from the Ultramarines 3rd and 8th Companies.

Tigurius' gift would perhaps be treated with suspicion and perceived as the stigmata of unholy associations, yet none who have witnessed the Chief Librarian in battle can find cause to doubt his allegiance. When the call to war comes, Tigurius is oft to be found in the Ultramarines' vanguard. Amid the fury of battle the Chief Librarian's silent manner falls from him like a shroud, replaced by the vigour of a warrior born. So it was on the world of Boros. Focusing his psychic might, Tigurius sent hellfire coursing through the Ork horde and led the charge that saw the wearied 4th Company victorious over a far more numerous foe.

Tigurius has recently turned his talents to divining the threat of the Tyranids. His predictions about their movements have been so accurate that it would appear he has tapped into the Tyranid Hive Mind – a feat that has driven lesser individuals quite mad. If this is true then Tigurius will have proved himself the most powerful psyker in the Imperium.

	WS	BS	S	T	W	I	A	Ld	Sv
Varro Tigurius	5	4	4	4	2	4	2	10	3+

SPECIAL RULES
And They Shall Know No Fear, Combat Tactics, Independent Character.

Master Psyker: Tigurius knows all the Psychic powers available to Space Marine Librarians (see page 57).

Gift of Prescience: If your army contains Tigurius, you can choose to re-roll any reserve rolls – even successful ones.

WARGEAR
Hood of Hellfire: The Hood of Hellfire functions as a psychic hood and, furthermore, allows Tigurius to use three psychic powers each turn.

Rod of Tigurius: The Rod of Tigurius is a master-crafted force weapon.

> "Each path must be chosen with care,
> Lest disaster swallow us whole."
>
> Varro Tigurius
> Ultramarines Chief Librarian

ORTAN CASSIUS
ULTRAMARINES CHAPLAIN, MASTER OF SANCTITY

Chaplain Cassius is the oldest active member of the Ultramarines Chapter. What little of his skin can be seen amid the life-sustaining bionics is gnarled and battle-scarred, and his one good eye burns with unfulfilled vengeance. Though Cassius is close on four centuries of age, his arm remains strong, his aim remains true and his sturdy presence within the Ultramarines battlelines fills the hearts of his younger brethren with pride and valour. His impassioned words have carried the Ultramarines forward into battle on a thousand, thousand worlds, firing his Battle-Brothers with his own deeply-held passion and belief.

Cassius can recall tales of the first Tyrannic War when he fought alongside Marneus Calgar (always "young Calgar" to Cassius) to purge Ultramar of the horrific denizens of Hive Fleet Behemoth. In the final stages of the war, Cassius accompanied the attempt to rescue the doomed 1st Company at the polar fortress of Macragge. At great cost of life the Tyranid invaders were hunted down and exterminated, though it was too late for the Veterans of the 1st Company who had long since laid down their lives for their brethren. Few of Cassius' companions emerged unscathed from the terrible close quarters fighting, and the Chaplain himself was laid low by a rampaging Carnifex, sustained only by a formidable strength of will until the chapter's Apothecaries could tend his ruined body.

After a long convalescence, during which much of his shattered form was rebuilt with bionics, Cassius returned to his duties, filled with new fire and purpose. The ancient Chaplain had been blessed with revelation as he lay dying in the ichor-stained ice. He believed that the Tyranid menace was no mere physical threat. The aliens were Mankind's rightful punishment for their lack of vigilance, and in Cassius' eyes there was no greater calling than to purge them from the galaxy.

To this end, the grizzled Chaplain petitioned Lord Macragge for the authority to forge a new body of Ultramarines, chosen from the survivors of the Tyrannic wars. Cassius believed that only these Space Marines, men who had been tested as he had, could truly understand the threat posed by the Tyranids.

Though secretly thoughtful of the strength of Cassius' newfound fervour, Calgar acceded to the request. The Chapter Master's sanction given, Cassius pulled together his corps of Tyrannic War Veterans. Though Cassius' recruits were initially few in number, each fresh clash with the Tyranid Hive Fleets provides new followers to his cause.

As the movement has grown, Cassius has become ever more withdrawn and his followers an ever more influential faction within the Ultramarines. Though this is perhaps a minor deviation from the Codex Astartes, Lord Macragge tolerates his mentor's divergence. Calgar knows that there shall yet be another reckoning between the Ultramarines and the Tyranids, and that Cassius' followers may then be the key to final victory.

	WS	BS	S	T	W	I	A	Ld	Sv
Ortan Cassius	5	4	4	6	2	4	2	10	3+

SPECIAL RULES
Combat Tactics, Feel No Pain, Independent Character.

Honour of the Chapter, Liturgies of Battle:
See page 58 for details.

WARGEAR
Infernus: This is a master-crafted combi-flamer, lovingly crafted and modified by Cassius himself. Note that the boltgun is loaded with hellfire rounds and will therefore wound any model on a 2+.

"The blasphemy of the Tyranids is such that only one solution is acceptable. Extermination. There can only be two sides in such a fight – choose carefully, lest you and I find ourselves on different sides."

Chaplain Cassius
Ultramarines Master of Sanctity

TORIAS TELION
BROTHER-SERGEANT OF THE ULTRAMARINES 10th COMPANY

Sergeant Telion has marched to war under the command of three successive Chapter Masters and has trod more battlefields than most of the Chapter's Captains. Indeed, no less than four of the current Ultramarines Captains learnt their skills under Telion's watchful eye and rightly accredit their success to the peerless tutelage they received at his grizzled hands.

Having been awarded fully two-score battlefield commendations, including the Iron Skull, the Imperial Laurel and a dozen Marksman's Honour badges, Telion has earnt a position in the Ultramarines Honour Guard several times over. Nonetheless, he chooses to remain in the Scout Company, where by example and experience he can forge the future warriors of the Chapter.

Telion has mastered all of the martial disciplines of the Space Marines over his three centuries of service. Having fought eye-to-eye and blade-to-blade with Mankind's most fearsome enemies, Telion has taken the measure of each and found them wanting. He is a master of brawl, parry and stance. Few gambits of brute strength or elegant skill can penetrate Telion's guard, and fewer opponents can hope to defend themselves against the Sergeant's precise and controlled blows.

Yet however formidable Telion might be as a close-quarter foe, his skills of mêlée are nothing as to those he practices at range. He can take account of environmental interferences, such as wind or gravity, like few others and use bolter or sniper rifle to deliver a killing shot far beyond the official range. Two of his many Marksman's Honour badges were earnt for such feats at the relief of Pallia, where a pair of extreme-range bolter shots ended the lives of both the Commander and Ethereal of a Tau reconnaissance force. With the death of their leaders, the invaders lost all resolve and were easy prey for the oncoming Ultramarines.

Much of Telion's marksmanship is innate, a quirk produced from the merging of latent talent and gene seed, but under his guidance even the rawest Scout can achieve a level of expertise worthy of the most experienced Captain.

That the Ultramarines can boast the most skilled marksmen of any Space Marine Chapter is credited in large part to Telion, whose admonishments and precepts on the subject of war at a distance have become legendary far beyond Ultramar. Indeed, Telion has been seconded to several Chapters with close ties to the Ultramarines, so that his knowledge and unique skills can more widely benefit the immortal Emperor's cause.

	WS	BS	S	T	W	I	A	Ld	Sv
Sergeant Telion	5	6	4	4	1	4	2	9	4+

SPECIAL RULES
And They Shall Know No Fear, Combat Tactics, Stealth, Acute Senses, Infiltrate, Move Through Cover, Scout.

Eye of Vengeance: Wounds caused by Telion's Shooting attacks are allocated by his controlling player, rather than the opposing player.

Voice of Experience: Telion can forgo making a Shooting attack of his own to guide a Battle-Brother's shot. If Telion does not make a shooting attack, one friendly model in his squad can use his Ballistic Skill of 6. You must declare you are using this ability before either Telion or the beneficiary fire any shots.

WARGEAR
Stalker Pattern Boltgun: Telion commonly carries a boltgun equipped with a targeter and loaded with silenced shells. It can be fired with the following profile:

Range	Strength	AP	Type
36"	4	5	Heavy 2 Rending, Pinning

ANTARO CHRONUS
BROTHER-SERGEANT OF THE ULTRAMARINES ARMOURY

Antaro Chronus is the most gifted of all the Ultramarines tank commanders. While most such warriors dedicate themselves to the mastery of a particular vehicle, Chronus' abilities extend to almost any tank in the armoury of the Adeptus Astartes. Few other commanders can match the precision of his bombardments when at the helm of a Whirlwind or Vindicator. No living man can hope to be as coldly precise when unleashing the baleful weaponry of a mighty Predator.

For a Space Marine to be assigned to serve in the armoury is an honour indeed, and to do so is to be entrusted with command of the Chapter's most valuable weapons of war. It is a transition that few Battle-Brothers are able to make, for the crew must suppress their physical self and adopt the adamantium behemoth's form as their own. A crewman must act as decisively and instinctively with the tank as he would with his own limbs. The tank's sensors and viewfinders become the commander's eyes and ears, its weapons are his fists and rage, and its armour his skin.

Chronus takes such skill one step further. He knows the capabilities and limits of every weapon system in every tank, and is cognisant of which of those mechanisms can be bypassed or jury-rigged in the event of damage.

So it was that Chronus kept the Predator *Rage of Antonius* battleworthy during the closing actions of the Damnos Incident, despite suffering several broadside hits from Necron gauss cannons. That the *Rage* survived at all was the cause of much wonderment in the Techmarines who repaired the tank's extensive damage at the campaign's end. That Chronus not only managed to complete his mission goal of destroying the Necron phase generator, but also forced the Necron War Cell into full retreat before the *Rage of Antonius'* systems went into shutdown, was seen as nothing short of miraculous. Such a feat has often been imitated by other Ultramarines tank crews, but never bettered.

For his actions on Damnos and a hundred other worlds, Sergeant Chronus was anointed as the 'Spear of Macragge' – a pre-Heresy title awarded to the Ultramarines' pre-eminent tank commander.

As the Spear, it is Chronus' duty to lead the Chapter's armoured assaults, and his privilege to choose the chariot in which he rides to battle. It is a unique position of authority within the Ultramarines, for it means that although Sergeant Chronus has command over some fifty Brother-Marines, he himself is not subject to the orders of a Captain and answers in all things only to Lord Macragge.

	WS	BS	S	T	W	I	A	Ld	Sv
Antaro Chronus	4	5	4	4	1	4	2	9	3+

SPECIAL RULES
Tank Commander: Chronus is always bought as an upgrade and starts the game as commander of a Space Marine tank (see the army list). Use the tank commander model of Chronus to represent this.

Chronus' tank ignores any Crew Shaken or Crew Stunned results and can use his Ballistic Skill of 5.

If the tank suffers a Wrecked or Explodes! result, roll a D6. On a 1 or 2, Chronus is slain. If the result is 3 or more, Chronus leaps clear at the last second – when the damage has been resolved, place him within 2" of the vehicle's position. If Chronus' vehicle has been destroyed he has the above profile and following special rules for the remainder of the game: And They Shall Know No Fear, Combat Tactics, Independent Character. He may not take command of a different tank.

"The roar of engines, the recoil of cannons.
That is where the true joy of battle lies."

Brother-Sergeant Chronus
The Spear of Macragge

PEDRO KANTOR
CHAPTER MASTER OF THE CRIMSON FISTS

Pedro Kantor has served as the master of the Crimson Fists for almost a century, and his record of service goes back another 250 years. He first rose to prominence at the Battle of Melchitt Sound, where, as sergeant, he led the crucial boarding action against the Ork Kill Kroozer, *Da Growla*. The Kroozer was disabled in the attack, allowing the Crimson Fists' Strike Cruiser, *the Crusader*, to break the Ork line of battle and scatter the greenskin fleet into the detritus-clogged outer system.

When Waaagh! Snagrod hit Rynn's World, Kantor was one of a handful fortunate enough to survive the rogue missile strike that levelled the Crimson Fists' fortress monastery. Kantor witnessed the rippling explosions that tore the heart from his Chapter, but set aside his grief to consolidate what power he still commanded. Weighing up his options, Kantor resolved to make for New Rynn City, where a small force of Crimson Fists stood as sentinels alongside the local garrison. The trek took ten days through a landscape choked with rampaging Ork warbands. During the daylight hours Kantor and his men were forced to seek shelter where they could – lying up against the ruins of a farm one day, hiding out in an abandoned quarry the next. Kantor arrived at New Rynn City wearied to the bone, and his armour slick with the blood of slain Orks. Scarce half of the Crimson Fists who had

embarked upon the journey survived to reach the city gates, and not a man amongst them arrived without a score of wounds. Yet still their resolve never faltered. No sooner had Kantor arrived than the greenskins came to New Rynn City in force. What the Orks found before them was no faltering garrison, but a vengeful and determined force of Space Marines whose fury had been well and truly roused. Under Kantor's determined leadership, New Rynn City remained inviolate, and eighteen months later became the staging area for the offensive that drove the Orks from Rynn's World.

In the aftermath of the fighting, Kantor was presented with a choice few Chapter Masters have ever had to make. Rynn's World had been saved, but the Crimson Fists were a shadow of their former glory. He could lead the remnants of his decimated force in a vainglorious last stand, determined to slaughter as many of the enemy as possible before succumbing to their overwhelming numbers, or he could marshal his resources and look to the eventual rebuilding of the Chapter.

It is to Pedro Kantor's eternal credit, and a mark of his superior character as a leader of men, that he chose the latter path. In these dark times, the Imperium can ill afford the loss of such a Chapter as the Crimson Fists.

	WS	BS	S	T	W	I	A	Ld	Sv
Pedro Kantor	6	5	4	4	3	5	3	10	3+

SPECIAL RULES
And They Shall Know No Fear, Combat Tactics, Orbital Bombardment, Independent Character.

Chapter Tactics: If you include Pedro Kantor then all units in your army exchange the **Combat Tactics** special rule for the **Stubborn** universal special rule and your Sternguard Veteran squads gain the **Hold The Line!** special rule detailed below. If more than one character in your army has the **Chapter Tactics** special rule, you must choose which version will apply.

Hold the Line! If your army includes Pedro Kantor, your Sternguard Veteran squads are scoring units.

Inspiring Presence: All friendly units within 12" of Pedro Kantor receive +1 Attack whilst he lives. This bonus does not apply to Kantor, and does not stack with the similar bonus from a Chapter Banner.

WARGEAR
Dorn's Arrow: This ancient and venerated storm bolter has the following profile:

Range	Strength	AP	Type
24"	4	4	Assault 4

DARNATH LYSANDER
CAPTAIN OF THE IMPERIAL FISTS 1ˢᵗ COMPANY

Even for a Space Marine, Darnath Lysander has led a long and bloody career. As sergeant he was credited with the successful defence of Colonial Bridge and hailed as the vanquisher of the heretics of Iduno. As Captain of the 2nd Company he led the storming of the Eldar cruiser *Blood of Khaine* and rescued the Haddrake Tor planetstrike from disaster. For two centuries afterwards, Lysander led the Imperial Fists' 1st Company with distinction, earning the highest praises his Chapter could bestow.

Then, in the latter years of M40, the Strike Cruiser *Shield of Valour* was lost to the Warp, taking Lysander and a good portion of the 1st Company with it. Initially the Imperial Fists kept vigil, hoping that the Warp would give up its prize. But as the decades and centuries passed, no trace could be found of the *Shield of Valour* and the lost Captain did not return. In a sombre ceremony, Lysander's name was added to the roster of the fallen and his statue was raised in the hall of heroes.

Nearly a thousand years later the *Shield of Valour* re-entered normal space in outer orbit of Malodrax, an Iron Warriors stronghold on the western fringes of the Eye of Terror. Instantly ravaged by the full firepower of three orbital fortresses, the *Shield of Valour* was swiftly disabled. The handful of survivors, Lysander amongst them, were incarcerated and subjected to weeks of torture at the hands of his Chapter's hated foes. That Lysander survived at all is ascribed to incredible tenacity and a dauntless refusal to accept defeat. Within a month of his capture, though his body was broken and bloodied from the torments inflicted upon him, Lysander broke free of his restraints. Unarmoured, and initially with no weapons save for bare hands and righteous fury, Lysander and his fellows tore a bloody path through the streets of Malodrax's planetary capital, stole a shuttle, and escaped.

It is difficult to say which emotion ran strongest amongst the Imperial Fists' Chapter Council when they learnt that Lysander still lived – joy that one of their greatest heroes had been returned to them, or fear that his travails had left Lysander tainted and broken. For six months or more, Lysander stoically bore an exhaustive investigation in which every fragment of his body and mind were tested against Chapter records. Though the Chapter's Apothecaries and Librarians exerted every technique at their command, no trace of corruption, physical or spiritual, could be found. To the deafening cheers of his Battle Brothers – the oldest of which had not been born when the *Shield of Valour* was lost – Lysander was restored as the 1st Company's Captain.

Within six months of his return to power, Lysander led the Imperial Fists in the assault that laid waste to Malodrax, repaying in blood the indignities and tortures meted out in its dungeons. Before the dust had settled on Malodrax, Lysander was on the move once again. Gathering to him warriors from across the Imperium, Lysander vowed to scour the Iron Warriors from the galaxy once and for all. His crusade continues to this day.

	WS	BS	S	T	W	I	A	Ld	Sv
Darnath Lysander	6	5	4	4	4	5	3	10	2+

SPECIAL RULES
And They Shall Know No Fear, Combat Tactics, Independent Character, Eternal Warrior, Bolster Defences (see page 71 for details).

Bolter Drill: Lysander has never lost the skills that made him the most efficient squad sergeant the Imperial Fists have ever known. Any models in a squad Lysander has joined can re-roll failed 'to hit' rolls when shooting with heavy bolters, storm bolters, bolters, and bolt pistols.

Chapter Tactics: If you include Lysander then all units in your army exchange the combat tactics special rule for the stubborn universal special rule. If more than one character in your army has the Chapter tactics special rule, you must choose which version will apply.

WARGEAR
The Fist of Dorn: This is a master-crafted thunder hammer. All hits from the Fist of Dorn are resolved at Strength 10 and add +1 to rolls on the vehicle damage table.

KAYVAAN SHRIKE
SHADOW CAPTAIN OF THE RAVEN GUARD 3ʳᵈ COMPANY

Captain Shrike made his name during the early months of the Targus campaign. The Raven Guard 3ʳᵈ Company was one of many Imperial units assigned to the assault on Targus VIII, tasked with the elimination of the Orks' orbital defences. Striking hard and fast, Shrike's force accomplished its mission, only to become stranded when their extraction Thunderhawk was destroyed in near orbit.

Undaunted by his predicament, Shrike led a campaign of destructive havoc behind the Ork lines. For two years the Raven Guard 3ʳᵈ struck at the Waaagh! wherever it showed weakness, destroying fuel dumps, ammunition stores and supply lines, all the while providing invaluable targeting and intelligence data to orbiting naval vessels. Shrike and his men were untouchable, able to strike at the Orks' brutal war machine with seeming impunity, inflicting catastrophic damage before slipping away into the shadowed ruins of the hive cities.

By the time Shrike had extracted his Company from the ruins of Targus VIII he was hailed a hero systemwide. After his subsequent assaults on Ork conquests in the Donara and Yakhee systems, Shrike became nothing less than a saviour. Amongst the besieged ruins of Aldeb, Sulphuron and a dozen other worlds, desperate men beseeched the Immortal Emperor to send Shrike to deliver them from the terror of Waaagh! Skullkrak. Fleet Commanders and Generals of the Imperial Guard pleaded with the Master of the Raven Guard to assign Captain Shrike to their sector of the campaign. But if the sombre Captain was aware of either petition, he gave no sign.

Under Shrike's direction, the Raven Guard 3ʳᵈ continues to assail Waaagh! Skullkrak. They go wherever they are most needed, not to battlezones where Imperial Commanders struggle to contain the Ork menace, but to worlds whose populations have been abandoned to their fates by an overstretched and uncaring Imperium. Shrike and his men are legends on these worlds, as revered as the greatest heroes of old.

On every planet under threat from the Orks, Guardsmen grasp their guns tighter and fight more fiercely, knowing that every minute they hold out is a minute in which the Raven Guard 3ʳᵈ might arrive to deliver them from a hopeless battle. Meanwhile, beyond the ravaged defences, Skullkrak's Boyz keep a wary eye on the shadows cast by ruin and undergrowth, knowing that Shrike and his Company might be lurking in the darkness, just waiting for the correct moment to strike.

	WS	BS	S	T	W	I	A	Ld	Sv
Kayvaan Shrike	6	5	4	4	3	5	3	10	3+

SPECIAL RULES
And They Shall Know No Fear, Combat Tactics, Independent Character.

See, But Remain Unseen: Shrike (and models in his squad) benefit from the infiltrate special rule (see the Warhammer 40,000 rulebook).

Chapter Tactics: If you include Kayvaan Shrike then all units in your army exchange the **Combat Tactics** special rule for the **Fleet** universal special rule. If more than one character in your army has the Chapter Tactics special rule, you must choose which version will apply.

WARGEAR
The Raven's Talons: These are a pair of master-crafted lightning claws. They also bestow the **Rending** special rule on Shrike's close combat attacks.

> "Wherever you tread, tread lightly. We are closer than you think, and our blades are sharp."
>
> Captain Kayvaan Shrike
> Raven guard 3ʳᵈ Company

VULKAN HE'STAN
FORGEFATHER OF THE SALAMANDERS

According to the ancient lore of the Salamanders, the Primarch Vulkan left behind nine artefacts – nine technological relics for his children to find and wield if they proved worthy. Vulkan scattered these artefacts throughout the galaxy, both to prevent them from falling into the hands of Mankind's enemies, but also because he knew that even the grandest prize was as nothing were it to be seized without challenge. Since Vulkan's disappearance, seven thousand and more years ago, the Salamanders have appointed one from amongst their number to seek the Primarch's lost legacy. This is a quest handed down through the Forgefathers, the greatest heroes of the Chapter, and, at the close of the 41st Millennium, it is a burden borne by Captain He'stan.

He'stan had served with distinction for nearly a century when the Chapter Council commanded he set down his burdens as commander of the 4th Company and don the mantle of Forgefather. As He'stan relinquished his old titles and duties, so too did he set aside his forename, for the rituals of the Salamanders dictate that he who shall walk in Vulkan's footsteps shall bear his name, and bear it with pride.

In the pursuance of his quest, He'stan has walked a crooked and winding path through the galaxy, guided from system to system by clues inked within the Tome of Fire. Though he no longer commands a company of his own, He'stan can draw upon any and all of the Salamanders' resources to aid in his search. Though some information can be gained through trade and negotiation, such opportunities are rare.

Many of the worlds He'stan must visit are in the hands of traitorous humans, alien invaders or worse. Clues can only be unearthed at such places once they have been scoured clean by boltgun and chainsword, and the Salamanders do not hesitate to bring their full might to bear if such is required. The Salamanders would endure any woe and suffer any loss to retrieve the Primarch's gifts, for they believe that he will return to them only when all nine artefacts have finally been recovered.

Only four of the nine does He'stan seek – the others have been found through the travails of previous Forgefathers. He'stan himself is the keeper of three: the Spear of Vulkan, a blade that burns so brightly as to set even ceramite ablaze, Kesare's Mantle, a legendary drakescale cloak, and the Gauntlet of the Forge, whose molten rage none can endure.

The other two recovered gifts remain on Prometheus, for they are valuable beyond measure. One is the forgeship *Chalice of Fire*, whose vast manufactorums provide the Salamanders with their weapons of war. The other is the Eye of Vulkan, a spacebound defence laser assembly that stands eternal vigil over the Salamander's fortress monastery. Of the remaining artefacts, the Engine of Woes, the Obsidian Chariot, the Unbound Flame and the Song of Entropy, only the names are known. Size, form and location are locked within the Tome of Fire, there to be uncovered as the Primarch's prophecies reveal themselves.

	WS	BS	S	T	W	I	A	Ld	Sv
Vulkan He'stan	6	5	4	4	3	5	3	10	2+

SPECIAL RULES
And They Shall Know No Fear, Combat Tactics, Independent Character.

Chapter Tactics: If you include He'stan then all units in your army lose the **Combat Tactics** special rule. Instead, all thunder hammers in your army will count as master-crafted, and all flamers, heavy flamer, meltaguns and multimeltas count as twin-linked. If more than one character in your army has the **Chapter Tactics** special rule, you must choose which version will apply.

WARGEAR
Kesare's Mantle: The adamantium-hard drake scales of this cloak grant He'stan a 3+ invulnerable save.

The Gauntlet of the Forge: This armoured gauntlet can be fired as a heavy flamer.

The Spear of Vulkan: This is a master-crafted relic blade.

KOR'SARRO KHAN
CAPTAIN OF THE WHITE SCARS 3rd COMPANY

Kor'sarro Khan is the White Scars' Master of the Hunt, the fifty-first individual to hold that honorific since the days of the Great Jaghatai Khan. This title is unique to the White Scars Chapter. They, above all other Chapters, seek the blood of an adversary who, through quirk of fate or artifice, has battled them and lived to tell the tale. Such enemies cannot be allowed to glory in their small victories of survival. Every twenty-five years, at the height of the Rites of Howling, the Master of the Hunt is despatched to seek out one such foe and bring their severed head back to the White Scars fortress monastery as trophy and proof.

As Captain of the 3rd Company, Khan can draw upon many resources in pursuit of his prey, and often embarks upon a hunt with companions chosen from the Battle-Brothers under his command. A pursuit can take months or years as Khan tracks his quarry from warzone to warzone and world to world. Though the hunt may be postponed as wars and other duties interfere, it is never abandoned. Sooner or later the quarry is tracked, cornered and beheaded.

Kor'sarro's return to Chogoris is a time of great celebration and moonlit feasting, for it marks the passing of a hated nemesis. When the carousal is done, Kor'sarro surrenders the prey's severed head to the High Chaplain, who takes up a brand from the flames and burns the eyes from the dead skull. The hymn of vengeance is sung as the flesh burns and peels, and the quarry's name is struck from the roster of the hunt. The head itself is masked in silver and set upon a lance, its hollow gaze destined to forever stare out over the approach to the fortress monastery. The White Scars' citadel is high in the Khum Karta mountains; the road is long, yet the silvered heads of the slain line every pace of its passage.

Over his years as Master of the Hunt, Kor'sarro Khan has brought nearly a score of quests to a successful conclusion. Some of the White Scars' greatest foes, such as the Daemon Prince Kernax Voldorius and the Eldar pirate lord Varaliel, had evaded previous Masters of the Hunt only to have their heads severed by Kor'sarro's blade.

> "Surround yourself with the greatest warriors at your command, or cower in the deepest and darkest hole you can find. It matters not. I shall take your head for the Great Khan and for the Emperor."
>
> Kor'sarro Khan
> White Scars 3rd Company

	WS	BS	S	T	W	I	A	Ld	Sv
Kor'sarro Khan	6	5	4	4	3	5	3	10	3+

SPECIAL RULES
And They Shall Know No Fear, Combat Tactics, Independent Character.

Master of the Hunt: Kor'sarro Khan, and models in his unit, benefit from the hit and run and furious charge special rules (see the Warhammer 40,000 rulebook).

Chapter Tactics: If you include Kor'sarro Khan then all units in your army exchange the **Combat Tactics** special rule for the ability to outflank. If you choose to do this, all dedicated transports also gain the ability to outflank – see the **Reserves** mission special rule. If more than one character in your army has the **Chapter Tactics** special rule, you must choose which will apply.

WARGEAR
Moondrakkan: The bike Moondrakkan was originally commissioned for the fourth Master of the Hunt. Moondrakkan is a Space Marine Bike (see page 100 for details). If riding Moondrakkan, Kor'sarro Khan has the ability to run in the Shooting phase and has the fleet special rule (see the rulebook for details).

Moonfang: This is an ancient power sword and a relic of the White Scars Chapter. Any rolls to wound on which Kor'sarro scores a 6 will cause Instant Death, regardless of the target's Toughness.

THE LEGION OF THE DAMNED
ACCURSED CRUSADERS, FORGED IN THE FIRES OF VENGEANCE

Of all the legends of the Imperium, the strangest by far is that of the Legion of the Damned. These silent warriors are Space Marines in appearance, their black armour adorned with chilling images of bones and fire, yet they are not of any Chapter under the Emperor's sun. Most eyewitnesses dispute even the Legionnaires' mortality, for an eerie glow suffuses their sable armour and a halo of ghostly fire dances about their feet. There are many corroborated accounts of Legionnaires enduring firepower that would annihilate mortal men. The most notable of these reports came from the Keyan battlezone, where a half dozen Legion of the Damned walked unharmed from the volcano cannon blast that claimed four Predators and two-score Space Marines. The bolters carried by the Legionnaires, though in aspect no different to those borne by other Space Marines, discharge flaming projectiles that can pierce the strongest armour. Nothing, not Chaos Chosen, rockcrete bastion nor boiling lava can stay the spectral wrath of the Legion.

The nature and origin of the Legion of the Damned is a topic much debated by the Imperial scholars. Some believe the Legion to be the survivors of the lost Fire Hawks Chapter, transmuted into a new and terrible form by the Warpstorm that claimed their vessel.

Others consider the Legion to be an extension of the Emperor's superhuman will, time-lost saviours or even the vengeful and immortal spirits of Space Marines slain in the Imperium's many wars. In the course of their investigations, several Inquisitors have tried to capture or intercept the Legion of the Damned, but all have failed. Some have even been present on the same battlefield as the Legion, but events always inexplicably conspire to prevent the Inquisitors getting close to their quarry, leaving them nothing more than frustrated witnesses to the event.

Who, or what, guides the Legion of the Damned is an enigma to all save maybe the beneficent Emperor himself. They appear only in the times of greatest need, coalescing unexpectedly out of the fires of a desperate battlefield to turn a disaster into victory. The Damned Legionnaires fear no foe, and they fight with a chill precision that few mortal warriors can match, passing through the bloody ground like vengeful ghosts. Terror is their harbinger and oblivion their gift. When the battle is done and the foe eliminated, the Legion of the Damned depart as suddenly as they had arrived. They seek neither reward nor thanks from those they have saved, and leave only the bodies of the slain and an enduring mystery in their wake.

	WS	BS	S	T	W	I	A	Ld	Sv
Damned Sergeant	5	4	4	4	1	4	2	10	3+
Damned Legionnaire	4	4	4	4	1	4	2	10	3+

SPECIAL RULES
Fearless, Slow and Purposeful.

Unyielding Spectres: The Legion of the Damned are impervious to even the deadliest weaponry. Their saving throw is invulnerable.

Aid Unlooked For: The Legion of the Damned always start the game in reserve and always arrive by **Deep Strike**, even in missions that do not normally use these rules. Note that the Legion of the Damned are renowned to arrive wherever they are most needed, so you can re-roll the deep strike scatter dice if you wish.

> "Never before or since have I seen fighting such as I witnessed when that host fell upon the Orks. Seizing the moment, I regrouped my Company and led them once more into the fray, yet there was little work for us, for the greenskins lacked stomach for the fight. Soon we secured the great bastion once more and without further loss. Of the dark brotherhood there was no sign."
>
> Varro Tigurius
> Ultramarines Chief Librarian

IDAEUS' LAST COMMAND

In 999.M41, the taint of Chaos was detected on the world of Thracia, and Imperial forces rapidly moved to meet the threat. Half the planetary garrison had been corrupted. Worse still, there were reports indicating the presence of Night Lords Chaos Space Marines.

Loyalist forces drove the poorly-armed traitors before them until advancing Imperial Guard units were in position to launch a full offensive against the capital city of Mercia. Before the assault could be launched, six bridges on the Imperial right flank needed to be destroyed in order to prevent the Emperor's forces from being attacked on the march. Atmospheric electrical storms prevented demolition by orbital strike, but the bridges were believed to be held by under-strength rebel units and thus vulnerable to ground assault. Detachments of Ultramarines were deployed via Thunderhawk Gunships to capture and destroy each bridge with melta charges.

Bridge Two-Four - a gargantuan structure of rockcrete slabs and adamantium girders, and whose girth could easily accommodate the passage of a Baneblade super-heavy tank - was the lynchpin of the entire operation, and its destruction was assigned to the Ultramarines 4th Company. After a brief fire fight, the rebel garrison was swept aside. The bridge, and both approaches, were captured. As Techmarines rigged the bridge for detonation, the bulk of Idaeus' Company secured the eastern approach, keeping keen watch for Chaos forces advancing through the mist-shrouded plains to the east.

Within minutes, shells began dropping in the midst of the Space Marines. As the first explosions split the air, a massive Chaos counter-attack loomed out of the mist and thrust towards the bridge. The Ultramarines' gambit had been anticipated by the Night Lords, and now a considerable force was bearing down on the 4th Company's position. Though his forces were heavily beset, Idaeus knew that to fall back with his mission unfinished was to expose the right flank of the main Imperial army.

Under Idaeus' steady leadership, the 4th Company fell back before the oncoming horde, spending their lives to buy time so that the Techmarines could complete their sabotage. With the charges set, Idaeus pulled his men back across the bridge and signalled for Thunderhawk exfiltration as he prepared to detonate the breaching charges. The Ultramarines fell back in good order but, before the bridge could be destroyed, the Techmarine carrying the detonators was obliterated by a direct hit from an artillery shell. Worse yet, as the Thunderhawk swept in behind the Ultramarines position, concealed Hydra flak tanks blew it from the sky.

With the mission undone and their retreat severed, the Ultramarines occupied the bunkers and gun nests at the western end of the bridge and prepared to hold their position to the last man. Idaeus sent warning to the Imperial army and ordered another Thunderhawk to extract his men. For the rest of the night, the servants of Chaos assaulted across the bridge, and each time were repulsed by disciplined waves of bolter fire. As dawn approached, a lull in the fighting gave Idaeus the opportunity to despatch a raiding party in an attempt to detonate the explosives manually. The gambit ended in failure - none of those men were seen again until dawn.

As the sun rose, Rhino transports in the colours of the Night Lords pushed across the debris-strewn bridge. Ultramarines prisoners taken during the night were nailed to the hulls, their rib-cages cracked open and spread wide. Brimming with rage, Idaeus led a countercharge onto the bridge's ravaged arches. Some say that the Captain's wrath that day was such that he tore the foe apart with his bare hands, and none can argue that the Night Lords' attack was defeated more swiftly than the defenders had any right to expect. Overcome by the Ultramarines' valourous rage, the Night Lords fell back once more, leaving the corpses they had so mercilessly despoiled in the hands of the Ultramarines. The attack was defeated, but there was no doubt there would be many more before the day was out. Less than a fifth of the Ultramarines who had begun the operation were still alive and Idaeus knew that one more push would see them defeated. He ignored the pleas of his sergeants and set off alone in a suicidal attempt to blow the bridge.

Sprinting through the bullet-chased and smoke haunted rubble, Idaeus reached the first of the demolition charges just as the retrieval Thunderhawk touched down beyond the bridge's western approach and out of range of the enemy anti-aircraft positions. Triggering the comms-net, Idaeus ordered the remaining Ultramarines to retreat under the command of Sergeant Uriel Ventris as the Night Lords began yet another assault. The surviving Ultramarines withdrew under fire to the Thunderhawk and Idaeus waited until the last possible second before detonating the first charge. In a catastrophic chain reaction, the remaining charges exploded, destroying Idaeus, the bridge and much of the Night Lords' oncoming assault wave in a searing blast that shook the earth for leagues around.

Though the cost had been high, the attack across bridge two-four had been thwarted. Its right flank secure, the Imperial army moved on Mercia and crushed all resistance in a matter of days. Within two months, the planet had been brought under Imperial control once again.

WARGEAR

This section of Codex: Space Marines lists the weapons and equipment used by the Space Marines, along with the rules for using them in your games of Warhammer 40,000.

Weapons and equipment that can be used by more than one type of model or unit are detailed here, while equipment that is unique to a single model or unit (including wargear carried by named special characters) is detailed in the appropriate entry in the Forces section.

For example, bolters are ubiquitous and carried by many models, and so are detailed in this section. The Cyclone missile launcher, however, is unique to Terminators. While you will find a page reference here, the rules are detailed in the Terminators entry.

WEAPONS

Assault Cannon

The rapidly rotating, multiple barrels of an assault cannon unleash a storm of shells, each one capable of shredding a man. The sheer volume of fire means that an assault cannon can be turned against infantry or even vehicles, where the overwhelming salvo of shells is capable of shredding even the heaviest armour.

Range	Strength	AP	Type
24"	6	4	Heavy 4 Rending

Astartes Grenade Launcher

See the Scout Bikers entry on page 67.

Auxiliary Grenade Launcher

The auxiliary grenade launcher is a tubular device that fires pre-primed and pre-loaded grenades. It is commonly fixed onto another weapon, such as a bolter, combi-weapon or even a power fist, but more esoteric shoulder- and wrist-mounts have been employed in the past. Such devices are rare and as such are normally only utilised by command personnel and veterans.

An auxiliary grenade launcher can be fired in addition to another weapon. Each time an auxiliary grenade launcher fires, the controlling player can choose which type of grenade is being used.

Krak

Range	Strength	AP	Type
12"	6	4	Assault 1

Frag

Range	Strength	AP	Type
12"	3	6	Assault 1, Blast

Boltgun

The boltgun, or bolter, fires small missiles, or 'bolts'. Each self-propelled bolt explodes with devastating effect once it has penetrated its target, blowing it apart from the inside.

Range	Strength	AP	Type
24"	4	5	Rapid Fire

Bolt Pistol

Bolt pistols are smaller versions of bolters. They are perfect side arms for Space Marines and are wielded alongside the chainsword by Assault Marines.

Range	Strength	AP	Type
12"	4	5	Pistol

Chainfist

See the Terminators entry on page 64.

Chainsword or Combat Blade

Space Marines utilise an array of close combat weapons, from the combat blades wielded by Scouts to the chainswords carried by Assault Marines. All are equally deadly in the hands of a Space Marine.

Both chainswords and combat blades are close combat weapons, as described in the Assault Phase chapter of the Warhammer 40,000 rulebook.

Combi-Weapons

Combi-weapons are bolters that have been specially modified by the Chapter's most skilled artisans. Each has been expertly converted to house another weapon, either a meltagun, plasma gun or flamer. This extra weapon carries only a limited charge, allowing the bearer a single shot, perfect for emergencies and shots of opportunity.

A Space Marine armed with a combi-weapon (combi-meltagun, combi-plasma gun or combi-flamer) can choose to fire either the bolter, or the secondary weapon, each with the profile listed elsewhere in this section. The bolter can be fired every turn, but the secondary weapon can only be fired once per battle (a combi-plasma gun can, of course, Rapid Fire). You cannot fire both weapons in the same turn.

Conversion Beamer

See the Master of the Forge entry on page 70.

Crozius Arcanum

See the Chaplain entry on page 58.

Cyclone Missile Launcher

See the Terminators entry on page 64.

Digital Weapons

Digital weapons are concealed lasers fitted into finger rings, bionic implants or the knuckles of a glove. They lack the power to be used at range, but can be triggered in close combat to take advantage of an exposed weakness while the enemy fends off the main attack.

A model armed with digital weapons can re-roll a single failed roll to wound in each Assault phase.

Flamer

Flamers spew a highly volatile cloud of liquid chemicals that ignites on contact with the air. Flamers are primarily used to scour the enemy from defended positions, their belches of superheated vapour slaughtering the defenders in a fiery conflagration.

Range	Strength	AP	Type
Template	4	5	Assault 1

Force Weapon

See the Warhammer 40,000 rulebook.

Frag Grenade

Frag grenades are explosive devices that are hurled at the enemy prior to an assault. The storm of shrapnel from the exploding frag grenades drives opponents further into cover for a few precious moments while the attackers close in.

Frag grenades are assault grenades, as described in the Warhammer 40,000 rulebook.

Heavy Bolter

An enormous version of the boltgun, the heavy bolter fires fist-sized bolts at the enemy with a staggering rate of fire.

Range	Strength	AP	Type
36"	5	4	Heavy 3

Heavy Flamer

The heavy flamer is the ultimate weapon for sweeping fortifications clear and purging the ranks of the enemy at close quarters.

Range	Strength	AP	Type
Template	5	4	Assault 1

Krak Grenade

Krak grenades are armour piercing bombs, designed to crack open the armoured hulls of enemy vehicles. Though they lack the explosive force of melta bombs or other specialised demolition charges, they are small and easy to carry, making them ideal weapons of opportunity.

See the Vehicles chapter of the Warhammer 40,000 rulebook for details of using krak grenades.

Lascannon

There are few finer weapons for tank hunting than the lascannon. Within the gun is a laser chamber that charges an energy blast capable of shattering any enemy vehicle. The lascannons used by Space Marine forces vary, from the man-portable variants carried by Devastator squads, to the godhammer pattern lascannons borne by the Land Raider.

Range	Strength	AP	Type
48"	9	2	Heavy 1

Lightning Claws

Lightning claws are heavily armoured gauntlets with long, slashing talons sheathed in a rippling power field. Used most effectively in pairs, lightning claws slice through armour, flesh and bone with terrifying effectiveness.

See the Assault Phase chapter of the Warhammer 40,000 rulebook for the rules for using lightning claws.

Master-Crafted Weapons

Master-crafted weapons are the product of years of careful labour by the most accomplished artisans in the Chapter. A weapon that has been manufactured with such dedication will be superior to any other weapon of its type.

A master-crafted weapon allows the bearer to re-roll one failed roll to hit per player turn when using the weapon.

Meltabomb

Meltabombs are subatomic charge-powered demolition munitions, capable of melting through even the most heavily armoured targets. They are much bulkier than krak grenades, with a more sophisticated detonation mechanism. Space Marine Assault squads carry melta bombs to destroy enemy tanks and bunkers.

See the Vehicles chapter of the Warhammer 40,000 rulebook for details of using meltabombs.

Meltagun

Meltaguns are lethal anti-armour weapons, used by Space Marines when undertaking assaults against heavily fortified defence lines and bunkers. Most effective at very short range, the meltagun is capable of reducing rock, metal and living material to molten slag or ash.

Range	Strength	AP	Type
12"	8	1	Assault 1, Melta

Missile Launcher

The standard heavy weapon for Space Marine Tactical squads, missile launchers can fire either krak or frag missiles. Frag missiles are designed to wreak havoc amongst lightly armoured infantry, while krak missiles can challenge the most heavily armoured targets.

Each time a missile launcher fires, the controlling player can choose which type of missile is being used.

Krak

Range	Strength	AP	Type
48"	8	3	Heavy 1

Frag

Range	Strength	AP	Type
48"	4	6	Heavy 1, Blast

Multi-melta

A larger, more destructive version of the meltagun, a multi-melta is perfect for destroying bunkers and tanks.

Range	Strength	AP	Type
24"	8	1	Heavy 1, Melta

Plasma Cannon

Plasma cannons fire a plasma 'bolt' that explodes on impact, generating the destructive heat of a small sun. Plasma cannons are prone to overheating, and can prove as deadly to the wielder as the target.

Range	Strength	AP	Type
36"	7	2	Heavy 1 Blast, Gets Hot!

Plasma Gun

Smaller than the plasma cannon, this fires several compact 'pulses' of plasma energy.

Range	Strength	AP	Type
24"	7	2	Rapid Fire Gets Hot!

Plasma Pistol

Plasma pistols are the smallest variant in the plasma weapon family. The destructive fury is undiminished, although the range and rate of fire are less.

Range	Strength	AP	Type
12"	7	2	Pistol, Gets Hot!

Power Fist

A power fist is an armoured gauntlet surrounded by a disruptive energy field. It is used to deliver crushing blows, capable of smashing the thickest armour asunder.

See the Assault Phase chapter of the Warhammer 40,000 rulebook for details of using power fists.

Power Weapon

A power weapon (typically a sword or axe, but sometimes a glaive, halberd or mace) is sheathed in the lethal haze of a disruptive energy field, capable of tearing through all manner of materials with ease.

See the Assault Phase chapter of the Warhammer 40,000 rulebook for details of using power weapons.

Relic Blade

Relic blades are two-handed swords or axes sheathed in an armour-sundering power field. Most have their origins in the dark days of the Horus Heresy, although some have been crafted in the long centuries since, in commemoration of other momentous events. Only a Space Marine of long and faultless service can earn the right to wield a relic blade

A relic blade counts as a power weapon whose hits are resolved at Strength 6. Due to its size and weight, a model wielding a relic blade cannot get an extra attack for an additional close combat weapon.

Shotgun

See the Scouts entry on page 66.

Sniper Rifle

See the Scouts entry on page 66.

Storm Bolter

A storm bolter resembles two boltguns attached side by side. The storm bolter is capable of withering fire without hindering manoeuvrability, enabling the bearer to charge headlong into combat, firing on his enemy all the while.

Range	Strength	AP	Type
24"	4	5	Assault 2

Thunder Hammer

Thunder hammers release a terrific blast of energy when they strike an opponent. Thunder hammers are often paired with storm shields, combining superb protection and lethal offensive capabilities.

See the Assault Phase chapter of the Warhammer 40,000 rulebook for details of using thunder hammers.

OTHER EQUIPMENT

Cluster Mines
See the Scout Bikers entry on page 67.

Combat Shield
A combat shield is a lighter version of a storm shield that is fitted to the arm of the wearer. This leaves the user's hand free to wield a pistol or other weapon, substituting a measure of defence for increased versatility. The combat shield confers a 6+ invulnerable save.

Camo Cloak
Space Marine Scouts often wear camo cloaks – loose garments woven from light absorbing material, that imitate nearby terrain. So garbed, Scouts are almost impossible to see at long distance, and make for difficult targets when in cover of any kind.

A model wearing a camo cloak has the stealth universal special rule.

Chapter Banner
See the Honour Guard entry on page 53.

Company Standard
See the Command squad entry on page 55.

Hellfire Rounds
These are specially modified bolter rounds, originally designed for slaying Tyranid bio-monstrosities. Each hellfire round replaces the bolt's standard explosive charge with chamber of bio-acid that eats through flesh with a voraciousness impossible to survive. If a model carries hellfire rounds, replace their boltgun's profile (including a boltgun on a Space Marine bike) with the following.

Range	Strength	AP	Type
24"	X	5	Rapid fire Poisoned (2+)

Note that Hellfire rounds can only be used in a boltgun.

Hellfire Shells
See the Scouts entry on page 66.

Iron Halo
See the Chapter Master entry on page 52.

Jump Pack
A jump pack enables the wearer to make great bounding leaps across the battlefield or even to fly short distances.

Models equipped with jump packs are jump infantry, as described in the Warhammer 40,000 rulebook. In addition, Space Marines wearing jump packs can be dropped from low-flying Thunderhawk Gunships, using their jump packs to swoop down on to the battlefield. To represent this they can be kept in reserve and arrive using the deep strike rules (see the Mission Special Rules section of the Warhammer 40,000 rulebook).

Locator Beacon
See the Scout Bikers entry on page 67.

Psychic Hood
See the Librarian entry on page 56.

Rosarius
See the Chaplain entry on page 58.

Narthecium
See the Command squad entry on page 55.

Servo-arm
See the Techmarine entry on page 71.

Servo-harness
See the Techmarine entry on page 71.

Signum
The signum is a special form of communication device that can access a myriad of useful targeting data, allowing a more accurate concentration of fire. A model can use a signum in lieu of making a shooting attack of his own. If he does so, one model in his squad is Ballistic Skill 5 for the remainder of the Shooting phase. Declare that the signum is being used before any rolls to hit are made.

Space Marine Bike
Space Marine bikes are fitted with powerful engines and bulletproof tyres. Each bike is a versatile fighting platform capable of firing its armament on the move and launching devastating charges into combat. Models equipped with Space Marine bikes follow all of the rules for bikes as described in the Warhammer 40,000 rulebook. Space Marine bikes are fitted with a twin-linked bolter.

Storm Shield

A storm shield is a solid shield that has an energy field generator built into it. The energy field is capable of deflecting almost any attack, even blows from lascannons and power weapons.

A model with storm shield has a 3+ invulnerable save. A model equipped with a storm shield can never claim the +1 Attack bonus for being armed with two close combat weapons in an assault.

Teleport Homer

Teleport homers emit a powerful signal enabling Space Marine Strike Cruisers to lock on to them with their teleportation equipment. By utilising this signal, the risk of missing the intended mark is greatly reduced, as are the dangers of more serious accidents. If Terminators wish to teleport onto the battlefield via deep strike and choose to do so within 6" of a model carrying the homer, then they won't scatter. Note that the teleport homer only works for units that are teleporting, not for units entering play using jump packs, drop pods or other means of transport. Also note that the homer must already be on the table at the start of the turn for it to be used.

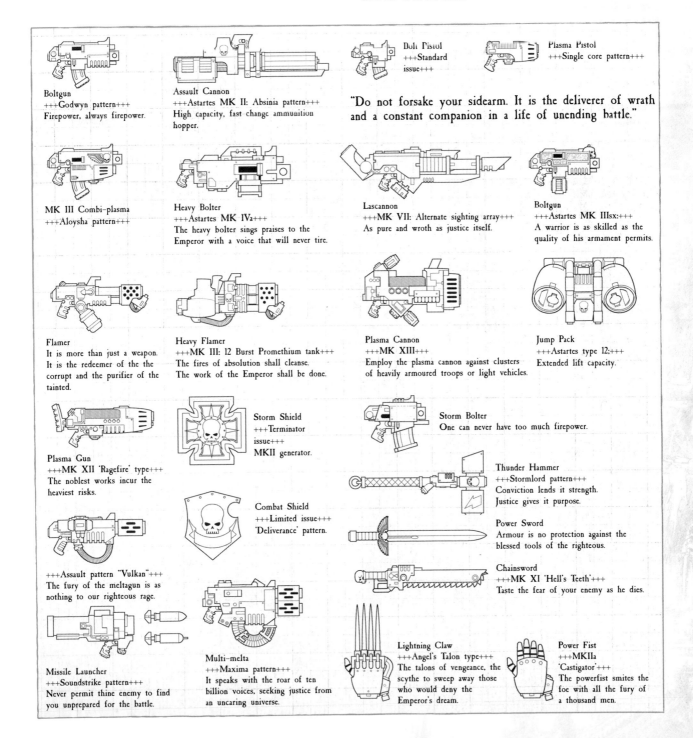

Boltgun
+++Godwyn pattern+++
Firepower, always firepower.

Assault Cannon
+++Astartes MK II: Absinia pattern+++
High capacity, fast change ammunition hopper.

Bolt Pistol
+++Standard issue+++

Plasma Pistol
+++Single core pattern+++

"Do not forsake your sidearm. It is the deliverer of wrath and a constant companion in a life of unending battle."

MK III Combi–plasma
+++Aloysha pattern+++

Heavy Bolter
+++Astartes MK IVa+++
The heavy bolter sings praises to the Emperor with a voice that will never tire.

Lascannon
+++MK VII: Alternate sighting array+++
As pure and wroth as justice itself.

Boltgun
+++Astartes MK IIIsx:+++
A warrior is as skilled as the quality of his armament permits.

Flamer
It is more than just a weapon. It is the redeemer of the the corrupt and the purifier of the tainted.

Heavy Flamer
+++MK III: 12 Burst Promethium tank+++
The fires of absolution shall cleanse. The work of the Emperor shall be done.

Plasma Cannon
+++MK XIII+++
Employ the plasma cannon against clusters of heavily armoured troops or light vehicles.

Jump Pack
+++Astartes type 12;+++
Extended lift capacity.

Plasma Gun
+++MK XII 'Ragefire' type+++
The noblest works incur the heaviest risks.

Storm Shield
+++Terminator issue+++
MKII generator.

Storm Bolter
One can never have too much firepower.

Combat Shield
+++Limited issue+++
'Deliverance' pattern.

Thunder Hammer
+++Stormlord pattern+++
Conviction lends it strength. Justice gives it purpose.

Power Sword
Armour is no protection against the blessed tools of the righteous.

+++Assault pattern "Vulkan"+++
The fury of the meltagun is as nothing to our righteous rage.

Chainsword
+++MK XI 'Hell's Teeth'+++
Taste the fear of your enemy as he dies.

Missile Launcher
+++Soundstrike pattern+++
Never permit thine enemy to find you unprepared for the battle.

Multi–melta
+++Maxima pattern+++
It speaks with the roar of ten billion voices, seeking justice from an uncaring universe.

Lightning Claw
+++Angel's Talon type+++
The talons of vengeance, the scythe to sweep away those who would deny the Emperor's dream.

Power Fist
+++MKIIa 'Castigator'+++
The powerfist smites the foe with all the fury of a thousand men.

ARMOUR

Artificer Armour

Though the two are superficially similar in appearance, artificer armour is as far beyond power armour as power armour is beyond the carapace used by Space Marine Scouts and elite Imperial Guard formations. Indeed, cunningly wrought damage control mechanisms and superdense construction materials ensure that most suits of artificer armour offer a degree of protection rivalling that of Tactical Dreadnought armour.

A suit of artificer armour is an incredibly valuable relic, often having belonged to several great heroes of the Chapter. Many elements of the suit will have been repaired or replaced over the years and its heraldry amended for each bearer, but it is still held to be the same suit of armour and venerated as such.

Due to its rarity, to wear a suit of artificer armour is an honour afforded only to the mightiest warriors of a Chapter – typically its Chapter Masters, Captains and members of the Honour Guard. Techmarines also wear a form of artificer armour. These are rarely as old and venerable as the other suits, but are power armour substantially modified and improved upon by several generations of Techmarines. Such suits contain a bewildering array of mechanical interfaces and built-in servo-tools, the better to aid the Techmarine in his duties.

Models equipped with artificer armour receive an armour save of 2+.

Power Armour

Power armour is the standard protection for Space Marine warriors and its distinctive outline casts fear into the enemies of Mankind. Made from thick ceramite plates and electrically motivated fibre bundles that replicate and enhance the movements of the wearer, power armour offers some of the best protection the Imperium can provide. Models equipped with power armour receive an armour save of 3+.

Scout Armour

Scout armour is formed of thick plates of carapace armour, easily capable of stopping a bullet. Less cumbersome and noisy than power armour, scout armour is ideal for the subtle infiltration work that its wearers embark upon and allows a greater freedom of motion. Models with Scout armour receive a 4+ armour save.

Terminator Armour

Also known as Tactical Dreadnought armour, Terminator armour is the best protection a Space Marine can be equipped with. Designed for close-quarters fighting aboard Space Hulks and other confined areas, Terminator armour is capable of withstanding almost any attack. The ceramite plates can deflect most conventional assaults, whilst the Crux Terminatus on every Terminator's shoulder plate serves as a ward capable of turning aside even attacks from power weapons or melta fire. It is even said that Terminator armour can withstand the titanic energies at a plasma generator's core, and that this was in fact the armour's original purpose.

Due to the powerful exoskeleton and power sources built into their armour, models in Terminator armour have the relentless universal special rule.

On the other hand, this armour is somewhat cumbersome, so Space Marine Terminators are not able to pursue a more lightly armoured foe when they flee. Terminators cannot perform a Sweeping Advance.

A model wearing Terminator armour has a 2+ armour save and a 5+ invulnerable save.

Any model wearing Terminator armour can be teleported onto the battlefield. They may always start the game in reserve and arrive using the deep strike rules, even if it is not part of the mission being played.

Terminators count as two models for the purposes of transport capacity, and cannot embark Rhinos or Razorbacks.

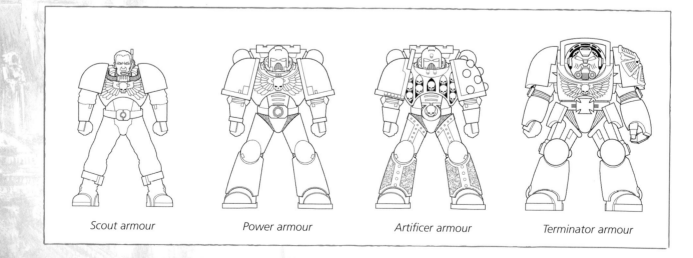

Scout armour   Power armour   Artificer armour   Terminator armour

VEHICLE ARMOURY

Autocannon

Autocannons fire large calibre, high velocity shells. They are employed in the turret mounts of Predator Destructors, and are also carried, as a linked pair, on Dreadnoughts.

Range	Strength	AP	Type
48"	7	4	Heavy 2

Cerberus Launcher

See the Land Speeder Storm entry on page 75.

Deathwind Launcher

See the Drop Pod entry on page 69.

Demolisher Cannon

See the Vindicator entry on page 80.

Dozer Blade

Dozer blades are heavy ploughs, blades, rams, or scoops, used to clear obstacles from the vehicle's path, Vehicles equipped with dozer blades can re-roll a failed Difficult Terrain test.

Extra Armour

Some Space Marine vehicle crews add additional armour plating to their vehicles to provide extra protection. Vehicles equipped with extra armour count Crew Stunned results on the Vehicle Damage tables as a Crew Shaken result instead.

Flamestorm Cannon

See the Land Raider Redeemer entry on page 83.

Frag Assault Launchers

See the Land Raider Crusader entry on page 82.

Hunter-killer Missile

Hunter-killer missiles are commonly fitted to Imperial vehicles. These single-use weapon systems allow vehicles such as Rhinos to engage enemy armoured vehicles that would otherwise far outmatch them.

A hunter-killer missile is a krak missile with unlimited range that can only be used once per battle. They are fired at Ballistic Skill 4. They are treated as an additional weapon.

Hurricane Bolters

See the Land Raider Crusader entry on page 82.

Ironclad Assault Launchers

An Ironclad assault launcher is loaded with a variety of anti-personnel grenades that disorient the enemy and drive them from cover.

A Dreadnought with Ironclad assault launchers counts as being armed with both defensive and assault grenades.

Jamming Beacon

See the Land Speeder Storm entry on page 75.

Storm Bolter

Pintle-mounted storm bolters are weapons fitted to Space Marine vehicles to provide additional fire support.

Pintle-mounted storm bolters are treated as an additional defensive weapon, with the profile of a normal storm bolter. See the storm bolter entry for details.

Searchlight

Searchlights are often fitted to Space Marine vehicles, so that the foe may not use darkness as an ally.

Searchlights are used where the night fighting rule is in effect. If a vehicle has a searchlight it must still use the night fighting rules to pick a target but, having acquired a target, will illuminate it with the searchlight. For the rest of the Shooting phase, any other unit that fires at the illuminated unit does not use the night fighting special rule. However, a vehicle that uses a searchlight, can be targeted during the following enemy turn, as if the night fighting rules were not in effect, as the enemy can see the searchlight.

Seismic Hammer

See the Dreadnought entry on page 65.

Smoke Launchers

Smoke launchers are used to temporarily obscure the vehicle behind concealing clouds of smoke, allowing it to cross open areas in greater safety. See the vehicles section of the Warhammer 40,000 rulebook for details.

Typhoon Missile Launcher

See the Land Speeder entry on page 74.

Whirlwind Multiple Missile Launcher

See the Whirlwind entry on page 79.

FOUNDING A CHAPTER

You've chosen to continue the Emperor's mission and protect Mankind, so it's time to assemble an army and lead your Space Marines to victory. Let's take a look at a few things to bear in mind.

Space Marines are an elite army, perhaps the most elite army in Warhammer 40,000. Space Marines have access to all manner of troop types, tanks and characters, from neophyte Scouts and stalwart Tactical squads, to fearsome war engines such as Dreadnoughts, Thunderfire Cannon and Land Raiders. With this diversity comes plenty of tactical options, but there are a few basics to bear in mind as you begin your collection.

THE BASICS

The standard force organisation chart includes two compulsory Troops units. These are the backbone of your force. Not only do Troops units bear a large burden of the fighting, they are also used for seizing objectives – a crucial role in many missions. Space Marines have a substantial advantage in this area, simply because their Troops units are more durable than most other units in the game!

Space Marines have two Troops units to choose from, but what is lost in variety is made up for in versatility. Even with only basic equipment, Tactical squads and Scout squads can perform a wide range of roles, able to fight at range and in bloody close combat with equal skill. Better still, as every model comes with krak grenades as standard, Tactical Marines and Scouts can take on all but the most heavily armoured vehicle once they get close enough!

Both types of squad can be further refined to a particular role if you wish, with heavy and specialist weapons chosen to deal with particular foes. From the armour penetrating plasma gun to the anti-tank precision of the lascannon, each of these upgrade weapons has its own role. If you're undecided as to how your squads should be equipped, a missile launcher is a sensible place to start. With a choice of frag and krak ammunition, for dealing with infantry or tanks respectively, a missile launcher will always wreak havoc, regardless of the nature of your foe.

MIGHTY HEROES

With your Troops chosen, you'll need one or two HQ choices to lead your army. There are many HQ choices in a Space Marine army, and it can be said that each falls into one of two categories: leader or support.

Leader HQ choices are powerful fighters, able to tear through enemies at range or in close combat. Captains and Chapter Masters are the leaders of the Space Marine army, with formidable battle skills and a broad range of wargear options to further refine their deadliness. Each also has the option for a retinue unit – a Command Squad or Honour Guard respectively – to further increase the raw combat might of your army. On the other hand, Librarians, Chaplains and Masters of the Forge are all support HQ choices. These are best employed to complement or augment the abilities of another unit. A Chaplain, for example, boosts a unit's close combat prowess and makes it less likely to retreat, while a Librarian can harness his mind to project blasts of eldritch lightning, enhance his combat prowess or weaken that of his foe.

EXPANDING YOUR CHAPTER

Once you've decided on your HQ and Troops units, the more specialist units of the army become available for recruitment. Fast Attack, Elites and Heavy Support units all bring something unique to your army, whether through impenetrable armour, unique abilities, specialist weaponry or a mix of all three. In a standard organisation chart you're limited to three picks from each category, but you shouldn't think of this as too much of a restriction. In truth, it's really a guideline to help you pick a balanced and effective army. Everything in the Space Marine army is fantastic – in fact, pretty much any unit in the army can fight any other unit in the game with at least a fair chance of victory. But such splendour doesn't come cheap. There are only so many points to go around, and you'll have to pick your army to a plan. The more you specialise in Land Raider, Predator and Whirlwind tanks in Heavy Support, say, the less points you'll have to spend on the incredibly manoeuvrable and swift-moving Bike Squads and Land Speeders from the Fast Attack section.

There are three example Space Marine armies on the following pages, each chosen to a value of 1,500 points – a popular size of army for an evening's worth of gaming. Each has been chosen to a particular theme. The Ultramarine army is truest to a 'standard' Space Marine strike force, with a solid core of Tactical Marines and an even mix of Elites, Fast Attack and Heavy Support. Such an army contains a balance of firepower, assault troops and armoured support and is prepared to defeat all-comers. By contrast, the Salamanders example army is a stalwart defensive force, with plenty of heavy weaponry and well-armoured units, such as Terminators. The Salamanders army can both unleash and endure massive amounts of firepower, but manoeuvres relatively slowly. Finally, the White Scars army is a lightning-fast assault force, able to seize ground and objectives at the expense of some heavy firepower. All of these themes are viable and battle-winning in their own right. As you play more games you'll discover which balance of units suits you best, and discover your own tactics for victory.

PAINTING YOUR STRIKE FORCE

There are many Space Marine Chapters detailed in this book, such as the Ultramarines, the Crimson Fists and the White Scars. On the following pages you'll find painted examples from more than thirty different Space Marine Chapters, each with their own heraldry, colours and markings. If you don't want to paint your army as one of these famous Chapters, but rather want to create your own heroes of the Imperium, the examples given in this book should prove a great source of inspiration. Further guidance on painting your army can be found in the How to Paint Citadel Miniatures and How to Paint Space Marines books.

Your Space Marine army will likely never stop growing – there are always fresh tactics to try and new models to collect. Additional models give you the option to fight battles that last not merely an hour or an evening, but become a whole day, or even a weekend's, worth of gaming. That said, you don't have to use all of your miniatures at once – having a wide selection of units from which to choose is a joy all of its own.

Ultramarines Strike Force 'Vengance'

Salamanders Strike Force 'Magma Storm'

White Scars Strike Force 'Iceblade'

SPACE MARINE COMMANDERS

Marneus Calgar, Lord Macragge,
Master of the Ultramarines.

Marneus Calgar wearing the
Armour of Antilochus.

Captain Cato Sicarius of the
Ultramarines 2nd Company.

Ultramarines Captain
with lightning claws.

Ultramarines Honour Guard
with Chapter Banner.

Ultramarines Honour Guards with relic blades and boltguns.

Ultramarines Chapter Champion
with power sword.

Ultramarines Captain
with power weapon and
storm shield.

Ultramarines Captain with
power weapon and storm bolter.

Ultramarines Captain with
power sword.

Ultramarines Captain with
thunder hammer.

Ultramarines Captain with
combi-plasma and power fist.

Ultramarines Captain with
lightning claw and plasma pistol.

Ultramarines Captain with
storm bolter and chainsword.

Raven Guard Captain with
power fist and jump pack.

Pedro Kantor, Master
of the Crimson Fists.

Captain Lysander of the Imperial Fists.

Crimson Fist Captain.

Captain Shrike of the Raven Guard.

HEROES OF THE SPACE MARINES

*Ultramarines Chaplain
with jump pack.*

*Raven Guard Chaplain with bolt
pistol and Crozius Arcanum.*

*Salamanders Chaplain in
Terminator armour.*

*Ultramarines
Chaplain Cassius.*

*Chief Librarian Tigurius of
the Ultramarines.*

*Exorcists Librarian
with plasma pistol.*

Salamanders Librarian.

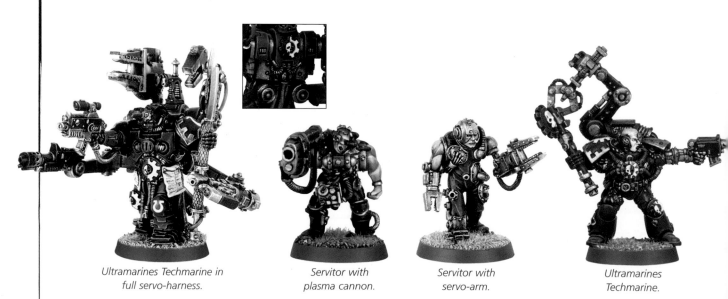

*Ultramarines Techmarine in
full servo-harness.*

*Servitor with
plasma cannon.*

*Servitor with
servo-arm.*

*Ultramarines
Techmarine.*

COMMAND SQUADS

Ultramarines Veteran with Company Banner.

Ultramarines Apothecary.

Ultramarines Veteran with boltgun.

Ultramarines Company Champion.

Ultramarines Veteran with plasma gun.

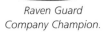

Crimson Fists Apothecary.

Salamanders Company Champion.

Howling Griffons Apothecary.

Mentors Company Champion.

Raven Guard Company Champion.

A Salamanders Captain leads his Command squad into battle.

TACTICAL SPACE MARINES

Ultramarines Sergeant with chainsword and bolt pistol.

Ultramarines Sergeant with chainsword.

Ultramarines Sergeant with boltgun.

Space Marine with meltagun.

Space Marine with flamer.

Ultramarines Space Marines with boltguns – note the differing colours of the shoulder trims that denote each Space Marine's Company.

Relictors Sergeant.

Raven Guard Sergeant.

Doom Legion Space Marine.

Brazen Claws Space Marine.

Blood Ravens Space Marine.

Eagle Warriors Space Marine.

Hawk Lords Space Marine.

White Consuls Space Marine.

Invaders Space Marine.

Legion of the Damned Space Marine.

ASSAULT SPACE MARINES

Ultramarines Sergeant with plasma pistol.

Ultramarines with bolt pistol and chainsword.

Ultramarines Sergeant with thunder hammer.

Raven Guard Assault Marine.

Exorcists Assault Marine.

Doom Eagles Assault Marine.

Salamanders Assault Marine.

Crimson Fists Assault Marine.

SPACE MARINE DEVASTATORS

Ultramarines Devastator with missile launcher.

Ultramarines Devastator with multimelta.

Ultramarines Devastator with plasma cannon.

Ultramarines Devastator with heavy bolter.

Ultramarines Devastator Sergeant with signum.

Crimson Fists Devastator.

Storm Lords Devastator.

Silver Skulls Devastator.

Salamanders Devastator.

Death Spectres Devastator.

SPACE MARINE VETERANS

*Space Marine Sternguard Veterans
are the masters of the short-range firefight.*

*Ultramarines Sternguard
Veteran with combi-melta.*

*Ultramarines Sternguard
Veteran Sergeant
with storm bolter and
power sword.*

*Silver Skulls
Vanguard Veteran.*

Ultramarines Vanguard Veterans.

*Ultramarines Sternguard
Veteran with boltgun.*

*Vanguard Veterans
equipped with
jump packs excel at
lightning assaults.*

*Red Templars ▶
Vanguard Veteran.*

*Iron Fists ▶
Vanguard Veteran
with relic blade.*

*Eagle Warriors Sternguard
Veteran with power fist.*

*Iron Hands
Sternguard Veteran.*

*White Scars
Vanguard Veteran
with lightning claws.*

*Sons of Orar
Sternguard Veteran.*

SPACE MARINE TERMINATORS

Ultramarines Terminator with cyclone missile launcher and chainfist.

Ultramarines Terminator with storm bolter and chainfist.

Ultramarines Terminator with assault cannon and power fist.

Ultramarines Terminator Sergeant with power sword.

Iron Lords Terminator with thunder hammer and storm shield.

Salamanders Terminator with lightning claws.

Crimson Fists Terminator with heavy flamer and power fist.

THUNDERFIRE CANNON

Techmarine with servo-harness

ARMOURED TRANSPORT

Chapter symbol

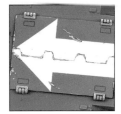

Tactical designation

▲ Ultramarines Rhino.

▲ Ultramarines Razorback.

Razorbacks can carry a variety of
weaponry, such as the twin-linked
lascannon shown above.

Chapter symbol.

Battle damage detail.

▲ Raven Guard Razorback.

BIKE SQUADRONS

Ultramarines Biker.

Ultramarines Biker with meltagun.

Raven Guard Biker with meltagun.

White Scars Sergeant on bike.

Hawk Lords Biker.

Red Templars Biker Sergeant.

Ultramarines Attack Bike with multi-melta.

Ultramarines Attack Bike with heavy bolter.

▶ *White Scars Attack Bike with heavy bolter.*

SCOUTS

Sergeant Telion of the Ultramarines Chapter.

Ultramarines Scout with boltgun.

Ultramarines Scout with heavy bolter.

Ultramarines Scout with missile launcher.

Ultramarines Scout with sniper rifle.

Crimson Fists Scout.

Raven Guard Scout.

Genesis Chapter Scout Sergeant.

Aurora Chapter Scout.

Iron Knights Scout with shotgun.

Ultramarines Scout Biker with shotgun.

Ultramarines Scout Biker Sergeant.

Ultramarines Scout Biker with Astartes grenade launcher.

Revilers Scout Biker.

Novamarines Scout Biker.

Brazen Claws Scout Biker Sergeant.

DREADNOUGHTS

Salamanders Dreadnoughts commonly bear icons of flame and lava – the sigils of their lost Primarch, Vulkan.

Ultramarines Dreadnought with twin-linked lascannon and missile launcher.

Salamanders Dreadnought with twin-linked lascannon and power fist with heavy flamer.

Salamanders Dreadnought with multi-melta and power fist with heavy flamer.

Ultramarines Venerable Dreadnought.

Raven Guard Dreadnought with assault cannon and power fist with storm bolter.

Crimson Fists Dreadnought with twin-linked lascannon and missile launcher.

LAND SPEEDERS

Ultramarines Land Speeder Tornado.

Raven Guard Land Speeder Tornado.

Salamanders Land Speeder with multi-melta.

White Scars Land Speeder.

Ultramarines Land Speeder and Land Speeder Typhoon.

ARMOURED SUPPORT

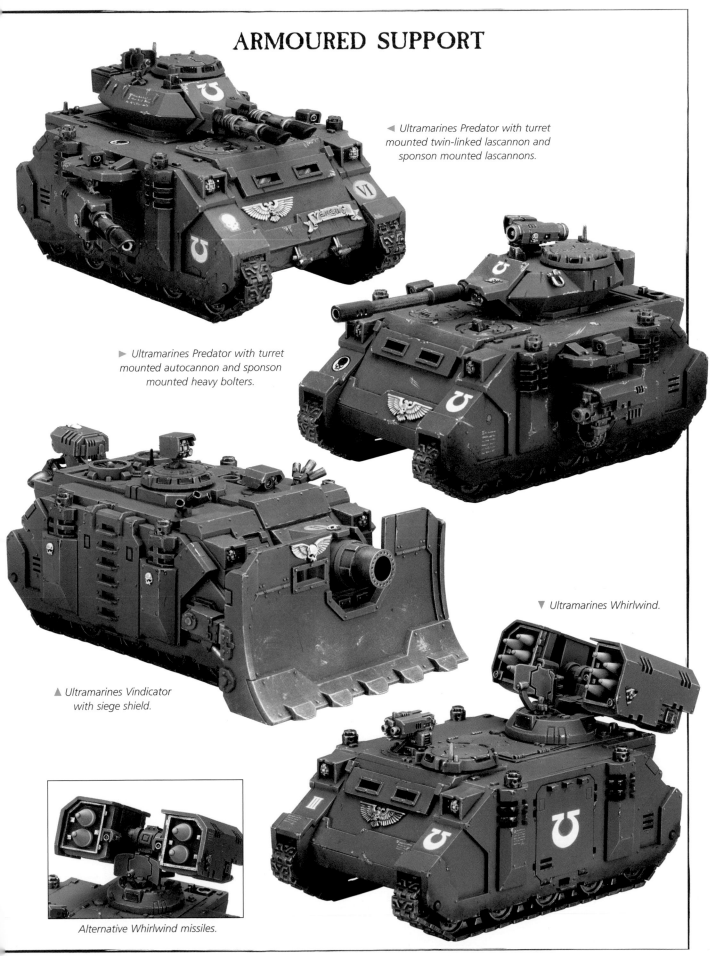

◄ *Ultramarines Predator with turret mounted twin-linked lascannon and sponson mounted lascannons.*

► *Ultramarines Predator with turret mounted autocannon and sponson mounted heavy bolters.*

▲ *Ultramarines Vindicator with siege shield.*

▼ *Ultramarines Whirlwind.*

Alternative Whirlwind missiles.

LAND RAIDERS

The Land Raider's twin-linked lascannons are fearsome anti-tank weapons.

▲ ► *Brother-Sergeant Chronus of the Ultramarines Chapter.*

Land Raider Crusader armed with a twin-linked assault cannon and anti-infantry hurricane bolters.

The Land Raider Redeemer's flamestorm cannons make it a truly fearsome foe at close range.

MAGRAGGE

Marneus Calgar's personal Land Raider bears his heraldry and murals representing his greatest victories.

DROP POD

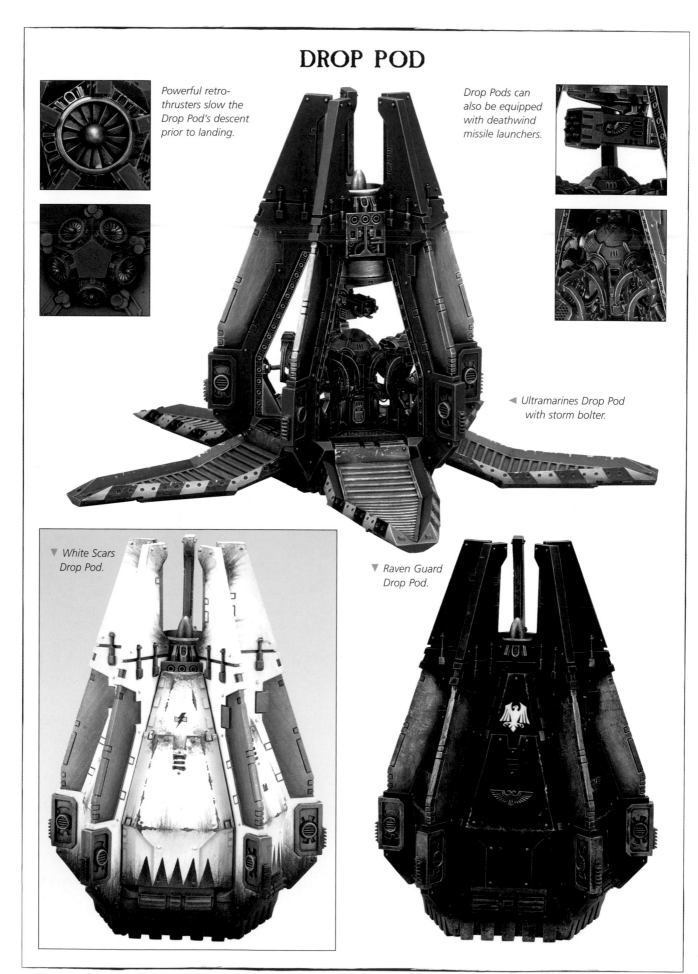

Powerful retro-thrusters slow the Drop Pod's descent prior to landing.

Drop Pods can also be equipped with deathwind missile launchers.

◀ Ultramarines Drop Pod with storm bolter.

▼ White Scars Drop Pod.

▼ Raven Guard Drop Pod.

SPACE MARINE ARMY LIST

The following pages contain an army list that enables you to field a Space Marines army and fight battles using the scenarios included in the Warhammer 40,000 rulebook. It also provides you with the basic information you'll need in order to field a Space Marines army in scenarios you've devised yourself, or that form part of a campaign.

The army list allows you to pick an army based on the troops that could be fielded by a Space Marines Battle Company, with attached support drawn from other companies in the Chapter.

The army list is split into five sections. All the squads, vehicles and characters in the army are placed into one of these depending upon their role on the battlefield. Each model is also given a points value, which varies depending on how effective that model is in battle. Before you choose an army, you will need to agree with your opponent upon a scenario and the total number of points each of you will spend. Then you can proceed to pick your army.

USING A FORCE ORGANISATION CHART

The army lists are used in conjunction with the force organisation chart from a scenario. Each chart is split into five categories that correspond to the sections in the army list, and each category has one or more boxes. Each grey-toned box indicates that you may make one choice from that section of the army list, while a dark-toned box indicates a compulsory selection. We've included the chart used for Standard Missions opposite.

MISSIONS & POINTS

These army lists are primarily designed for use with the Standard Missions from the Warhammer 40,000 rulebook. They may also be used with any other missions that use the Force Organisation charts, but please note that play balance may be effected if they are used for anything other than a Standard Mission.

USING THE ARMY LIST

Before putting your army together for a game, agree with your opponent on the size of each force. Many players like to play games of 1,500 points per side, which provides around two hours of play, or the best part of an afternoon or evening. Look in the relevant section of the army list and decide what unit you want to have in your army, how many models there will be in it, and which upgrades you want (if any). Any upgrades that are taken must be shown on the model. Once this is done, subtract the points value of the unit from your total points, and then go back and make another choice. Continue doing this until you have spent all your points. Then you're ready to do battle!

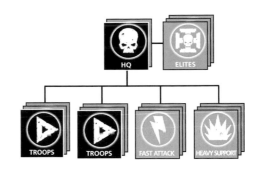

STANDARD MISSIONS

COMPULSORY	OPTIONAL	OPTIONAL
1 HQ	1 HQ	3 Fast Attack
2 Troops	4 Troops	3 Heavy Support
	3 Elites	

ULTRAMARINES AND OTHER CHAPTERS

This army list is based first and foremost around the Ultramarines, but can also be used to collect an army that follows the Codex Astartes. Use the Space Marines army list presented on the following pages and paint your miniatures using one of the colour schemes shown in this book (or make up the colours and heraldry yourself).

You'll notice that the named characters in the Space Marines army list are drawn from several different Chapters, but they can still be used in the same army if you wish. This can represent the common occurrence of different Space Marine Chapters fighting alongside one another. Alternatively, you can use the model and rules for a named character to represent a mighty hero of a different Chapter – for example, using the rules and model for Marneus Calgar as the Chapter Master of the Imperial Fists, or a Space Marine Chapter of your own design – you just need to come up with a new name.

This is a perfect way to personalise your army – just make sure your opponent is aware of what everything counts as.

ARMY LIST ENTRIES

Each entry in the army list represents a different unit that you can use in a game. More information about the background and rules for the troops, vehicles and equipment in the army lists can be found on pages 51-95, while information and examples of the Citadel Miniatures you will need to represent the troops, vehicles and equipment used in the lists can be found on pages 97-103.

Each unit entry in the army list is split into seven sections:

---

(1) **ASSAULT SQUAD** .... 100 Points   Page 60

	WS	BS	S	T	W	I	A	Ld	Sv
Space Marine Sergeant	4	4	4	4	1	4	2	9	3+
Space Marine	4	4	4	4	1	4	1	8	3+

(2) **Unit Composition:**
- 4 Space Marines
- 1 Space Marine Sergeant

(3) **Unit Type:**
- Jump infantry

(4) **Wargear:**
- Power armour
- Chainsword
- Bolt pistol
- Frag and krak grenades
- Jump pack

(5) **Special Rules:**
- And They Shall Know No Fear
- Combat Squads
- Combat Tactics

(6) **Dedicated Transport:**
- The Squad may remove its jump packs to count as Infantry. It may then have a Drop Pod or Rhino for free. Note that upgrades must be bought as normal. (see page 135 for points costs).

(7) **Options:**
- May include up to five additional Space Marines: .... +18 pts per model
- For every five models in the squad one Space Marine may replace his bolt pistol with one of the following:
  - a flamer .... +10 pts
  - a plasma pistol .... +15 pts
- The Space Marine Sergeant may replace his bolt pistol and/or chainsword with:
  - a storm shield .... +15 pts
  - a plasma pistol .... +15 pts
  - a power weapon or lightning claw .... +15 pts
  - a power fist .... +25 pts
  - a thunder hammer or pair of lightning claws ..... +30 pts
- The Space Marine Sergeant may take:
  - melta bombs .... +5 pts
  - a combat shield .... +5 pts

---

(1) **Unit Profile:** At the start of each entry you will find the name of the unit, the profile of any models it can include, and the points cost of the unit without any upgrades. For example, the entry shown above is for an Assault Squad that costs 100 points.

(2) **Unit Composition:** Where applicable, this entry lists the number and type of models that make up the basic unit. For example, the 100 point Assault Squad shown above is made up of a Space Marine Sergeant and four Space Marines.

(3) **Unit Type:** This entry refers to the Warhammer 40,000 Unit Type Rules chapter. For example, a unit may be Infantry, Vehicle or Jump Infantry, and be subject to a number of rules regarding movement, shooting, assault etc. If the Unit Type box includes the word 'Unique' you may only include one of this unit in your army.

(4) **Wargear:** This entry details the equipment the models in the squad entry carry. The cost for all of these models and all of their equipment is included in the points cost with the unit profile.

(5) **Special Rules:** Any special rules that apply to the unit are listed here. These special rules are explained in further detail in the Forces section. Some refer to the Universal Special Rules section of the Warhammer 40,000 rulebook. For example, the Assault Squad shown above benefits from the 'And They Shall Know No Fear' and 'Combat Squads' Special Rules, which are detailed in the Space Marines Army Special Rules on page 47, as well as the Deep Strike Scenario Special Rule, which can be found in the Warhammer 40,000 rulebook

(6) **Transport:** This last entry refers to any transport vehicles the unit may take. These have their own entry on page 135. The Transport Vehicles section of the Warhammer 40,000 rulebook explains exactly how these dedicated transports work.

(7) **Options:** This section lists all of the upgrades you may add to the unit if you wish to do so. If a model is equipped with something listed in the Unit Upgrades section then you must pay the points for it – you may not take an upgrade unless a model in the unit actually has it. Some units have additional options regarding how they may be chosen or fielded, often depending on whether an associated special character is taken. Where an option states that you may exchange one weapon 'and/or' another, you may replace either, neither or both provided you pay the stated points cost.

HQ

MARNEUS CALGAR, LORD MACRAGGE .... 250 Points

Page 84

	WS	BS	S	T	W	I	A	Ld	Sv
Marneus Calgar	6	5	4	4	4	5	4	10	3+

Unit Composition:
- 1 (Unique)

Unit Type:
- Infantry

Wargear:
- Power armour
- Power sword
- Iron Halo
- Gauntlets of Ultramar

Special Rules:
- And They Shall Know No Fear
- Combat Tactics
- Independent Character
- Titanic Might
- God of War
- Orbital Bombardment
- Eternal Warrior

Options:
- Replace power armour with Armour of Antilochus .... +15 pts

Master of the Ultramarines:
If your army includes Marneus Calgar, you may take three Honour Guard squads, rather than the usual one allowed for a Chapter Master (see page 131). Only one squad may carry the Chapter Banner. These units do not count against your HQ allowance.

CAPTAIN CATO SICARIUS .... 200 Points

Page 85

	WS	BS	S	T	W	I	A	Ld	Sv
Cato Sicarius	6	5	4	4	3	5	3	10	2+

Unit Composition:
- 1 (Unique)

Unit Type:
- Infantry

Wargear:
- Mantle of the Suzerain
- Talassarian Tempest Blade
- Plasma pistol
- Frag and krak grenades
- Iron Halo

Special Rules:
- And They Shall Know No Fear
- Combat Tactics
- Independent Character
- Rites of Battle
- Surprise Attack!
- Battle-forged Heroes

CHIEF LIBRARIAN TIGURIUS .... 230 Points

Page 86

	WS	BS	S	T	W	I	A	Ld	Sv
Varro Tigurius	5	4	4	4	2	4	2	10	3+

Unit Composition:
- 1 (Unique)

Unit Type:
- Infantry

Wargear:
- Power armour
- Bolt pistol
- Hood of Hellfire
- Frag and krak grenades
- Rod of Tigurius

Special Rules:
- And They Shall Know No Fear
- Combat Tactics
- Independent Character
- Master Psyker
- Gift of Prescience

Psychic Powers:
- Smite
- Force Shield
- The Avenger
- Might of Ancients
- Null Zone
- The Gate of Infinity
- Vortex of Doom
- Quickening
- Machine Curse

CHAPLAIN CASSIUS .... 125 Points

Page 87

	WS	BS	S	T	W	I	A	Ld	Sv
Ortan Cassius	5	4	4	6	2	4	2	10	3+

Unit Composition:
- 1 (Unique)

Unit Type:
- Infantry

Wargear:
- Power armour
- Crozius Arcanum
- Rosarius
- Bolt pistol
- Infernus
- Frag and krak grenades

Special Rules:
- Independent Character
- Combat Tactics
- Honour of the Chapter
- Liturgies of Battle
- Feel no Pain

HQ

CHAPTER MASTER PEDRO KANTOR ....175 Points

Page 90

	WS	BS	S	T	W	I	A	Ld	Sv
Pedro Kantor	6	5	4	4	3	5	3	10	3+

Unit Composition:
- 1 (Unique)

Unit Type:
- Infantry

Wargear:
- Power armour
- Dorn's Arrow
- Power fist
- Frag and krak grenades
- Iron Halo

Special Rules:
- And They Shall Know No Fear
- Combat Tactics
- Independent Character
- Orbital Bombardment
- Inspiring Presence
- Chapter Tactics

Master of the Crimson Fists:
If your army includes Pedro Kantor, you may also include one Honour Guard squad (see page 131 for details). This unit does not count against your HQ allowance.

CAPTAIN DARNATH LYSANDER ....200 Points

Page 91

	WS	BS	S	T	W	I	A	Ld	Sv
Darnath Lysander	6	5	4	4	4	5	3	10	2+

Unit Composition:
- 1 (Unique)

Unit Type:
- Infantry

Wargear:
- Terminator armour
- The Fist of Dorn
- Storm shield

Special Rules:
- And They Shall Know No Fear
- Combat Tactics
- Independent Character
- Bolter Drill
- Eternal Warrior
- Chapter Tactics
- Bolster Defences

SHADOW CAPTAIN KAYVAAN SHRIKE ....195 Points

Page 92

	WS	BS	S	T	W	I	A	Ld	Sv
Kayvaan Shrike	6	5	4	4	3	5	3	10	3+

Unit Composition:
- 1 (Unique)

Unit Type:
- Jump infantry

Wargear:
- Power armour
- Frag and krak grenades
- Bolt pistol
- The Raven's Talons
- Jump pack
- Iron Halo

Special Rules:
- And They Shall Know No Fear
- Combat Tactics
- Independent Character
- See, But Remain Unseen
- Chapter Tactics

FORGEFATHER VULKAN HE'STAN ....190 Points

Page 93

	WS	BS	S	T	W	I	A	Ld	Sv
Vulkan He'stan	6	5	4	4	3	5	3	10	2+

Unit Composition:
- 1 (Unique)

Unit Type:
- Infantry

Wargear:
- Artificer armour
- Frag and krak grenades
- Bolt pistol
- Kesare's Mantle
- The Spear of Vulkan
- Digital weapons
- The Gauntlet of the Forge

Special Rules:
- And They Shall Know No Fear
- Combat Tactics
- Independent Character
- Chapter Tactics

KOR'SARRO KHAN ....160 Points

Page 94

	WS	BS	S	T	W	I	A	Ld	Sv
Kor'sarro Khan	6	5	4	4	3	5	3	10	3+

Unit Composition:
- 1 (Unique)

Unit Type:
- Infantry

Wargear:
- Power armour
- Frag and krak grenades
- Bolt pistol
- Moonfang
- Iron Halo

Options:
- Moondrakkan +45 pts

Special Rules:
- And They Shall Know No Fear
- Combat Tactics
- Independent Character
- Master of the Hunt
- Chapter Tactics

Mounted Assault:
If Kor'sarro Khan rides Moondrakkan, Space Marine Bike squads of at least five models may be taken as Troops choices.

HQ

SPACE MARINE CHAPTER MASTER ....125 Points Page 52

	WS	BS	S	T	W	I	A	Ld	Sv
Chapter Master	6	5	4	4	3	5	3	10	3+

Unit Composition:
- 1 Chapter Master

Unit Type:
- Infantry

Wargear:
- Power armour
- Chainsword
- Bolt pistol
- Frag and krak grenades
- Iron Halo

Special Rules:
- And They Shall Know No Fear
- Combat Tactics
- Independent Character
- Orbital Bombardment

Options:
- Replace bolt pistol and/or chainsword with:
  - a boltgun .... *free*
  - a storm bolter .... *+3 pts*
  - a combi-flamer, -melta or -plasma .... *+10 pts*
  - a storm shield, power sword, lightning claw or plasma pistol .... *+15 pts*
  - a power fist .... *+25 pts*
  - a relic blade .... *+30 pts*
  - a thunder hammer .... *+30 pts*
- Replace power armour with artificer armour .... *115 pts*
- Take melta bombs .... *+5 pts*
- Take digital weapons .... *+10 pts*
- Take hellfire rounds .... *+10 pts*
- Take auxiliary grenade launcher .... *+15 pts*
- Replace power armour, bolt pistol, chainsword, frag and krak grenades with Terminator armour with storm bolter and power sword .... *+40 pts*
- Replace Terminator armour's storm bolter with:
  - combi-flamer, -melta or -plasma .... *+5 pts*
  - lightning claw .... *+10 pts*
  - thunder hammer .... *+20 pts*
- Replace Terminator armour's power sword with:
  - lightning claw .... *+5 pts*
  - power fist or storm shield .... *+10 pts*
  - thunder hammer or chainfist .... *+15 pts*
- If Terminator armour is not chosen, may have one of the following:
  - Jump pack .... *+25 pts*
  - Space Marine bike .... *+35 pts*

HONOUR GUARD SQUAD ....115 Points Page 53

You may include one Honour Guard squad for every Chapter Master in your army. This unit does not count against your HQ allowance.

	WS	BS	S	T	W	I	A	Ld	Sv
Chapter Champion	5	4	4	4	1	4	3	10	2+
Honour Guard	4	4	4	4	1	4	2	10	2+

Unit Composition:
- 1 Chapter Champion
- 2 Honour Guards

Unit Type:
- Infantry

Wargear:
- Artificer armour
- Power weapon
- Frag and krak grenades
- Boltgun
- Bolt pistol

Special Rules:
- And They Shall Know No Fear
- Combat Tactics
- Honour or Death (Chapter Champion only)

Dedicated Transport:
- May select a Drop Pod, Rhino or a Razorback (see page 135 for points values).

Options:
- May include up to seven additional Honour Guards .... *+35 pts per model*
- The Chapter Champion may replace his boltgun with:
  - a combat blade .... *free*
- The Chapter Champion may replace his power sword with:
  - a thunder hammer .... *+15 pts*
- The Chapter Champion may take:
  - digital lasers .... *+10 pts*
- Any model may take:
  - a relic blade .... *+15 pts per model*
  - auxiliary grenade launcher .... *+15 pts per model*
- One Honour Guard may carry the Chapter Banner: .... *+25 pts*

HQ

SPACE MARINE CAPTAIN ....100 Points

Page 54

	WS	BS	S	T	W	I	A	Ld	Sv
Captain	6	5	4	4	3	5	3	10	3+

Unit Composition:
- 1 Captain

Wargear:
- Power armour
- Chainsword
- Bolt pistol
- Frag and krak grenades
- Iron Halo

Unit Type:
- Infantry

Special Rules:
- And They Shall Know No Fear
- Combat Tactics
- Independent Character

Mounted Assault:

If your army includes a Captain on Space Marine bike, Space Marine Bike squads of at least five models may be taken as Troops choices.

Options:
- Replace bolt pistol and/or chainsword with:
  - a boltgun ....*free*
  - a storm bolter ....*+3 pts*
  - a combi-flamer, -melta or -plasma ....*+10 pts*
  - a storm shield, power sword, lightning claw or plasma pistol ....*+15 pts*
  - a power fist ....*+25 pts*
  - a relic blade ....*+30 pts*
  - a thunder hammer ....*+30 pts*
- Replace power armour with artificer armour.................*+15 pts*
- Take melta bombs...*+5 pts*
- Take digital weapons...*+10 pts*
- Take hellfire rounds..*+10 pts*
- Take auxiliary grenade launcher............................*+15 pts*
- Replace power armour, bolt pistol, chainsword, frag and krak grenades with Terminator armour with storm bolter and power sword...*+40 pts*
- Replace Terminator armour's storm bolter with:
  - combi-flamer, -melta or -plasma..................*+5 pts*
  - lightning claw...*+10 pts*
  - thunder hammer...*+20 pts*
- Replace Terminator armour's power sword with:
  - lightning claw...*+5 pts*
  - power fist or storm shield............................*+10 pts*
  - thunder hammer or chainfist............................*+15 pts*
- If Terminator armour is not chosen, may have one of the following:
  - Jump pack...*+25 pts*
  - Space Marine bike...*+35 pts*

COMMAND SQUAD ....115 Points

Page 55

You may take one Command Guard squad for every Space Marine Captain in your army (including Captain Sicarius, Captain Lysander, Shadow Captain Shrike and Kor'sarro Khan). This unit does not count against your HQ allowance.

	WS	BS	S	T	W	I	A	Ld	Sv
Company Champion	5	4	4	4	1	4	2	9	3+
Apothecary	4	4	4	4	1	4	2	9	3+
Veteran	4	4	4	4	1	4	2	9	3+

Unit Composition:
- 4 Veterans
- 1 Apothecary

Unit Type:
- Infantry

Wargear:
- Power armour
- Chainsword
- Frag and krak grenades
- Boltgun or bolt pistol
- The Apothecary also has a narthecium

Special Rules:
- And They Shall Know No Fear
- Combat Tactics

Dedicated Transport:
- May select a Drop Pod, Rhino or a Razorback (see page 135 for points values)

Unit Options:
- One Veteran may carry the Company Standard: .....*+15 pts*
- One Veteran may be upgraded to a Company Champion with a power weapon and combat shield: ....*+15 pts*
- The entire squad may ride Space Marine bikes: ......*+90 pts*

Model Options:
- Any Veteran may replace his chainsword and/or bolt pistol with:
  - a storm bolter ....*+3 pts*
  - a flamer ....*+5 pts*
  - a meltagun ....*+10 pts*
  - a combi-flamer, -melta or -plasma..................*+10 pts*
  - a plasma gun, power sword or lightning claw ...*+15 pts*
  - a power fist ....*+25 pts*
  - a thunder hammer ....*+30 pts*
- Any Veteran may replace his bolt pistol with:
  - a plasma pistol...*+15 pts*
- Any Veteran may have the following:
  - melta bombs...*+5 pts*
  - a storm shield...*+15 pts*

HQ

SPACE MARINE LIBRARIAN ....100 Points

Page 56

	WS	BS	S	T	W	I	A	Ld	Sv
Librarian	5	4	4	4	2	4	2	10	3+

Unit Composition:
- 1 Librarian

Unit Type:
- Infantry

Wargear:
- Power armour
- Boltgun or bolt pistol
- Frag and krak grenades
- Force weapon
- Psychic hood

Special Rules:
- And They Shall Know No Fear
- Combat Tactics
- Independent Character
- Psyker

Psychic Powers:
A Librarian has any two of the following powers:
Smite, Force Dome, Machine Curse, Quickening, Null Zone, The Avenger, Might of Ancients, The Gate of Infinity, Vortex of Doom.

Options:
- Upgrade to an Epistolary..................................+50 pts
- Replace boltgun with:
  - a storm bolter..+3 pts
  - a combi-flamer, -melta or -plasma.............+15 pts
  - a plasma pistol.......................................+15 pts
- May replace power armour, boltgun, frag and krak grenades for Terminator armour and:
  - no additional weapon...............................+25 pts
  - a storm bolter...+30 pts
  - a combi-flamer, -melta or -plasma.............+35 pts
  - a storm shield...+40 pts
- If Terminator armour is not chosen, may have one of the following:
  - Jump pack...+25 pts
  - Space Marine bike....................................+35 pts

SPACE MARINE CHAPLAIN ....100 Points

Page 58

	WS	BS	S	T	W	I	A	Ld	Sv
Chaplain	5	4	4	4	2	4	2	10	3+

Unit Composition:
- 1 Chaplain

Unit Type:
- Infantry

Wargear:
- Power armour
- Boltgun or bolt pistol
- Frag and krak grenades
- Rosarius
- Crozius Arcanum

Special Rules:
- Combat Tactics
- Independent Character
- Liturgies of Battle
- Honour of the Chapter

Options:
- Replace boltgun with:
  - a storm bolter..+3 pts
  - a combi-flamer, -melta or -plasma.............+15 pts
  - a power fist..+15 pts
  - a plasma pistol.......................................+15 pts
- Take melta bombs..+5 pts
- Take digital weapons...................................+10 pts
- May replace power armour, boltgun, frag and krak grenades for Terminator armour and:
  - a storm bolter...+30 pts
  - a combi-flamer, -melta or -plasma.............+35 pts
- If Terminator armour is not chosen, may have one of the following:
  - Jump pack...+15 pts
  - Space Marine bike....................................+35 pts

MASTER OF THE FORGE ....100 Points

Page 70

	WS	BS	S	T	W	I	A	Ld	Sv
Master of the Forge	4	5	4	4	2	4	2	10	2+

Unit Composition:
- 1 Master of the Forge

Unit Type:
- Infantry

Wargear:
- Artificer armour
- Servo-harness
- Boltgun or bolt pistol
- Frag and krak grenades

Special Rules:
- And They Shall Know No Fear
- Combat Tactics
- Independent Character
- Blessing of the Omnissiah
- Bolster Defences

Options:
- Replace servo-harness and boltgun with:
  - conversion beamer ....+20 pts
- Replace boltgun with:
  - a storm bolter ....+5 pts
  - a combi-flamer, -melta or -plasma.............+10 pts
  - a plasma pistol ....+15 pts
- Take digital weapons ....+10 pts
- Take either:
  - a power sword ....+15 pts
  - a thunder hammer ....+30 pts
- May ride a Space Marine bike ....+35 pts

Lord of the Armoury:
If you include a Master of the Forge in your army, Dreadnoughts, Venerable Dreadnoughts and Ironclad Dreadnoughts may be taken as Heavy Support choices as well as Elites choices.

TROOPS

TACTICAL SQUAD .... 90 Points   Page 59

	WS	BS	S	T	W	I	A	Ld	Sv
Space Marine Sergeant	4	4	4	4	1	4	2	9	3+
Space Marine	4	4	4	4	1	4	1	8	3+

Unit Composition:
- 4 Space Marines
- 1 Space Marine Sergeant

Unit Type:
- Infantry

Wargear:
- Power armour
- Bolt pistol
- Frag and krak grenades
- Boltgun

Special Rules:
- And They Shall Know No Fear
- Combat Squads
- Combat Tactics

Dedicated Transport:
- May select a Rhino or a Razorback. If the squad numbers ten models, may take a Drop Pod (see page 135 for points costs).

Options:
- May include up to five additional Space Marines: ......+16 pts per model
- If the squad numbers ten models, one Space Marine may replace his boltgun with one of the following:
  - a flamer..free
  - a meltagun..+5 pts
  - a plasma gun...+10 pts
- If the squad numbers ten models, one Space Marine may replace his boltgun with one of the following:
  - a heavy bolter, multi-melta or a missile launcher..........free
  - a plasma cannon..+5 pts
  - a lascannon..+10 pts
- The Space Marine Sergeant may replace his boltgun and/or bolt pistol with:
  - a chainsword..free
  - a combi-melta, -flamer or -plasma.....................+10 pts
  - a storm bolter...+10 pts
  - a plasma pistol...+15 pts
  - a power weapon...+15 pts
  - a power fist...+25 pts
- The Space Marine Sergeant may take:
  - melta bombs...+5 pts
  - teleport homer...+15 pts

SCOUT SQUAD .... 75 Points   Page 66

	WS	BS	S	T	W	I	A	Ld	Sv
Scout Sergeant	4	4	4	4	1	4	2	9	4+
Scout	3	3	4	4	1	4	1	8	4+

Unit Composition:
- 4 Scouts
- 1 Scout Sergeant

Unit Type:
- Infantry

Wargear:
- Scout armour
- Bolt pistol
- Boltgun
- Frag and krak grenades

Special Rules:
- And They Shall Know No Fear
- Combat Squads
- Combat Tactics
- Infiltrate
- Move Through Cover
- Scouts

Options:
- May include up to five additional Scouts....................
  ....+13 pts per model
- Any model may replace his boltgun with:
  - a shotgun, combat blade or sniper rifle...............free
- One Scout may replace his boltgun with a heavy bolter (with hellfire shells) or a missile launcher.....................+10 pts
- The Scout Sergeant may replace his boltgun and/or bolt pistol with:
  - a combi-melta, -flamer or -plasma.....................+10 pts
  - a plasma pistol...+15 pts
  - a power weapon...+15 pts
  - a power fist...+25 pts
- The Scout Sergeant may take:
  - melta bombs...+5 pts
  - teleport homer...+15 pts
- The squad may have camo cloaks................+3 pts per model

SERGEANT TELION .... 50 Points   Page 88
One Scout squad in the army may replace its Scout Sergeant with Sergeant Telion.

	WS	BS	S	T	W	I	A	Ld	Sv
Sergeant Telion	5	6	4	4	1	4	2	9	4+

Unit Type:
- Infantry

Wargear:
- Scout armour
- Bolt pistol
- Frag and krak grenades
- Stalker Pattern Boltgun

Special Rules:
- And They Shall Know No Fear
- Combat Tactics
- Infiltrate
- Move Through Cover
- Scouts
- Acute Senses
- Eye of Vengeance
- Voice of Experience
- Stealth

DEDICATED TRANSPORTS

Certain Space Marine units have the option of selecting a dedicated transport vehicle. These vehicles do not use up any Force Organisation chart selections, but otherwise function as separate units. See the Vehicles section of the Warhammer 40,000 rulebook for details of how transport vehicles operate.

RHINO ....35 Points   Page 76

| | BS | Armour | | |
		F	S	R
Rhino	4	11	11	10

Unit Composition:
• 1 Rhino

Unit Type:
• Vehicle (Tank)

Wargear:
• Storm bolter
• Smoke launchers
• Searchlight

Transport Capacity:
• Ten models

Options:
• May take any of the following:
  - a storm bolter ....+10 pts
  - a hunter-killer missile ....+10 pts
  - a dozer blade ....+5 pts
  - extra armour ....+15 pts

Special Rules:
• Repair

RAZORBACK ....40 Points   Page 77

| | BS | Armour | | |
		F	S	R
Razorback	4	11	11	10

Unit Composition:
• 1 Razorback

Unit Type:
• Vehicle (Tank)

Wargear:
• Twin-linked heavy bolter
• Smoke launchers
• Searchlight

Transport Capacity:
• Six models

Options:
• Replace twin-linked heavy bolters with:
  - twin-linked heavy flamer ....+25 pts
  - twin-linked assault cannon ....+35 pts
  - twin-linked lascannon ....+35 pts
  - lascannon and twin-linked plasma gun: ......+35 pts
• May take any of the following:
  - a storm bolter ....+10 pts
  - a hunter-killer missile ....+10 pts
  - a dozer blade ....+5 pts
  - extra armour ....+15 pts

DROP POD ....35 Points   Page 69

| | BS | Armour | | |
		F	S	R
Drop Pod	4	12	12	12

Unit Composition:
• 1 Drop Pod

Unit Type:
• Vehicle (Open-topped)

Wargear:
• Storm bolter

Transport Capacity:
• Twelve models, one Dreadnought or one Thunderfire Cannon

Options:
• Replace storm bolter with deathwind missile launcher ....+20 pts
• Take a locator beacon ....+10 pts

Special Rules:
• Inertial Guidance System
• Immobile
• Drop Pod Assault

ELITES

TERMINATOR SQUAD .... 200 Points

Page 64

	WS	BS	S	T	W	I	A	Ld	Sv
Terminator Sergeant	4	4	4	4	1	4	2	9	2+
Terminator	4	4	4	4	1	4	2	9	2+

Unit Composition:
- 1 Terminator Sergeant
- 4 Terminators

Unit Type:
- Infantry

Wargear:
- Terminator armour
- Storm bolter
- Power sword (Terminator Sergeant)
- Power fist (Terminators)

Special Rules:
- And They Shall Know No Fear
- Combat Squads
- Combat Tactics

Options:
- May include up to five additional Terminators:
  ....+40 pts per model
- For every five models in the squad, one Terminator may choose one of the following options:
  - replace his storm bolter with a heavy flamer............+5 pts
  - replace his storm bolter with an assault cannon..+30 pts
  - take a cyclone missile launcher................................+30 pts
- Any Terminator may replace his power fist with a chainfist:
  ....+5 pts per model

Dedicated Transport:
- One Terminator squad in the army may select a Land Raider of any type as a dedicated transport. (see Heavy Support for points costs).

TERMINATOR ASSAULT SQUAD .... 200 Points

Page 64

	WS	BS	S	T	W	I	A	Ld	Sv
Terminator Sergeant	4	4	4	4	1	4	2	9	2+
Terminator	4	4	4	4	1	4	2	9	2+

Unit Composition:
- 1 Terminator Sergeant
- 4 Terminators

Unit Type:
- Infantry

Wargear:
- Terminator armour
- Lightning claws

Special Rules:
- And They Shall Know No Fear
- Combat Squads
- Combat Tactics

Options:
- May include up to five additional Terminators:
  ....+40 pts per model
- Any model may replace his lightning claws with a thunder hammer and storm shield:................................free

Dedicated Transport:
- One Terminator Assault Squad in the army may select a Land Raider of any type as a dedicated transport. (see Heavy Support for points costs).

STERNGUARD VETERAN SQUAD .... 125 Points

Page 63

	WS	BS	S	T	W	I	A	Ld	Sv
Space Marine Sergeant	4	4	4	4	1	4	2	9	3+
Veteran	4	4	4	4	1	4	2	9	3+

Unit Composition:
- 1 Space Marine Sergeant
- 4 Veterans

Unit Type:
- Infantry

Wargear:
- Power armour
- Boltgun
- Bolt pistol
- Special issue ammunition
- Frag and krak grenades

Special Rules:
- And They Shall Know No Fear
- Combat Squads
- Combat Tactics

Options:
- May include up to five additional Veterans:+25 pts per model
- The Space Marine Sergeant may replace his bolt pistol and/or his boltgun with:
  - a chainsword..free
  - a power weapon or lightning claw....................+15 pts
  - a plasma pistol..+15 pts
  - a power fist..+25 pts
- The Space Marine Sergeant may take:
  - melta bombs..+5 pts
- Any model may replace his boltgun with:
  - a storm bolter, combi-melta, -flamer or -plasma ...+5 pts
- Two Veterans may replace their boltguns with:
  - a flamer, meltagun, heavy bolter, a multi-melta or a missile launcher................................+5 pts
  - a plasma gun, plasma cannon or heavy flamer....+10 pts
  - a lascannon..+15 pts

Dedicated Transport:
- May select a Drop Pod, Rhino or a Razorback (see page 135 for points costs).

ELITES

VENERABLE DREADNOUGHT ....165 Points Page 65

	WS	BS	S	F	S	R	I	A
				Armour				
Venerable Dreadnought	5	5	6	12	12	10	4	2

Unit Composition:
• 1 Venerable Dreadnought

Unit Type:
• Vehicle (Walker)

Wargear:
• Multi-melta
• Dreadnought close combat weapon (with built in storm bolter)
• Smoke launchers
• Searchlight

Special Rules:
• Venerable

Options:
• Replace storm bolter with heavy flamer:........................+10 pts
• Replace multi-melta with:
   - twin-linked heavy flamer...................................free
   - twin-linked heavy bolter.................................+5 pts
   - twin-linked autocannon.................................+10 pts
   - plasma cannon or assault cannon...................+10 pts
   - twin-linked lascannon.................................+30 pts
• Replace Dreadnought close combat weapon with
   - twin-linked autocannon or missile launcher:.........+10 pts
• Take extra armour..+15 pts

Dedicated Transport:
• May select a Drop Pod (see page 135).

DREADNOUGHT ....105 Points Page 65

	WS	BS	S	F	S	R	I	A
				Armour				
Dreadnought	4	4	6	12	12	10	4	2

Unit Composition:
• 1 Dreadnought

Unit Type:
• Vehicle (Walker)

Wargear:
• Multi-melta
• Dreadnought close combat weapon (with built in storm bolter)
• Smoke launchers
• Searchlight

Options:
• Replace storm bolter with heavy flamer:........................+10 pts
• Replace multi-melta with:
   - twin-linked heavy flamer:...............................free
   - twin-linked heavy bolter:...............................+5 pts
   - twin-linked autocannon:.................................+10 pts
   - plasma cannon or assault cannon...................+10 pts
   - twin-linked lascannon.................................+30 pts
• Replace Dreadnought close combat weapon with:
   - twin-linked autocannon or missile launcher:.........+10 pts
• Take extra armour...+15 pts

Dedicated Transport:
• May select a Drop Pod (see page 135).

IRONCLAD DREADNOUGHT ....135 Points Page 65

	WS	BS	S	F	S	R	I	A
				Armour				
Ironclad Dreadnought	4	4	6	13	13	10	4	2(3)

Unit Composition:
• 1 Ironclad Dreadnought

Unit Type:
• Vehicle (Walker)

Wargear:
• Seismic hammer (with built in meltagun)
• Dreadnought close combat weapon (with built in storm bolter)
• Smoke launchers
• Searchlight
• Extra armour

Special Rules:
• Move through cover

Options:
• Replace storm bolter with heavy flamer........................+10 pts
• Replace meltagun with heavy flamer........................+5 pts
• Replace Dreadnought close combat weapon and storm bolter with a hurricane bolter...................free
• Replace seismic hammer with a chainfist...................free
• Take up to two hunter-killer missiles...................+10 pts each
• Take Ironclad assault launchers........................+15 pts

Dedicated Transport:
• May select a Drop Pod (see page 135).

Space Marine Army List **137**

ELITES

TECHMARINE ....50 Points

Page 71

	WS	BS	S	T	W	I	A	Ld	Sv
Techmarine	4	4	4	4	1	4	1	8	2+

Unit Composition:
- 1 Techmarine

Unit Type:
- Infantry

Wargear:
- Artificer armour
- Servo-arm
- Boltgun or bolt pistol
- Frag and krak grenades

Special Rules:
- And They Shall Know No Fear
- Combat Tactics
- Independent Character
- Blessing of the Omnissiah
- Bolster Defences

Options:
- Upgrade servo-arm to a servo-harness ....+25 pts
- Replace boltgun with:
  - a storm bolter ....+3 pts
  - a combi-flamer, -melta or -plasma ....+10 pts
  - a plasma pistol ....+15 pts
- Take either:
  - a power weapon ....+15 pts
  - a thunder hammer ....+30 pts
- May have a Space Marine bike ....+35 pts

SERVITORS ....10 Points ....Page 72

You may include one unit of Servitors for every Techmarine or Master of the Forge in your army.

	WS	BS	S	T	W	I	A	Ld	Sv
Servitor	3	3	3	3	1	3	1	8	4+

Unit Composition:
- 1 Servitor

Unit Type:
- Infantry

Wargear:
- Servo-arm

Special Rules:
- Mindlock

Options:
- May include up to four additional Servitors
  ....+15 pts per model
- Up to two Servitors may replace their servo-arm with:
  - a heavy bolter ....+20 pts
  - multi-melta or plasma cannon ....+30 pts

LEGION OF THE DAMNED SQUAD ....155 Points

Page 95

	WS	BS	S	T	W	I	A	Ld	Sv
Damned Sergeant	5	4	4	4	1	4	2	10	3+
Damned Legionnaire	4	4	4	4	1	4	2	10	3+

Unit Composition:
- 1 Damned Sergeant
- 4 Damned Legionnaires

Unit Type:
- Infantry

Wargear:
- Bolt pistol
- Frag and krak grenades
- Boltgun

Special Rules:
- Fearless
- Unyielding Spectres
- Aid Unlooked For
- Slow and Purposeful

Options:
- May include up to five additional Damned Legionnaires:
  ....+30 pts per model
- The Damned Sergeant may replace his boltgun with:
  - a chainsword ....free
  - a combi-melta, -flamer or -plasma ....+10 pts
  - a storm bolter ....+10 pts
  - a plasma pistol ....+15 pts
  - a power weapon ....+15 pts
  - a power fist ....+25 pts
- One Damned Legionnaire may replace his boltgun with one of the following:
  - a flamer, meltagun or plasma gun ....+20 pts
- One Damned Legionnaire may replace his boltgun with one of the following:
  - a heavy bolter ....+10 pts
  - a missile launcher ....+15 pts
  - a plasma cannon ....+20 pts
  - a lascannon, multi-melta or heavy flamer ....+30 pts

FAST ATTACK

ASSAULT SQUAD ....100 Points Page 60

	WS	BS	S	T	W	I	A	Ld	Sv
Space Marine Sergeant	4	4	4	4	1	4	2	9	3+
Space Marine	4	4	4	4	1	4	1	8	3+

Unit Composition:
- 4 Space Marines
- 1 Space Marine Sergeant

Unit Type:
- Jump infantry

Wargear:
- Power armour
- Chainsword
- Bolt pistol
- Frag and krak grenades
- Jump pack

Special Rules:
- And They Shall Know No Fear
- Combat Squads
- Combat Tactics

Dedicated Transport:
- The Squad may remove its jump packs to count as Infantry. It may then have a Drop Pod or Rhino for free. Note that upgrades must be bought as normal. (see page 135 for points costs).

Options:
- May include up to five additional Space Marines:
  ....*+18 pts per model*
- For every five models in the squad one Space Marine may replace his bolt pistol with one of the following:
  - a flamer...*+10 pts*
  - a plasma pistol.....................................*+15 pts*
- The Space Marine Sergeant may replace his bolt pistol and/or chainsword with:
  - a storm shield......................................*+15 pts*
  - a plasma pistol.....................................*+15 pts*
  - a power weapon or lightning claw......*+15 pts*
  - a power fist..*+25 pts*
  - a thunder hammer or pair of lightning claws.........*+30 pts*
- The Space Marine Sergeant may take:
  - melta bombs...*+5 pts*
  - a combat shield....................................*+5 pts*

VANGUARD VETERAN SQUAD ....125 Points Page 62

	WS	BS	S	T	W	I	A	Ld	Sv
Space Marine Sergeant	4	4	4	4	1	4	2	9	3+
Veteran	4	4	4	4	1	4	2	9	3+

Unit Composition:
- 1 Space Marine Sergeant
- 4 Veterans

Unit Type:
- Infantry

Wargear:
- Power armour
- Bolt pistol
- Frag and krak grenades
- Chainsword (the Sergeant instead has a power sword).

Special Rules:
- And They Shall Know No Fear
- Combat Squads
- Combat Tactics
- Heroic Intervention

Dedicated Transport:
- If the squad does not have jump packs, it may select a Drop Pod, Rhino or a Razorback (see page 135 for points costs).

Options:
- May include up to five additional Veterans:
  ....*+20 pts per model*
- The Sergeant may replace his power sword with:
  - a lightning claw..................................*free*
  - a power fist..*+10 pts*
  - a thunder hammer or relic blade.........*+15 pts*
- Any model may replace his bolt pistol and/or chainsword with:
  - a storm shield......................................*+15 pts*
  - a plasma pistol.....................................*+15 pts*
  - a power weapon or lightning claw......*+15 pts*
  - a power fist..*+25 pts*
  - a thunder hammer................................*+30 pts*
- Any model may take:
  - melta bombs...*+5 pts*
- The entire squad may have jump packs:
  ....*+10 pts per model*

LAND SPEEDER SQUADRON ....50 Points per model Page 74

		Armour		
	BS	F	S	R
Land Speeder	4	10	10	10

Unit Composition:
- 1-3 Land Speeders

Unit Type:
- Vehicle (Fast, Skimmer)

Wargear:
- Heavy bolter

Special Rules:
- Deep Strike

Options:
- Any Land Speeder may replace its heavy bolter with:
  - heavy flamer..*free*
  - multi-melta...*+10 pts*
- Any Land Speeder may be upgraded with one of the following:
  - a Typhoon missile launcher...............*+40 point*
  - a Tornado pattern:
    - heavy flamer....................................*+10 pts*
    - heavy bolter.....................................*+10 pts*
    - multi-melta.......................................*+20 pts*
    - assault cannon.................................*+40 pts*

FAST ATTACK

SPACE MARINE BIKE SQUAD .... 90 Points

Page 68

	WS	BS	S	T	W	I	A	Ld	Sv
Biker Sergeant	4	4	4	4(5)	1	4	2	9	3+
Space Marine Biker	4	4	4	4(5)	1	4	1	8	3+
Attack Bike	4	4	4	4(5)	2	4	2	8	3+

Unit Composition:
- 1 Biker Sergeant
- 2 Space Marine Bikers

Unit Type:
- Bike

Wargear:
- Power armour
- Bolt pistol
- Frag and krak grenades
- Space Marine bike

Special Rules:
- And They Shall Know No Fear
- Combat Squads
- Combat Tactics

Options:
- May include up to five additional Space Marine Bikers .... +25 pts per model
- The Biker Sergeant may replace his bolt pistol with:
  - a plasma pistol .... +15 pts
  - a combi-melta, -flamer or -plasma .... +10 pts
  - a power weapon .... +15 pts
  - a power fist .... +25 pts
- The Biker Sergeant may take:
  - melta bombs .... +5 pts
- Up to two Bikers may replace their bolt pistols with:
  - a flamer .... +5 pts
  - a meltagun .... +10 pts
  - a plasma gun .... +15 pts
- Add one heavy bolter armed Attack Bike to the Squadron .... +40 pts
- The Attack Bike may upgrade its heavy bolter to a multi-melta .... +10 pts

ATTACK BIKE SQUAD .... 40 Points per model

Page 68

	WS	BS	S	T	W	I	A	Ld	Sv
Attack Bike	4	4	4	4(5)	2	4	2	8	3+

Unit Composition:
- 1-3 Attack Bikes

Unit Type:
- Bikes

Wargear:
- Power armour
- Bolt pistol
- Frag and krak grenades
- Space Marine bike
- Heavy bolter

Special Rules:
- And They Shall Know No Fear
- Combat Tactics

Options:
- Any Attack Bike may upgrade its heavy bolter to a multi-melta .... +10 pts

FAST ATTACK

LAND SPEEDER STORM .... 50 Points

Page 75

	BS	Armour F	S	R
Land Speeder Storm	3	10	10	10

Unit Composition:
- 1 Land Speeder Storm

Unit Type:
- Vehicle (Fast, Skimmer, Open-topped)

Wargear:
- Heavy bolter
- Jamming beacon
- Cerberus launcher

Transport Capacity:
- Five models (Scouts only)

Special Rules:
- Deep Strike
- Scouts

Options:
- Replace heavy bolter with:
  - heavy flamer .... +10 pts
  - multi-melta .... +15 pts
  - assault cannon .... +35 pts

SCOUT BIKE SQUAD .... 70 Points

Page 67

	WS	BS	S	T	W	I	A	Ld	Sv
Scout Biker Sergeant	4	4	4	4(5)	1	4	2	9	4+
Scout Biker	3	3	4	4(5)	1	4	1	8	4+

Unit Composition:
- 1 Scout Biker Sergeant
- 2 Scout Bikers

Unit Type:
- Bike

Wargear:
- Scout armour
- Bolt pistol
- Frag and krak grenades
- Space Marine bike
- Shotgun

Special Rules:
- And They Shall Know No Fear
- Combat Squads
- Combat Tactics
- Infiltrate
- Scouts

Options:
- May include up to seven additional Scout Bikers .... +20 pts per model
- The Scout Biker Sergeant may replace his bolt pistol with:
  - a plasma pistol .... +15 pts
  - a combi-melta, -flamer or -plasma .... +10 pts
  - a power weapon .... +15 pts
  - a power fist .... +25 pts
- The Scout Biker Sergeant may take:
  - melta bombs .... +5 pts
  - locator beacon .... +25 pts
- Up to three Bikers may replace their bike's twin-linked boltguns with an Astartes grenade launcher: .... +10 pts
- The squad may have cluster mines: .... +10 pts

Note that a squad that separates into two Combat Squads is still only treated as a single unit for the purposes of using cluster mines.

HEAVY SUPPORT

DEVASTATOR SQUAD .... 90 Points

Page 61

	WS	BS	S	T	W	I	A	Ld	Sv
Space Marine Sergeant	4	4	4	4	1	4	2	9	3+
Space Marine	4	4	4	4	1	4	1	8	3+

Unit Composition:
- 4 Space Marines
- 1 Space Marine Sergeant

Unit Type:
- Infantry

Wargear:
- Power armour
- Bolt pistol
- Frag and krak grenades
- Boltgun
- Signum (Sergeant only)

Special Rules:
- And They Shall Know No Fear
- Combat Squads
- Combat Tactics

Dedicated Transport:
- May select a Drop Pod, Rhino or a Razorback (see page 135 for pts costs).

Options:
- May include up to five additional Space Marines:
  .... +16 pts per model
- Up to four Space Marines may replace their boltguns with one of the following:
  - a heavy bolter, multi-melta or missile launcher ...... +15 pts
  - a plasma cannon .... +25 pts
  - a lascannon .... +35 pts
- The Space Marine Sergeant may replace his boltgun and/or bolt pistol with:
  - a chainsword .... free
  - a combi-melta, -flamer or -plasma .... +10 pts
  - a storm bolter .... +10 pts
  - a plasma pistol or power weapon .... +15 pts
  - a power fist .... +25 pts
- The Space Marine Sergeant may take:
  - melta bombs .... +5 pts

THUNDERFIRE CANNON .... 100 Points

Page 73

	WS	BS	S	T	W	I	A	Ld	Sv
Techmarine	4	4	4	4	1	4	1	8	2+

Unit Composition:
- 1 Techmarine Gunner
- 1 Thunderfire cannon

Unit Type:
- Artillery

Wargear:
- Artificer armour
- Bolt pistol
- Frag and krak grenades
- Servo-harness

Special Rules:
- And They Shall Know No Fear
- Combat Tactics
- Blessing of the Omnissiah
- Bolster Defences

Dedicated Transport:
- May select a Drop Pod (see page 135).

LAND RAIDER .... 250 Points

Page 81

	BS	Armour F	S	R
Land Raider	4	14	14	14

Unit Composition:
- 1 Land Raider

Unit Type:
- Vehicle (Tank)

Wargear:
- Twin-linked heavy bolter
- Two twin-linked lascannons
- Smoke launchers
- Searchlight

Transport Capacity
- Twelve models

Options:
- May take any of the following:
  - a storm bolter .... +10 pts
  - a hunter-killer missile .... +10 pts
  - a multi-melta .... +10 pts
  - extra armour .... +15 pts

Special Rules:
- Power of the Machine Spirit
- Assault Vehicle

LAND RAIDER CRUSADER .... 250 Points

Page 82

	BS	Armour F	S	R
Land Raider	4	14	14	14

Unit Composition:
- 1 Land Raider

Unit Type:
- Vehicle (Tank)

Wargear:
- Twin-linked assault cannon
- Two Hurricane Bolters
- Frag Assault Launcher
- Smoke Launchers
- Searchlight

Transport Capacity
- Sixteen models

Options:
- May take any of the following:
  - a storm bolter .... +10 pts
  - a hunter-killer missile .... +10 pts
  - a multi-melta .... +10 pts
  - extra armour .... +15 pts

Special Rules:
- Power of the Machine Spirit
- Assault Vehicle

HEAVY SUPPORT

LAND RAIDER REDEEMER · · · · · · · · · · 240 Points
Page 83

Armour

	BS	F	S	R
Land Raider	4	14	14	14

Unit Composition:
• 1 Land Raider

Wargear:
• Twin-linked assault cannon
• Two flamestorm cannons
• Frag Assault Launcher
• Smoke Launchers
• Searchlight

Unit Type:
• Vehicle (Tank)

Transport Capacity
• Twelve models

Special Rules:
• Power of the Machine Spirit
• Assault Vehicle

Options:
• May take any of the following:
 - a storm bolter +10 pts
 - a hunter-killer missile +10 pts
 - a multi-melta +10 pts
 - extra armour +15 pts

PREDATOR · · · · · · · · · · 60 Points
Page 78

Armour

	BS	F	S	R
Predator	4	13	11	10

Unit Composition:
• 1 Predator

Wargear:
• Autocannon
• Smoke launchers
• Searchlight

Unit Type:
• Vehicle (Tank)

Options:
• Replace autocannon with a twin-linked lascannon: +45 pts
• May take side sponsons with heavy bolters for +25 pts
 or with lascannons for +60 pts
• May take any of the following:
 - a storm bolter +10 pts
 - a hunter-killer missile +10 pts
 - a dozer blade +5 pts
 - extra armour +15 pts

WHIRLWIND · · · · · · · · · · 85 Points
Page 79

Armour

	BS	F	S	R
Whirlwind	4	11	11	10

Unit Composition:
• 1 Whirlwind

Wargear:
• Whirlwind multiple missile launcher
• Smoke launchers
• Searchlight

Unit Type:
• Vehicle (Tank)

Options:
• May take any of the following:
 - a storm bolter +10 pts
 - a hunter-killer missile +10 pts
 - a dozer blade +5 pts
 - extra armour +15 pts

VINDICATOR · · · · · · · · · · 115 Points
Page 80

Armour

	BS	F	S	R
Vindicator	4	13	11	10

Unit Composition:
• 1 Vindicator

Wargear:
• Demolisher cannon
• Storm bolter
• Smoke launchers
• Searchlight

Unit Type:
• Vehicle (Tank)

Options:
• May take any of the following:
 - a storm bolter +10 pts
 - a hunter-killer missile +10 pts
 - a dozer blade +5 pts
 - a siege shield +10 pts
 - extra armour +15 pts

BROTHER-SERGEANT CHRONUS · · · · · · · · · · 70 Points
Page 88

Chronus must be assigned to one tank in the army.

	WS	BS	S	T	W	I	A	Ld	Sv
Antaro Chronus	4	5	4	4	1	4	2	9	3+

Unit Composition:
• 1 (Unique)

Unit Type:
• Infantry

Wargear:
• Power armour
• Bolt pistol
• Frag and krak grenades
• Servo-arm

Special Rules:
• Tank Commander

SUMMARY

TROOP TYPES

	WS	BS	S	T	W	I	A	Ld	Sv	Page
Apothecary	4	4	4	4	1	4	2	9	3+	55
Attack Bike	4	4	4	4(5)	2	4	2	8	3+	68
Biker Sergeant	4	4	4	4(5)	1	4	2	9	3+	68
Captain	6	5	4	4	3	5	3	10	3+	54
Cato Sicarius	6	5	4	4	3	5	3	10	2+	85
Chaplain	5	5	4	4	2	5	2	10	3+	58
Chapter Champion	5	4	4	4	1	5	3	10	2+	53
Chapter Master	6	5	4	4	3	5	3	10	3+	52
Chronus	4	4	4	4	1	4	2	9	3+	89
Company Champion	5	4	4	4	1	4	2	9	3+	55
Damned Legionnaire	4	4	4	4	1	4	2	10	3+	95
Damned Sergeant	4	4	4	4	1	4	2	10	3+	95
Darnath Lysander	6	5	4	4	3	5	4	10	2+	91
Honour Guard	4	4	4	4	1	4	2	10	2+	53
Kayvaan Shrike	6	5	4	4	3	5	3	10	3+	92
Kor'sarro Khan	5	5	4	4	3	5	3	10	3+	94
Librarian	5	4	4	4	2	4	2	10	3+	56
Marneus Calgar	6	5	4	4	5	5	4	10	3+	84
Master of the Forge	4	5	4	4	2	4	2	10	2+	70
Ortan Cassius	5	4	4	4	2	4	2	10	3+	87
Pedro Kantor	6	5	4	4	3	5	3	10	3+	90
Scout	3	3	4	4	1	4	1	8	4+	66
Scout Biker	3	3	4	4(5)	1	4	1	8	4+	67
Scout Biker Sergeant	4	4	4	4(5)	1	4	2	8	4+	67
Scout Sergeant	4	4	4	4	1	4	2	9	4+	66
Sergeant Telion	5	5	4	4	2	4	2	9	4+	88
Servitor	3	3	3	4	1	3	1	8	4+	72
Space Marine	4	4	4	4	1	4	1	8	3+	var.
Space Marine Biker	4	4	4	4(5)	1	4	1	8	3+	68
Space Marine Sgt.	4	4	4	4	1	4	2	9	3+	var.
Techmarine	4	4	4	4	1	4	1	8	2+	71
Terminator	4	4	4	4	1	4	2	9	2+	64
Terminator Sergeant	4	4	4	4	1	4	2	9	2+	64
Varro Tigurius	5	4	4	4	2	4	2	10	3+	86
Veteran	4	4	4	4	1	4	2	9	3+	var.
Vulkan He'stan	6	5	4	4	3	5	3	10	2+	93

VEHICLES

	BS	Armour Front	Side	Rear	Page
Drop Pod	4	12	12	12	69
Land Raider	4	14	14	14	81
Land Raider Crusader	4	14	14	14	82
Land Raider Redeemer	4	14	14	14	83
Land Speeder	4	10	10	10	74
Land Speeder Storm	3	10	10	10	75
Predator	4	13	11	10	78
Razorback	4	11	11	10	77
Rhino	4	11	11	10	76
Vindicator	4	13	11	10	80
Whirlwind	4	11	11	10	79

	WS	BS	S	Armour Front	Side	Rear	I	A	Page
Dreadnought	4	4	6	12	12	10	4	2	65
Ironclad Dreadnought	4	4	6	13	13	10	4	2(3)	65
Venerable Dreadnought	5	5	6	12	12	10	4	2	65

ORDNANCE

Weapon	Range	Str.	AP	Type	Page
Demolisher	24"	10	2	Ord 1, Barrage	80
Orbital bombardment	X	10	1	Ord 1, Barrage	52
Whirlwind multiple missile launcher*					79
Vengeance	12-48"	5	4	Ord 1, Barrage	
Incendiary	12-48"	5	4	Ord 1, Barrage	
Castellan				Ignores Cover	

WEAPON TYPES

Weapon	Range	Str.	AP	Type	Page
Assault cannon	24"	6	4	Heavy 4, Rending	97
Astartes grenade launcher*					67
(Frag)	24"	3	6	Rapid Fire, Blast	
(Krak)	24"	6	4	Rapid Fire	
Autocannon	48"	7	4	Heavy 2	103
Auxiliary grenade launcher*					97
(Frag)	12"	3	6	Assault 1, Blast	
(Krak)	12"	6	4	Assault 1	
Bolt pistol	12"	4	5	Pistol	97
Boltgun	24"	4	5	Rapid Fire	97
Conversion beamer*					70
up to 18"	6	-	Heavy 1, Blast		
18"–42"	8	4	Heavy 1, Blast		
42"–72"	10	1	Heavy 1, Blast		
Cyclone missile launcher*					64
(Frag)	48"	4	6	Heavy 2, Blast	
(Krak)	48"	8	3	Heavy 2	
Deathwind launcher	12"	5	-	Heavy 1, Large Blast	69
Dragonfire bolts	24"	4	5	Rapid Fire Ignores Cover	63
Flamer	Template	4	5	Assault 1	98
Flamestorm	Template	6	3	Heavy 1	83
Heavy bolter	36"	5	4	Heavy 3	98
Heavy flamer	Template	5	4	Assault 1	98
Hellfire round	24"	X	5	Rapid Fire, Poisoned (2+)	100
Hellfire shell	36"	X	-	Heavy 1, Blast*, Poisoned (2+)	66
Kraken bolt	30"	4	4	Rapid Fire	63
Lascannon	48"	9	2	Heavy 1	98
Meltagun	12"	8	1	Assault 1, Melta	98
Missile launcher*					99
(Frag)	48"	4	6	Heavy 1, Blast	
(Krak)	48"	8	3	Heavy 1	
Multi-melta	24"	8	1	Heavy 1, Melta	99
Plasma cannon	36"	7	2	Heavy 1, Blast, Gets Hot!	99
Plasma gun	24"	7	2	Rapid Fire, Gets Hot!	99
Plasma pistol	12"	7	2	Pistol, Gets Hot!	99
Shotgun	12"	4	–	Assault 2	66
Sniper rifle	36"	X	6	Heavy 1, Sniper	66
Storm bolter	24"	4	5	Assault 2	99
Thunderfire cannon*					73
Surface	60"	6	5	Heavy 4, Blast	
Airburst	60"	5	6	Heavy 4, Blast Ignores Cover	
Subterranean	60"	4	-	Heavy 4, Blast, Tremor	
Typhoon Missile launcher*					74
(Frag)	48"	4	6	Heavy 2, Blast	
(Krak)	48"	8	3	Heavy 2	
Vengeance round	18"	4	3	Rapid Fire, Gets Hot!	63

* These weapons can fire in two or more different modes.
See the relevant page for details.